DOWN HOME WAYS

DOWN HOME WAYS

OLD-FANGLED SKILLS FOR MAKING HUNDREDS OF SIMPLE, USEFUL THINGS

JERRY MACK JOHNSON

GREENWICH HOUSE
Distributed by Crown Publishers, Inc.
New York

Copyright © MCMLXXVIII by Jerry Mack Johnson
All rights reserved.

This 1984 edition is published by Greenwich House, a division of Arlington House, Inc.,
distributed by Crown Publishers, Inc. by arrangement with Times Books.

Manufactured in the United States of America

Library of Congress Cataloging in Publication Data

Johnson, Jerry Mack.
    Down home ways.

    Reprint. Originally published: New York : Times Books, c1978.
    Includes index.
    1. Home economics.   2. Handicraft.   3. Cookery.
I. Title.
TX147.J64   1984   640   83-25430

ISBN: 0-517-433923

h g f e d c b

DESIGNED BY BETH TONDREAU
ILLUSTRATIONS BY A. PESCHKE

Dedicated to the folks who
passed these ways down to us
from all over our great land

CONTENTS

INTRODUCTION

There seems to be in all of us an elemental desire to create with our own labor something useful from the earth's materials. Nothing affords so much satisfaction in its ownership and use as a thing we have made ourselves. Said my teen-age daughter, upon learning of this book's subject matter, "Nothing rates with homemade."

The projects described in *Down-Home Ways* are neither regional nor limited to a particular category. They cover a wide geographic area and a broad scope of interests, ranging from adobe bricks to zucchini pickles. Each undertaking requires only moderate initial expense. You will not be encumbered with materials and equipment for which little or no genuine need exists. Instructions are presented as simply as possible and as nearly equivalent to old-time methods as feasible. Where we feel that some modern-day tool will reduce expenditure in time and energy, it is recommended.

Although many of the subjects are less than exhaustive, they are sufficiently complete as an introduction to projects that may be new to you. We suggest a thorough reading of all information until it is clearly understood prior to commencing work. Approach each undertaking with the conviction that there is a way to accomplish everything. You will be surprised, delighted, and satisfied with the results. If a better means of performing some step occurs to you, don't hesitate to improvise. These projects can serve as a starting point for your own experiments. You may be inspired to pursue some of them to greater lengths than indicated here, at which time extra equipment and special materials would be justified.

The subjects presented in *Down-Home Ways* may be undertaken as an economic necessity, an enjoyable pastime, or both. In their making, economy and pleasure are bound up together.

JERRY MACK JOHNSON
San Angelo, Texas

DOWN HOME WAYS

1

WAYS WITH WOOD

CURING AND SPLITTING WOOD

To cure wood for planking, proceed in this way: Melt paraffin in a double boiler, and paint all the logs on their cut ends with the melted paraffin. Then stack them off the ground on skids. Cover the wood with a tarpaulin, and leave it to season for one year.

After curing, logs may be transported to a sawmill for cutting into planks. The boards must be stored in a dark, dry place. Stack them flat, with strips of wood between them to permit air circulation.

Splitting hardwoods for firewood is particularly difficult. To make the task easier, cut logs to the desired length and stand them on end for five or six months. Then, when set on their opposite ends, they can be split readily, especially if you cut from the sides instead of in the center.

A precision-sharpened ax blade is a boon when cutting wood. One that has been too thinly sharpened may break; a too-thick blade tends to glance off the wood. Make an ax-bit gauge for keeping the original profile of a new blade. First, take a piece of sheet metal and place the ax head upright on it. Then draw around the cutting half of the head. Using sheet metal scissors, cut along the inside of the outline. Work slowly and carefully to achieve an accurate gauge. With a file or sandpaper, smooth any rough edges.

Insert the blade in the slot. If it fits smoothly, neither loosely nor too snugly, your gauge is precise.

Label each ax and its gauge with a matching number. When grinding or honing an ax blade, use the appropriate gauge to help you maintain its correct cutting profile.

MAKING A LASTING FIRE

To build a fire of low blaze that burns with steady heat and does not require constant attention, start with a bed of ashes reaching several inches above the andiron legs. Place a good-sized log, about 10 inches in diameter, against the back wall of the fireplace. Balance a smaller log on top of it. Now place a log just behind and against the andirons. The front and rear logs must be sufficiently bedded down in ashes to keep draft and flames from getting under them. Only their tops and faces should burn. Put paper and dry kindling wood in the center of the fireplace and light them. Gradually the logs at front and back will burn through. Move them to the middle of the fire and substitute new logs, well-embedded in ashes.

A fire constructed in this manner will use a minimum of wood. They will also have red-hot coals that can be covered over with ashes from the sides of the fireplace and will last through the night, even well into the following day. Uncover them and the fire can be rekindled. In country homes of old, fire and heat were maintained day after day in this way.

FURNITURE
Lamp Table

Large cable reels can be converted into lamp tables with little effort or expense. Ask utilities companies for one of these empty spools; they come in different sizes and are cost-free.

Buy a cheap floor lamp at a rummage sale or secondhand store, find a round piece of plywood in a scrap pile at a construction site, and purchase some paint.

Disassemble the reel and put aside the hardware. Then

sand the spool and paint or stain it to suit your taste, making the plywood and lamp parts the same color.

Reassemble the reel. Cut the center of the circular plywood to fit the circumference of the lamp shaft. Insert the lamp pole in the middle of the plywood top and the spool.

Utilize the bottom shelf as a circular bookcase.

Rustic Patio and Garden Furniture

For making rustic wooden furniture, select a hardwood. Oak is preferable, but any hardwood, such as beech or chestnut, will do. Thick branches about three inches in diameter are required for the main structure. Branches of this size, unwanted by orchardists, farmers, foresters, and lumber dealers, are generally consigned to the flames. So you may get your material simply for the asking or for a nominal fee. Inquire at orchards during spring pruning time. Consult the forest supervisor of a national forest. He is authorized to give away wood intended for private use. Or, if you live near a state forest, contact the state forester's office. Check in areas where land is being cleared for farming or building purposes.

In general, try to procure straight branches; however, irregularly shaped branches or roots can often be utilized interestingly in rustic furniture. Cut away all growths, twigs, and small branches from the main branch. Decide whether you want to retain or remove the bark on the poles. If you strip the bark, allow the timber to season for some weeks before staining and polishing it. Watch for areas of unusual grain in the wood, and plan a piece of furniture so as to set it off to advantage.

The easiest way to join the poles is by nailing them together with wrought-iron nails or flathead nails. While hammering, support the pieces from behind to facilitate nailing. A firm and attractive joining can be achieved by first shaping a smooth, concave area at the end of a horizontal pole to fit partially around the convex curve of the vertical pole to which it will be nailed. Use a wood chopper or ax to carve the concave curve. Always set nails deeply enough to avoid snagging your clothing.

When you connect sections of the furniture where stress will occur—for example, the seat support to the legs —use a stronger means of joining. Cut an opening in the vertical piece of timber, and insert, glue, and nail the end of the horizontal piece. A chair seat or table top can be constructed by lashing together the required number of poles (as in raft-making), which can be nailed together or to a back support.

For the most effective results, design your rustic furniture simply.

MAKING PINE TAR AND COUGH REMEDIES

Pine Tar: Wood Source and Extraction

Pine tar is contained in many cold remedies. Here is how to obtain this ingredient.

First, locate some yellow heart pine. Look for this greasy-looking, lemon-colored wood in damp places.

Cut it into slender, short pieces. Put them in a cast-iron pot, such as a Dutch oven. Wedge the wood splinters snugly into the pot so that they will remain in place when the vessel is inverted.

Take a flat board, larger than the iron pot, and scoop grooves in it with a knife. Make sure that the grooves are cut deeply enough to carry the flow of heavy tar. Lay one end of the board on a high enough pile of bricks or rocks to provide a slant after propping the other end with a container to catch the tar.

Invert the pot on the high end of the board, and cover it with a thick layer of clay. The clay will prevent the wood splinters from getting excessively hot and starting to burn. On the clay-covered pot, start a fire. In about ½ hour the wood should be hot enough to release tar. At first a watery, yellowish fluid will run along the grooves, but eventually it will become sticky and thick.

A Dutch oven packed with wood splinters should yield about three cups of pine tar. Scrape the thick syrup from the container and store it in jars.

Cough Remedies: Cough Syrup and Candy

* *PINE TAR COUGH SYRUP:* For a single dose of cough medicine, mix ½ teaspoon of pine tar with 3 teaspoons of honey. Blend thoroughly.

* RED CLOVER COUGH MEDICINE: Cough medicine can be made from red clover, which grows almost everywhere. Gather 1 cup of red clover blossoms. Put them in an earthenware crock, and add 2 cups of boiling water. Cover the crock. Allow the contents to steep until cool. Strain. Mix 1 tablespoon of honey with the liquid. To check the cough of a cold, take 1 teaspoonful.

* PINE TAR COUGH CANDY: Add 3 cups of water to 5 pounds of sugar. Boil to the hard snap. Spread in another container.

As it is cooling, add the following ingredients: 5 drops of pine tar (made by dissolving 1½ teaspoons of tar in 1 tablespoon of alcohol); 1½ teaspoons of oil of capsicum; and 1¾ teaspoons of oil of wintergreen. Work the mixture together with your hands until all substances are thoroughly blended. Keep the mass warm—near a fire—as you proceed. Roll the cough candy into round sticks, and continue rolling them until they are cold.

* HOARHOUND CANDY: Boil the downy, white leaves of the hoarhound plant in a small amount of water until juice is extracted. Strain it through cheesecloth. Depending upon the quantity of cough candy you desire, boil an amount of sugar in barely enough water to dissolve it. Blend in the juice. Using a spoon, work the sugar against the sides of the saucepan until it reaches a creamy, thick consistency. Pour into a buttered pan. When almost cool, it should be marked into squares and allowed to dry. (Or you can boil the sugar until candied, and then stir in dry, powdered hoarhound.) Put it in buttered tins to cool.

SAP GATHERING AND SYRUP AND SUGAR MAKING

Drown those golden pancakes in syrup of your own making.

Sap-gathering time ranges from mid-February to April (depending on where you live). It generally commences after the first good thaw. The most favorable days are sunny and warm, preceded by a frosty night. Preferred sap comes from sugar maples, but most maples produce sugar sap.

Fashioning a Spigot

Make a spigot for tapping trees from an elderberry stem. (Hollowed-out sticks of sumac and willow or stalks of bamboo and mullein can also be used as spouts.) Cut a piece about 5 or 6 inches in length. Push out the soft, pithy center with red-hot wire from a heated coat hanger. Sharpen one end of the stem to facilitate its insertion in the tree hole.

On the sunny side of a maple tree, bore a hole three feet from the ground using a brace and $7/16$-inch bit. The hole should be about 3 inchs deep and slant upward. After inserting the spigot, hammer in a nail above the spout for hanging the bucket. Make covers for the sap pails from tin or wood to protect the contents from rain, snow, dust, twigs, and insects.

Tapping Trees

You will need about 20 gallons of sap to make ½ gallon of syrup. One tapping of a tree that is no less than 12 inches in diameter will produce roughly 20 gallons of sap. Bore no more than one tap hole in a 12-inch trunk. An 18-inch tree will yield enough sap for two tap holes, a 24-inch tree enough for three buckets, and so on.

Making Maple Syrup

Collect the sap as soon as several gallons have flowed into the pails, for the juice will spoil if allowed to stand too long. To make syrup, boil down the sap. When white scum appears on the surface, scoop it out with a fine-meshed strainer. Although this step is not absolutely necessary, it will result in a cleaner product. Check continually to prevent the syrup's boiling over or scorching. If the foam starts to rise, add a little fresh sap and the contents will subside. Old-timers used to remedy the situation by tying a chunk of fat to one end of a stick and drawing it over the bubbles.

Watch for the liquid to attain the desired consistency. A candy thermometer will help you determine this. At the moment the sap starts to boil, read the temperature; when it increases by 7°, the proper sugar consistency has developed. The seething liquid generally becomes syrup at 219° F.

Fasten a double thickness of clean dishtoweling over the top of a bucket with clothespins. As you draw off the syrup, strain it through the cloth to remove impurities. You can also clarify it by letting it settle.

The syrup must be bottled or canned while hot to preserve its flavor. Store it in a cool place.

If you boil sap in the kitchen, be sure to have a fan above the stove to help eliminate the clouds of steam. You may find it more convenient to work outdoors with a large vessel—a big iron kettle or metal tub—set over a wood fire.

Making Maple Sugar

Making maple sugar entails further evaporation. If you allow the kettle's contents to reach 242° F., the result will be hard cake sugar. A temperature of 237° F. will result in a softer sugar.

To test for the hard sugar stage, let the syrup drip from the ladle. When it forms a fine thread, take the syrup from the fire. Permit it to cool for several minutes, and then stir it. The stirring will insure sugar of a finer grain. The syrup will begin to crystallize suddenly. Pour the mass into lightly greased molds and let stand. Muffin tins can serve as molds, if need be.

Maple Syrup Pie

½ cup boiling water   *3 tablespoons cold water*
1 cup maple syrup   *1 tablespoon butter*
3 tablespoons cornstarch   *chopped nuts*

Put the water and maple syrup in a saucepan; boil for five minutes. Mix the cornstarch and cold water. Use it as thickening for the boiling syrup. Stir in the butter.

Pour the mixture into a pastry-lined pie plate. Sprinkle the chopped nuts over it. Cover with pastry. Bake in a 400–degree oven for thirty minutes or until the crust is golden brown.

Maple Sugar Cough Remedy

Roast a lemon; be careful not to burn it. Slice it in two, and squeeze out the juice. Thoroughly blend in 3 tablespoons of powdered maple sugar. Take 1 teaspoonful to alleviate a cough due to a cold.

2

WAYS WITH PAINT AND PAPER

HOUSE PAINTING
Main Tasks

Painting a house consists of four main tasks:

* *SURFACE PREPARATION:* Some scraping, sanding, caulking, and priming may be necessary. For paint to adhere properly, underlying areas must be free of dirt and loose paint. Start by hosing down the outside walls of the house to remove soil; then scrape any cracked, chipped, or peeling places. Areas where the bare wood has been exposed need primer. If the patch is not large, however, two coats of paint will suffice. Recaulk doors, windowframes, and chimneys when necessary.

* *WINDOWS AND TRIM:* Save time by painting windows with care to avoid the job of scraping panes later. When doing trim on a house with overhanging eaves, you will be painting overhead, so wear a hat.

* **MAIN BODY OF HOUSE:** Using a wide brush, take long strokes, but don't overextend your reach when standing on a ladder.

* **CLEANING UP:** Pick up and dispose of any old caulking material, putty, or paint chips. Look over your work, and touch up places you have missed or failed to cover well.

Requirements for House Painting

* **PAINT:** Buy the best quality paint you can afford. The results of your labor will last longer and look better than when a cheaper product is used. Available types of paint are oil-based and water-based (latex). Water-based paint dries in roughly one hour so that two coats can be applied on the same day. Brushes can be cleaned with soap and water. Allow a drying time of forty-eight hours between coats of oil-based paint. Clean the brushes in spirits of oleum.

* **BRUSHES:** Some painters like a wide brush because of its extensive coverage. Others prefer one 2½ inches in width with a rounded handle. It easily covers narrow siding while its length permits reaching a wide swath. As time wears on, brushes of larger width tend to feel heavy. The better the brush, the better the results. One of nylon retains its shape and is easy to clean.

* **SPIRITS OF OLEUM:** Use it for cleaning brushes and thinning paint.

* **LADDERS:** Generally a 6- to 8-foot ladder and a 12- to 14-foot extension are sufficient.

* **DROPCLOTHS:** Protect shrubs and bushes from paint by draping them with old sheets or dropcloths of light canvas or plastic.

* **SCRAPERS:** Prepare surfaces with a 2-inch scraper that's been maintained in sharp condition with a file. A razor-blade scraper and putty knife will also come in handy.

* **RAGS**

* *NYLON STOCKINGS:* Paint that becomes scummy can be satisfactorily filtered through a piece of old nylon stocking. To prevent this condition in the first place, splash a small amount of oleum on the contents of the paint can before covering it at day's end.

* *WIRE:* Hang paint buckets on the ladder with the aid of coat-hanger wire. Suspend the pail on the side nearest your painting arm.

* *PAINTING CLOTHES:* Hat, shirt, and overalls (or pants) can be purchased cheaply at thrift stores. Overalls provide room for stowing cloths and tools. When working in warm weather, choose white garb to minimize the heat.

* *SHOES:* Footwear with steel shanks will make perching on a ladder more comfortable. Your feet won't tend to wrap around the rungs.

* *MASSAGE (optional):* At the end of a day's painting, you may welcome a massage to assuage aching muscles.

Paint Estimate

Here are some guidelines for estimating the amount of paint needed for a house:
* Figure the number of square feet of surface to be painted by finding the distance, in feet, around the outside of your house. Next, determine the average height to the eaves. (If there are gables, add 2 feet to this number.) Now multiply the first number (the distance around the house) by the second (the height to the eaves).
* Ask your paint dealer for the approximate coverage in square feet of each gallon of undercoat. Divide the total surface area by this number.
* Ascertain how many square feet are covered by 1 gallon of top coat; divide as indicated above.
* If the surface condition is uncommonly dry, porous, rough, or heavily textured, 20% more paint may be needed for the first coat.

Application of Paint

Begin painting under the eaves at the highest point and work downward. Guard against lap marks, the buildups where ending and beginning areas meet. Whenever possible, avoid painting in direct sunlight, which dries the coat too rapidly and can cause lap marks. If you do encounter a sunny spot, feather the ends of your brush strokes and draw the paint out to a thin, gradually fading streak.

When approached by flying, stinging insects (bees, hornets, etc.), yield ground. If the creature persists, have a knotted rag handy to flick at it in self-defense. The insect will be dazed long enough for you to make a safe retreat. It may be of some solace to know that you are less likely to be bothered by such pests in the morning. During the early hours of the day, flying insects are more sluggish in their activities.

MAKING PAPER

Paper from Plants

Paper can be made from all fibrous vegetation. One can prepare a wide assortment of paper, differing in texture and quality, from the various plants that grow in woods and meadows.

The most favorable time to gather your plants is toward summer's end or at the beginning of fall. Place them on a floor of stone, and keep them moist until they decompose.

Chop the rotted material into ½-inch-long pieces. Put them into a large vessel filled with water and add a good amount of caustic soda. Rub a thumb and forefinger together in the water. If enough soda is present, the water should feel greasy. Immediately after this test, wash your hand well, or the caustic soda can cause burns.

Paper intended for writing or painting has to be sized. Slowly heat the pulp. Use a thermometer to check the temperature. When it reaches 98° F., add gelatin for sizing. (Sizing— any thin, viscous substance—serves as a filler for porous materials, such as paper.) Boil for a minimum of three hours; be careful that the container does not boil dry.

Transfer the pulp to a pail. Wash the material until the water is clear, and pound it with your hands to press out the water. Put bleaching powder (chlorinated lime, available through building supply and hardware stores) into a large jug for mixing; then add water and stir. Allow to settle. Pour the bleach solution on the fibrous pulp. Let it stand for twelve hours, and stir now and then with a stick. When the material has become a pale fawn color, it has bleached sufficiently.

Once more, wash the material well and squeeze out the water. Cut the fibrous pulp into ½-inch pieces with scissors. In a large mortar, crush the pulp with a pestle until the fibers split lengthwise. You may pound the pulp on a stone slab with a heavy mallet if mortar and pestle are not available. Continue this procedure until the desired consistency is achieved. The longer the pulp is crushed, the smoother the paper will be.

To make but one sheet of paper at a time, put a nylon sieve, 10 inches in diameter, into a shallow pan of warm water. Place 3 cups of pulp in the sieve. Using your hand, spread it evenly on the sieve. Take the sieve from the pan and let any water drain off. Place it in a warm spot to dry.

Lift the dry sheet by slipping the tip of a knife beneath the edges of the paper. Its thickness will depend on the amount of pulp used. Repeat the process to make more sheets.

To prepare a greater number of sheets in a shorter time, make a wooden frame and nail a sheet of perforated zinc to it. Spread pulp evenly on the piece of zinc. Have some old blankets handy. Invert the frame and press the paper onto a wet blanket. Place another wet blanket on top in readiness to receive the next sheet. Continue alternating layers of blankets and paper sheets. Finally, place large, heavy stones atop the pile to press out the water. Now unstack the blankets, letting each sheet of paper dry on its blanket.

Paper from Paper Scraps

Paper can also be made from odds and ends of gift-wrapping paper, old magazines, junk mail, and newspaper. For equipment you will need an electric blender, a 5- by 7-inch picture frame (one that's 8 by 10 inches may also be used, but no larger), window screening the size of the frame, thumbtacks, a pile of newspapers, a 14½- by 10½- by 2-inch glass baking pan, two desk-sized white blotters, one wooden spoon, paper towels, and an iron.

Tear or cut the old paper in slender strips; loosely fill one-third of the blender with them. Pour water into the machine until it is two-thirds full. Blend the contents for four or five seconds. In the next step you can control the shade of your paper by introducing a preferred color; for example, if pink paper is desired, add strips of red. Blend once more. Produce texture by mixing in bits of colored thread, parsley, or even chili-pepper flakes.

Fashion a sieve by tacking the piece of screening to the frame. Place three stacks of newspapers in a row. Set the baking pan on one and a desk blotter on the next.

Pour the pulp into the baking pan, and add about 1 inch of water. Mix thoroughly with the wooden spoon. Holding the screen side of the frame uppermost and over the pan at a slight angle, spoon the pulp evenly on the sieve. Let excess water drip back into the pan.

Put a long edge of the sieve on the blotter, and quickly flip it over, pulp side down. With paper towels, blot up excess moisture, particularly at the edges of the frame, and carefully lift away the sieve. Immediately cover the soggy paper with the remaining blotter. Transfer the blotters protecting the moist paper to the last stack of newspapers.

Heat the iron at its wool setting, and press the blotter "sandwich" on both sides. Take away the top blotter; peel off the sheet of paper. If difficult to remove, it is still too damp. Iron directly on the paper until it is dry. Then lift it from the blotter.

Your tinted paper is ready for use.

WALLPAPER AND WALL STENCILING
Preparing Walls for Paper

Stretched on his deathbed, Oscar Wilde quipped, "My wallpaper is killing me—one of us must go!" If you have long felt that your wallpaper "must go," but have postponed replacing it to avoid the cost, consider making and hanging your own paper. The job is not difficult or expensive and the results are rewarding.

First, judge whether it is necessary to remove old paper before putting up new. Your decision depends on whether the present covering is firmly attached to the wall. Examine it closely. If no bulges exist and the seams are securely in place, new paper quite probably will adhere well. Should there be a few pieces of loose paper, snip them off and sand the edges. Unanchored seams can often be reglued.

When old paper is in an overall loose condition, it must be removed. Heavy types of wallpaper generally peel away with ease. Other kinds require sufficient moistening to soften the glue beneath. At that moment, scraping (use a wide-bladed putty knife, large case knife, or handscraper) or stripping should commence immediately, for it will quickly dry. Wetting and stripping but one section at a time is the most efficient procedure. To permeate the paper and soften the glue, use a wet sponge. You can also use a liquid wallpaper remover (available at paint dealers and hardware stores).

Once the paper has been taken off, wash the walls with vinegar and water or soda and water applied with a brush or large sponge. Then let the walls dry thoroughly. Prepare whitewashed walls by wetting them with a solution of 1 pound of alum to 2 gallons of water. Allow them to dry before papering.

Fill any holes or seams in the plaster or wallboard with patching plaster. When patching wallboard, it is advisable to use a primer-sealer over repaired places. The walls are now ready to receive your homemade paper.

Making Wallpaper

Wallpaper is believed to have been a Chinese invention. Europeans next adopted it, and by the seventeenth century the practice of covering walls with decorative paper became popular in North America.

Early wallpapers were designed by woodblock printing, handstamping, and the letterpress method. They were sometimes made to resemble fabrics that were the valuable wall coverings of the period.

To decorate your wallpaper with the simplest or the more complicated designs, use the rubbing technique described under "Gravestone Rubbings." Produce them on lining paper, which comes in the same width and length as ordinary wallpaper. Detail paper (used in architectural firms) will also serve. The motifs can overlap or be spaced in a chessboard, stripe, or diamond arrangement.

For your design to be most effective, rub it with varying amounts of pressure—lightly in some areas, heavily in others, sometimes using a mixture of the two. By such selective rubbing, you can develop certain areas of the design to greater prominence. Either one color or a pleasing combination of colors may be employed throughout.

Preparing Papering Paste

Prepare papering paste the day before it is needed so that it will be cold when applied. For fourteen rolls of wallpaper, 5 quarts of paste are required. Mix a bit more than 2 cups of wheat flour (rice flour or cornstarch can be substituted) with enough water to form a thin dough. Thin it down to avoid lumps. Heat 4 quarts of water. At the boiling point, pour in the thin hot batter. Stir constantly to prevent burning until the boiling point is reached once more. Then empty the vessel into a tin pail, and allow the paste to stand until the following day. To insure a lump-free paste, strain and press it through coarse muslin.

Hanging Wallpaper

Hang your wallpaper in the customary manner. Climb a ladder, and hold plain lining paper up to the ceiling while a helper below marks it along the baseboard with any blunt instrument. Cut along this mark. Use it as a pattern, cutting a sufficient number of decorated strips for walls that have no doors or windows.

Lay some boards, a sheet of scrap plywood, or an old door across widely spaced sawhorses, chair backs, or barrels. Place a wallpaper strip face down on this work surface, and evenly apply the papering paste with a whitewash brush. When the paper is sticky rather than wet, press the upper end just up to the ceiling, beginning at a corner, and work downward. Smooth out any wrinkles and large bubbles by moving a clean cloth from the center outward to the sides. Don't be concerned about smaller bubbles; they will dry smooth. Place the next strip so that its edge abuts on the first piece but does not overlap it.

Do not attempt to cut paper to fit around windows and doors prior to putting it up. Hang it in the usual way, and upon reaching the obstruction, paper right over the edge. Then trim around doors and windows by cutting diagonally up to and a little beyond their corners, which you can indicate with your finger as you feel them through the paper.

Fold back the excess paper, mark the edge, and cut it off.

Remove light fixtures, switch plates, thermostat covers, etc. Papering under instead of around them makes a much simpler and neater job. Mark the paper in these areas; then trim out the holes and replace the items.

Old-time paperhangers advise brushing an even coat of paste on walls instead of wallpaper, moistening the backs of strips with a water-soaked sponge, and then hanging them.

Preparing Walls for Stenciling

If you prefer painted walls to wallpaper but want them decorated, employ the technique of stenciling.

First, prepare walls with a coat of latex paint. Those that have been whitewashed will require scraping with a blunt-edged tool to remove any loose lime. You will find a hoe handy for this job. Next, go over the walls with sandpaper tacked to a large piece of wood that has a handle attached to it. Wash them down with a sponge. After they are dry, fill all cracks and breaks with plaster of Paris. Then apply the latex in white or in some pastel shade as the background for your stenciled pattern. Latex is preferable to oil-based paint. With its use, any necessary touching up will not be as evident as it would be with oil-based paint.

Stencil Designs

Select your stencil designs. You will find books containing patterns at the library or in art supply stores. You may enjoy creating original designs of your own. Using carbon paper, trace your motifs on waxed stencil paper or yellow stencil paper (available at paint and art stores).

Cut the stencils with a single-edged razor blade. Work on a glass surface. This step requires great care, for any errors will show up when you apply pigments to the wall.

Plan the layout of your stencils by measuring the design and the wall space it will occupy. Position it according to the number of times it will occur in that area.

More than one color may be incorporated in a design. Use oil-based, semigloss paints for the stenciling work. If you intend to mix your own paints, be sure to prepare enough for the whole room, thus insuring uniformity of tone.

Methods for Applying Stencils

Choose either of the following methods for applying wall stencils:

* STENCIL-BRUSH METHOD: Cut your stencils from waxed stencil paper. As they must be cleaned with turpentine between each application of pigments, it is convenient to make more than one set. Hold the stencil on the wall with masking tape. Apply pigments with round stencil brushes. Dip the brush into the paint; wipe off any excess on a rag or newspaper. Very little paint is needed. More can be added if necessary, but too much cannot be removed. Painting from the outside of the hole toward the center, rub the paint on the wall through each stencil opening. Make certain that the opening is completely filled with color before going on to another. Smudges, fuzzy edges, or other imperfections should be corrected with the background paint with a watercolor brush. Old-time stencilers generally used this method.

* WATERCOLOR-BRUSH METHOD: Cut stencils from inexpensive yellow stencil paper. This method will require no more than one set of stencils, and you won't need to tape them on the wall. Using one as a guide, hold it in place as you lightly but clearly outline the design with a hard lead pencil. You may want to sketch the designs throughout the room before beginning to paint. Set the stencils aside, and carefully paint in the drawn motifs with small watercolor brushes. This simplified method of stenciling was used during the fifteenth and sixteenth centuries in France.

Wall stenciling adapts to any decor, from Early American to modern.

If you intend to cover plaster walls in oil-based paint without stenciling, first brush them with a thin glue sizing (prepared by dissolving 4 ounces of glue in 1 gallon of boiling water over low heat). When wall surfaces are covered with several coats of whitewash, make and apply the following glue sizing: In 2½ gallons of water, dissolve 10 ounces of glue. In another vessel, mix 9 pounds of bole—a reddish-colored, easily pulverized clay available in paint stores—with sufficient water to produce a creamlike consistency, and strain it through cheesecloth. Add the moist bole to the glue sizing, and stir in 2 pounds of gypsum. Strain the mixture through cheesecloth. Dilute it with water for brushing on walls. When it is dry, apply the oil-based paint.

GRAVESTONE RUBBINGS
History of Rubbing Technique

The technique of rubbing is thought to have originated in China around 300 B.C. The practice spread throughout the Chinese empire and eventually the entire Far East. In the beginning, it served as a means to disseminate the written word prior to the invention of the printing press. Literature and edicts of emperors were incised on stone tablets and then reproduced on paper by rubbing. Eventually, pictures were carved in stone expressly for the purpose of being copied in this way. Later, archaeologists employed the method to record early tomb carvings.

Choice of Gravestones

You can use this ancient technique to create decorative pictures for your walls. Surfaces or objects to rub are almost limitless: brasses, architectural reliefs, medals, coins, any incised designs, bark, leaves, flowers, etc.

Perhaps some of the most unusual and interesting rubbings can be made on gravestones in old burial grounds. Those dating before 1800 are hand carved and represent the first sculpture of colonial settlers. As such, they are a unique expression of primitive American art. The stone slabs with their carved motifs and religious symbols were intended for instruction of the generally illiterate public in matters of man's mortality, his relation to God, and the blessings of heaven, thus reflecting religious attitudes of the times. Gradually, as Puritan faith became less strict, religious symbols were replaced by stylized portraiture. Details of dress currently in vogue and often the occupation or social status of the deceased were depicted by the stonecutter. These early craftsmen displayed an instinctive sense of design and expert workmanship. So, rubbings of tombstones several centuries old are both historically and artistically valuable.

While the philosophy of Puritans was revealed in symbols, views of the Old West were expressed in pithy epitaphs, always informative and sometimes amusing. Epitaphs in southern burial grounds often exceeded a single statement; they related a complete story of the circumstances leading to death in colorful local dialect, many times with primitive spellings.

Stonecutters, much in demand in more densely populated areas of colonial life, were master craftsmen. However, smaller towns throughout the country had to depend on woodcarvers or even shoemakers for tombstone carving. Their inexperience left us markers with entire words deleted or letters squeezed in at the end of a line, giving them a quaint appeal.

If you want to create and display such samples of your national heritage, follow these guidelines.

Essential Materials

The essential materials for making rubbings are few:

* *CLEANING AID:* piece of styrofoam, a soft hairbrush, or a rubber school eraser

* *PAPER:* butcher paper (long sheets are available at meat markets), detail paper (used by architects), rice paper, or any kind of thin, strong, linen-base paper

* *MASKING TAPE*

* *RUBBING MEDIUM:* black lumber-marking crayon or primary crayons (used in primary grades, they have a flat side to prevent their rolling off desks)

* *KNEELING PAD (optional):* carpet sample or foam-rubber pad

Surface Preparation

The time of year when you can work most comfortably and efficiently is early spring. By then winter has killed the weeds, and the sun and showers of a warmer season have not yet prodded the growth of grasses, briars, and branches, or roused snakes from their hibernation. The rains and snow of winter will have removed at least some moss from the surface of old gravestones.

If you find a heavy accumulation of moss or lichen on the stone's face, clean the surface gently but effectively with a small block of styrofoam, a child's nylon hairbrush, or a rubber eraser. (Never use a wire brush or harsh abrasives; old, weather-beaten markers are soft in texture and will erode easily.) By gently rubbing across the stone, most of the moss or other foreign matter will be removed. Where moss clings stubbornly, rub the area with a rag or sponge saturated with vinegar.

Rubbing Technique

After preparing the stone's surface, attach a large sheet of white or light-colored paper with masking tape in the center of all four sides, smoothing the paper from the middle outward before applying each strip. If more pieces are needed to make the sheet adhere tightly, position them midway between the original tape.

Remove the paper wrapper from the crayon (brown or black is most effective) and, using the flat side, work from the center outward. Establish the entire design lightly. The inscription and decorative motifs will spring into relief on your paper. Raised areas beneath the sheet will be registered by the crayon; depressed areas will remain white. Then, using firmer pressure and working from the edges inward, repeat the procedure.

Check your reproduction at a distance for uniformity of color. Correct weaker areas.

Now that your print is complete, remove it by peeling the tape from the paper toward the stone. To reproduce other surfaces, from coins to manhole covers, follow essentially the same method.

Framing the Rubbing

Set off your rubbing to best advantage with a rustic picture frame. An abandoned, weather-beaten farm building will provide appropriate material (with the owner's permission, of course). Usually, you can have a few rough-textured boards for very little or nothing at all. Select boards that are relatively straight. Don't be concerned about nail holes; they will only enhance the rustic look of the finished product.

Before making the frame, dry any wet wood for several days or more. You may want to add to the frame's weather-beaten appearance with the application of a light-gray, semi-transparent shingle stain. Brush in the direction of the grain.

3

WAYS WITH FIBERS AND FABRIC

PLANT DYES AND DYEING FIBERS

Plants offer an almost infinite source of pigments for dyeing fibers, yarns, and fabrics. Wool has traditionally been the most common textile in Europe and North America, where large areas are suited to sheep raising. Thus, over the centuries, plant dyes were developed chiefly for that fiber.

You should first experiment with wool, which is easier to color than other natural fibers because of its greater compatibility with plant dyes. However, you can toss samples of any kinds of material into the dye bath along with the wool in order to observe their reaction to a specific dye.

The beginner should start by dyeing fibers or yarns, not cloth. Dyeing a quantity of cloth requires greater skill. Through the use of fibers and yarns, you will learn which plants give dye and amass a repertory of colors.

For initial experiments, we recommend unraveling some discarded, white knitted garment, washing the wool well, and winding it into skeins. If no such garment is available, a hank of white wool from the five-and-ten-cent store will do. Check

24

to see that no man-made fibers have been incorporated with it.

General Information for Dyeing

* Use steel or unchipped enamel vessels of 1½-gallon capacity for dyeing and plastic pails for rinsing.
* Use soft water for the dye bath and rinses.
* Stir with a glass or stainless steel rod. A peeled stick (be sure it is smooth) may be used. Since wood absorbs some dye, use a different stick for each color.
* You may want to wear rubber gloves while working.
* Wash all plants before use to eliminate dirt or chemical sprays.
* Loosely tie the wool in skeins with string so that the dye can reach all areas.
* Thoroughly wet yarn or wool fibers before immersing them in the dye bath lest the dye take unevenly.
* Use a dairy thermometer to check the temperature of the dye bath.
* Never dry fibers or yarn in direct sunshine.

Certain plants will dye well only in the presence of a mordant—metallic salts that fix the coloring. The following dye recipes for beginners use substances generally available in any locality and in any season. They all produce dyes that do not require mordants. However, you probably have some mordants on hand in your home—vinegar, salt, and cream of tartar. Though not essential to the success of these dyes, a very small pinch of cream of tartar added to the dye pot before introducing the wool will enliven the color.

Dye Sources and Shades
Dye Source: Blueberries
Shades: Pink to Purple

1 ounce wool, separated into 5 skeins and tied with string	*¾ pound blueberries* *½ gallon soft water*

Crush about ¾ pound of blueberries (they may be fresh, dried, or canned) in an unchipped enamel pan or one of steel. Since the berries will yield juice, add something less than

½ gallon of soft water. Rainwater is preferable, but hard water can be softened with 1 tablespoon of vinegar or a commercial water softener. Bring to a simmer; continue simmering for thirty minutes.

Strain the vessel's contents into a plastic pail, discarding the berries. Pour the liquor back into the dye pot. When it is comfortable to the touch (100°–120° F.), immerse the clean and completely wetted wool. Bring to a simmer and continue simmering for thirty minutes, gently moving the wool around with a peeled stick.

Lift a skein from the pot, and allow it to drip into the bath for a few seconds. First rinse it in hot water and gently squeeze out excess water. Then give it a cooler rinse, again squeezing gently. Dry it on a rod suspended on hooks. Now and then turn the skein during drying, and give it a gentle pull to stretch it. Clip or tie on a label indicating the dye source, number of the recipe, and the mordant used, if any. This skein will probably be pink.

Simmer the wool remaining in the pot for thirty minutes longer. Remove another skein. Rinse, label, and hang to dry.

Simmer the rest of the skeins for another hour. Take out a skein. It will be considerably darker than the previous two.

Continue the same procedure until all skeins have been dyed.

Dye Source: Yellow Onionskins
Shades: Gradations of Yellow

1 ounce wool, divided	*onionskins*
into 5 skeins	*(outer skins)*
2 handfuls yellow	*½–1 gallon soft water*

Put 2 handfuls of yellow onionskins in ½ to 1 gallon of soft water. Bring to a simmer; simmer for thirty to sixty minutes. Cover to confine the odor. Add water to compensate for whatever amount boils away.

Strain the dye bath, discarding the onionskins. Return the liquid to the vessel. When it is cool enough to touch comfortably, put in the clean, completely wetted wool. Slowly bring to a simmer. Gently stirring the wool about, simmer for fifteen minutes.

Remove a skein and allow it to drain over the pot for a few seconds. Rinse it in hot water and squeeze. Then give it a cooler rinse and squeeze again. Label and hang to dry.

Simmer the remaining wool for fifteen minutes more. Remove another skein. Rinse, label, and hang to dry.

Simmer the rest of the wool for an additional fifteen minutes. Remove a skein. It should be much stronger in color than the other two.

Continue as already directed until all the skeins have been dyed.

Dye Source: Turmeric Powder
Shades: Yellow to Brilliant Yellow

1 ounce wool,	*1 ½ teaspoons turmeric*
separated into	*powder*
5 skeins	*½–1 gallon soft water*

To develop a yellow to brilliant yellow color, accompanied by less aroma than the previous recipe, use 1½ teaspoons of turmeric powder, commonly found on most kitchen spice shelves. Bring ½ to 1 gallon of soft water to hand heat (100° –120° F.) as you stir in the powder. Introduce the completely wetted wool. Gradually bring to a simmer. Simmering for two minutes, gently stir the wool around.

Lift out a skein, and let it drip over the pot a few seconds. Rinse the wool in hot water and gently squeeze it. Then squeeze it again in cooler water. Lable and dry the skein.

Simmer the wool remaining in the pot for two minutes more. Remove another skein. Rinse, label, and hang to dry.

Continue simmering the rest of the wool for a few minutes more, and follow the same procedure. A brilliant yellow can be achieved in ten minutes.

Uses for Dyed Fibers

After a number of dyed skeins have accumulated, they can be used in many interesting ways: for decorative embroidery, for crocheting small individual squares that can be sewed or crocheted together, in appliqué, patchwork, samplers, free hangings, cushions, clothes, and in macramé.

The experienced dyer will probably wish to plan a project in advance and dye the necessary quantity of yarn.

Perhaps these first attempts at dyeing yarn will instill you with the desire to try your hand at dyeing cloth and to experiment further with dyes requiring mordants.

An intriguing number of substances provide dyes—bark, pine cones and needles, nut hulls, berries, flowers, roots, cactus fruit, leaves, lichens, mollusk shells, and even insects. To learn more about natural dyes and the process of dyeing, enjoy the thrill of experimentation with these substances or any others that are available to you.

QUILTS

A quilt is a bedcover consisting of two layers of cloth with a filler of batting in between. The three layers are stitched together in patterns or lines.

Simple Quilt Frame

For a finished quilt to lie smoothly, it should be stretched on a wooden frame while its layers are being stitched together.

Construct a simple frame with the following materials:
* 4 boards—suggested dimensions: 1 inch by 4 inches by about 8½ feet in length
* 4 C-clamps
* 4 chairs of the same height

Scrap lumber would be suitable for this project, since the thickness and width of the wood are not crucial. Sand the boards until smooth to avoid splinters during quilting.

Place two boards parallel to one another on the floor. Lay the remaining two across them to form a square. Use the C-clamps to hold the frame together. Raise the frame and rest it on the tops of the chair backs at each corner. Securely fasten the corners to their supports with strips of cloth or rope.

In the middle of each board, make a permanent ink mark to use as a guide when attaching quilting material. Use thumbtacks to fasten the quilt fabric to the frame.

Tied Quilt

Covers with an underside of satin, nylon, or other slick fabrics tend to slide from the bed. Choose a nonslippery, closely woven material for the backing of a tied quilt. Sheets, cottons, and flannels are appropriate for the purpose. An old blanket (if it is thin, use two) provides a good filler. Scraps of fabric sewn together as patchwork or a colored sheet can be used for the top.

Check to see that the measurements of the top and backing are identical. Indicate the center of all four edges with a straight pin.

Now, match the center points on the fabric edges with those on the boards and fasten the backing to the frame. Working from the middle of the edges to their ends, tack the material to the stretcher.

Spread the filler smoothly on the taut backing. Then lay the top over the filler, and pin it to the backing. Adjust the C-clamps to keep the quilt taut.

Now begin tying. Space the ties evenly, with no more than two inches between each. Either stagger them or arrange them in rows. If the fabric pattern is geometric, it can serve as a guide for spacing your ties. To space them evenly on a scattered print, make a 9- by 12-inch grid of cardboard. Punch holes in it at regular intervals. Place the grid on the fabric, and through each hole put a pencil dot to indicate the spot for tying.

Thread your needle with a 3-foot length of string or yarn. Adjust the ends evenly to form a double strand, but do not make a knot.

Begin at the first pencil mark in an end row. When tying, work through the top of the quilt; have one hand beneath to insure that the needle penetrates all layers. Make a stitch as small as possible down and back up through the thicknesses of cloth, and leave a tail of thread 2 inches in length on the quilt's surface. Take another stitch directly over the first one. Then tie a firm square knot. Do not snip the thread. Continue to the next pencil mark and repeat the tying method until all the needle's yarn is used. Now go back and cut the thread midway between the pairs of ties. Leave the tails, which should be the same length if you have snipped the thread precisely halfway between ties. Trim any that are uneven.

After you have tied as far as you can reach from one end, work from the other as far as possible. Then free an end of the wooden stretcher. Removing tacks as necessary, roll the tied section around that board until you arrive at the untied area. Replace the clamps and be sure that the material is again pulled taut. Continue in this manner until the tying is completed.

Finish your tied quilt by turning raw edges of both top and bottom to the inside and blind-stitching all sides.

Crazy Quilt

To make a crazy quilt, empty all the fabric scraps from your ragbag. The scraps may be of any color or size. If you prefer that your quilt be washable, choose pieces that are colorfast and will shrink minimally. Iron them so that they are smooth and wrinkle free. Then group the scraps as to light and dark shades.

From some soft, loosely woven material, like muslin or cambric, cut a block sixteen inches square for a foundation. A full-sized quilt will require twenty such foundation blocks.

For sewing, use a short needle 1⅛ inches in length and white thread (#50 or #60), which is stronger than colored thread and tends to knot less.

Baste a 16-inch-square block of cotton or dacron batting to the foundation block. Dacron will make a fluffy quilt filling. Bulky to work with when fine stitching is required, it is particularly suitable for a crazy quilt, which does not call for delicate sewing. Batting can be bought in sheets.

Start by laying a fabric scrap on the batting in one corner. Fold under the edges on the sides bordering the edges of the block, and baste them in place. Repeat this procedure in the other three corners. Complete the block by placing patches with two basted edges on the unbasted edges of those patches already in the block. Begin in a corner. Working from left to right, use a hemming stitch to sew the patches in place. Produce a pleasing effect by choosing colors that harmonize or make an interesting contrast of light and dark hues. When the entire block is filled in, cover all patch seams with yarn. Use a simple embroidery stitch.

After all twenty blocks have been completed with patches of varying shapes and colors, it is time to "set" your quilt. First, sew the blocks in rows. Since your quilt will be four blocks wide and five long, you may make either four rows of five blocks each or five rows of four blocks each. Now sew the rows together. Make sure that all seams match. Tack the backing in the middle of alternate blocks with decorative stitches.

Finish your quilt by binding the three layers—patches, batting, and foundation—with bias tape purchased in a store or with bias strips you have cut yourself. You may make the bias strips from material that contrasts with the quilt or repeats a predominant color in it. Homemade binding is usually sturdier than store-bought tape.

Puffed Quilt

Making a puffed quilt is simple. Each puff is a square of velvet (you will find cotton velvet easier to use than slippery rayon velvet) or silk sewn to a muslin square and stuffed with batting. The puffs are then sewn together. A quilt of any size can be made by this method.

Cut 3-inch squares of velvet or silk (here's a chance to put those discarded or out-of-date silk ties to use) and 2¼-inch squares of muslin. Putting the wrong sides of the material together, pin the corners of the velvet or silk squares to those of the muslin squares. Pleat the excess velvet or silk on three of the square's sides and pin in place to the muslin. Through the fourth side, fill the puff with batting. Pleat this side and pin it in place. Baste around all sides. Stitch close to the edge.

Keeping the velvet–silk sides facing, and allowing for a ¼-inch seam, sew the puffs together. Then iron the seams open and make rows of either the desired width or length of the quilt.

Line the puffed quilt with some plain soft material. Finally, tack it on the back at regular intervals and catch the seams under the squares so that no tacking shows on top.

RUGS

Braided Cloth Rug

Before attempting to make a braided cloth rug, try a small sample one. In this way you will learn to do even work and to properly calculate the amount of needed materials. A larger rug may then be designed more accurately, insuring satisfactory results.

Assemble the following equipment and materials:
* 12 (or more) straight pins
* a few large safety pins
* 1 large needle for stitching braids or a bodkin—a thick, blunt needle—for lacing them
* 1 smaller needle for splicing strips
* scissors
* cloth strips, from 1 to 6 inches wide, the width depending upon the weight of the material and the intended rug design

Be sure all cloth is clean and well ironed. Roughly nine

ounces of fabric are needed for each square foot of a braided rug. Do not mix materials that have different degrees of shrinkage or varying rates of wear. If you are using old cloth, remove any weak areas.

Cut the material into even strips. When the material is of different weights, the width of strips should be relative to the thickness of the cloth. (Best results are obtained, however, when all the cloth is of uniform weight.) Cut thin cloth in 6-inch widths, medium cloth in 3-inch widths, and heavy cloth in 2½-inch widths. It is wise to use woven, rather than knitted, material. Because the warp is sturdier than the·weft, strips should be cut lengthwise on the material. For easy handling, make the strips between 1 and 1½ yards long. Fold the strips in half lengthwise, and iron them with their raw edges turned in.

To obtain a pleasing proportion of colors in a rug, arrange and rearrange the bundles of materials on the floor until the desired effect is reached.

Put three or more cloth strips on a safety pin—or fasten them to something stationary—for braiding. You could anchor the strips by closing a window on them. Begin with the left-hand strip. Bring it over the second one and under the third. If your braid is composed of more than three strips, continue in the same manner, placing the strip over the fourth strand and under the fifth. Eventually, you will learn to braid from both sides. Maintain an even braid by folding the outer strip as it is brought back rather than pulling it around as you would with a round cord. When nearly at the end of a strand, attach another by opening it out, cutting a bias at its end and the end of the new one, and sewing a smooth seam. Avoid having two joinings parallel to each other in the same braid.

Your first braid is the central one. Its length should equal the difference between the width and length of the completed rug. For example, a rug that's 36 inches by 48 inches would have a central braid of 12 inches. Indicate the center of your rug by attaching a safety pin at the starting point. In this way you can gauge whether you have an identical number of braided rows on each side and at each end.

In an oval rug, turn the end of the central braiding by easing it around and along its side. Avoid cupping. You can do this by pulling the inside strip a bit at the turn and stretching the outside one. When the opposite end is arrived at, the tips of the braid should be fastened in place with pins. The lengths of the parallel braids may then be sewed together.

In an oblong rug, the corners must be turned at each round. When flat strips are used, a good corner can be made by bringing the last strip of a braid to the point of turning back, over, and then under the other strips parallel to it. Follow the same procedure with the other strips; then commence braiding as for the straight braid. In the case of round strips, turn corners by easing the tension of the outside ones and drawing up the inside ones.

Sew the contiguous sides of the braids together with a slip stitch or blind stitch; the stitching should not be visible on either side. While sewing, keep the rug flat on a table top to maintain its proper shape. After sewing one side of the rug, braid as far as the next turn. Then sew the braid in place. By alternately sewing and braiding for only short distances, you'll find it easier to prevent cupping and make the braids fit smoothly together.

Add new color while working by fastening a new color, one strip at a time, to the braid. The most favorable effect is achieved when each series of a braid color forms a complete circle in an oval rug and a complete, rectangular stripe in an oblong rug. The border may be composed of colors located in the middle of the rug, but will be more interesting if they are of either brighter or darker hues. The size of the border will vary in proportion to the size of the rug's center according to the vividness of its color.

As your rug nears completion, especially when it is a large one, you may want to transfer it to the floor to keep it perfectly flat as you work.

When the rug has reached its planned dimensions, check for an even number of braids on all sides. Now snip the final braid at the rug's curve. Insert the ends of the braid beneath the last braiding row and pull it into shape, making the two oval rug ends match. Cut the ends of the last braid at uneven lengths so that they terminate at different places. Sew the ends of the strands firmly to the rug's edge.

For a stronger rug, you may fasten the braids together by lacing instead of stitching. Use a bodkin or safety pin for lacing. Thread the bodkin with a strip of material, or fasten the strip to a safety pin. Starting at the turn, lace the braids together. Do this by first sewing the tip of the lacing material to the braid. Now push the threaded bodkin or safety pin through the first loop on the side of the braid on the left, then over to the adjacent braid, and through the first loop on its side. Keep the lacing strand flat by folding it as it turns from loop to loop.

After aligning the braid loops, push the bodkin downward through the left loop, fold it back, and push it up through the right loop. Fold back once more and again pass the bodkin down through the left and up through the right side, thus lacing the two braid lengths together. Continue to braid and lace until the rug is completed. At the turns, extra lacing stitches will be required to avoid cupping. Instead of a strip of material for lacing, you may use a strong thin cord for a different effect.

Crocheted Rug

Crochet a low-cost rug quickly and easily by using fabric from cheap, secondhand clothing and a large crochet needle.

Explore resell shops and rummage sales for bathrobes, coats, and wide-skirted dresses with plenty of material in them. Whittle your crochet needle from a ¾-inch-thick wooden dowel, and smooth it with sandpaper.

Rip the garments into strips. Avoid having to sew short strips together by tearing the cloth one way to within ½ inch of the end; then reverse your direction and tear the opposite way. The kind of cloth determines the width of the strips. Those of cotton should be at least two inches wide; wool strips can be one inch in width. You won't need to hem them if you turn under the raw edges as you work.

Begin the rug with three chain stitches, and continue with a single crochet stitch in concentric circles. Occasionally, when the rug's edges start to curl up, make two single crochets in one stitch. When the end of one strip is reached, sew or tie on another. Keep loose ends on the underside.

4

WAYS WITH CLAY

ADOBE BRICKS

Adobe is derived from a wide variety of clayey soils, heavy in texture and composed of very fine grained material. The name designates the sun-dried bricks, the clay of which they are composed, and structures built of the stuff.

The word *adobe* comes from the Spanish *adobar,* to plaster. Its use as building material is said to have originated in northern Africa centuries ago. From there it was introduced into Spain. Not long after the discovery of America, Spanish conquerors brought the method to dry areas of the New World. Indians of Arizona and New Mexico began making adobe as early as the 1500's.

Adobe making is an uncomplicated procedure. Put simply, correct proportions of sand and suitable clay are combined and wet down, a small quantity of some fibrous material is added, and the whole is mixed thoroughly either in a machine or with bare feet.

Ingredients of Adobe Brick Mix

The chief components of adobe bricks are sand, clay, and a waterproofing substance. The sand acts as filler; the clay is the binder. Adobe brick mix generally contains more sand than clay. Clay content should be greater than 25% but less than 45%. Too little clay makes the dry bricks weak and crumbly; too much clay causes cracking as the bricks dry.

* *SAND:* Use sharp, coarse sand. If no natural sources of such sand are available, it can be purchased from a building supply company. (Avoid sand from ocean shores because of its salt content.)

* *CLAY:* Although many types of clay are usable in making adobe, one of high kaolin content is preferable. Such material not only is less sticky to handle than others, but also results in stronger bricks. To learn the location of kaolin clay deposits, consult local geologists or those connected with government offices, such as the Division of Mines and Geology.

* *STRAW:* The incorporation of straw in the mix causes the drying brick to shrink as a unit, thus preventing a considerable amount of cracking in the finished product. Cut the material in four-inch lengths. Straw can be bought at feed stores. Avoid using hay, if possible.

* *STABILIZER (waterproofing substance):* Use emulsified asphalt as a waterproofing agent, or stabilizer, so that the bricks will absorb only a small, safe percentage of water. (A stabilizer is required by the Uniform Building Code when adobe bricks are intended for construction of any type of building.) The liquid is available from road-paving companies or oil dealers.

If your bricks are to be used for outdoor walkways, garden walls, porch floors, and the like, Portland cement added to soil will produce strong bricks that will not be harmed by water. They will be very hard but not waterproof. (Bricks of this type would not comply with building code requirements and must not be used for inhabited structures.) Use 15% cement, and insure that it cures properly by keeping the bricks damp for several days.

Soil Testing

Test the suitability of soil for adobe–brick making in the following manner:

* Shovel away leaf mold, sod, and other organic matter from a small area of the test site.
* Dig a hole as deeply as you intend to go when excavating for soil. Mix the dirt removed from the hole so that all layers of earth are well blended.
* Put 8 ounces of the soil sample in a one-quart jar, and fill it with water. Add a teaspoon of table salt to speed settling of the clay. Shake the jar well, and let the contents settle for one hour or until the water is clear.
* Examine the jar's solid contents. You will see successive layers: lowermost will be small bits of rock; next will be sand, varying from coarse at the bottom to particles of silt size; the top layer will be clay, characterized by no perceptible particles. Rub some clay between your fingers. It should feel rather like soap and be free of grit.
* To determine clay–sand proportions, measure the height of the clay layer and estimate its percentage of the combined layers and the percentage occupied by the coarser layers. Clay material must range between 25 and 45%.

When the soil test indicates an excess in either clay or sand, you can procure high-clay soil or sand at a building materials outlet. Mix in the proper amount to correct whichever is deficient.

Making Test Bricks

If the soil tests properly, make a stiff mud with some of it and form several bricks of full size. Dry a few in the sun; dry others in shade. By so doing, you can determine which drying conditions are most favorable. Cracks will appear within the first few days if they are going to occur. A high degree of cracking can be remedied by shading the bricks or by adding more straw or sand.

Once the adobe drying test proves satisfactory, shape bricks that include emulsified asphalt to judge how much of it will be required.

Testing to Stabilize Bricks

* Fill a 1-cubic-foot box with loose soil that has already been tested and found acceptable for use. Record the number of shovelfuls required to fill the box.
* Empty the soil into a wheelbarrow. Hoe in sufficient water to form stiff mud.
* Gradually pour in ½ gallon of emulsified asphalt while continually blending it with the mud. Mix the whole thoroughly until you can no longer discern any asphalt. (A half-gallon of asphalt to 1 cubic foot of soil is a good ratio.)
* Shape the test bricks from the mud by hand. Make them some convenient size, perhaps 2 by 3 by 4 inches.
* Dry these bricks in a warm oven to shorten the drying time, which would be much longer in the sun.
* Immerse one of the dry bricks in water for a few hours. No softening should result, even at the edges. If softening does occur, repeat the test but this time use more stabilizer. Even though test results are good, follow the procedure again to determine if using less emulsified asphalt will bring equally satisfactory results.
* After determining the stabilizer–soil ratio, you can estimate what amount is needed for each mixer load according to the soil capacity of the machine in cubic feet. It's a good idea to use a bit more emulsified asphalt than the minimum required in testing, since conditions may alter somewhat during production. Always allow sufficient time for the stabilizer to thoroughly mix with the mud.

Molds

Make your molds from Douglas fir lumber. Besides being a strong wood, it holds screws and nails better than redwood or pine. Use fine-grained, finished wood. Rough lumber is difficult to separate from the wet bricks.

Molds range in size from eight inches square and two inches thick to two yards long, one foot wide, and 6 to 8 inches thick. However, the standard dimensions for an adobe brick are 4 by 7½ by 16 inches. So that the finished brick will be four inches thick, make the mold depth 4¼ inches to compensate for slight sagging of the mud as the mold is removed and to allow for some shrinkage during drying.

Cut four boards of the proper size and waterproof them.

For a stronger mold, fasten the boards with wood screws instead of nails. Reinforce each mold with two corner braces located diagonally from one another. Countersink them so that they are flush with the wood's surface.

At each end of the form, add wooden rectangles of a convenient size to serve as handles.

Tack a thin metal strip on the top edges of the form to prevent wear as your trowel scrapes away excess mud after the mold has been filled. For ease in separating the mold from the mud, either line the form with a thin sheet of tin or make the mold's bottom 1/16 inch wider on each side.

Making Adobe Bricks

Necessary Equipment:
* rectangular mason's trowel
* wooden molds
* pick (for hard earth)
* 2 shovels: a pointed one for digging soil; a square one for shoveling mud
* deep wheelbarrow
* containers for the stabilizer
* buckets
* large drum for storing water
* mechanical mud mixer equipped with paddles (A dough, plaster, or pug mixer works well; a concrete mixer is not satisfactory.)

This piece of equipment is essential if your bricks are intended for any type of building and will, therefore, require emulsified asphalt. For other purposes not requiring a stabilizer, the ingredients can be deposited in a pit and trampled and mixed with your bare feet.
* casting surfaces: You can cast bricks on flat ground, but a smooth surface is preferable. Use boards or scrap plywood supported on a framework of two-by-fours.
* shading material: If you plan to dry bricks out of the sun, provide shade with plywood supported several inches above the bricks.

Mixing

Break up any dirt chunks, and thoroughly mix the soil during excavation to create a homogeneous blend of the various layers of earth. Speed the breakdown of hard, stubborn clay masses by wetting the soil and keeping it covered with a sheet of plastic.

Now multiply the previously noted shovelfuls (required to fill the 1-cubic-foot box) by the cubic-foot capacity of the mixer. This quantity will be shoveled into the machine as you charge it.

To mix the mud, turn on the mixer and add most of the estimated amount of water required. Put in the soil and only enough additional water to form a stiff mud. After the paddles have beaten all lumps from the mud, gradually add the correct quantity of emulsified asphalt. Allow several minutes for this to be thoroughly mixed in. Lastly, add the straw. When it has been introduced, the mixer will labor due to the mud clotting and creating more resistance to the paddles. If left in too long, the straw tends to wrap about the paddles; therefore, just as soon as it is evenly dispersed throughout the mud, discharge the mixer's contents into a wheelbarrow.

Casting

Sprinkle the casting surface with sand or straw to keep the mud from adhering to it. Immerse the mold in water to avoid sticking; place it on the prepared casting surface. Fill the form with mud, making sure the corners are completely filled. Press the mud in with your hands. Using your trowel, strike the mold's contents even with its top. Now slowly and evenly lift the form from the fresh adobe brick. It is not necessary to let the mud set in the form before lifting it away.

After creating each adobe brick, plunge the mold into a tub of water to clear off any bits of clinging mud. Then proceed with making the next brick.

Drying and Curing Bricks

Freshly created adobe bricks must be allowed to dry evenly. During the initial four days, protect them from rain or foggy, cold weather with a sheet of scrap plywood supported several inches over them. Leave the ends open to the wind for further drying. Mild spring days are most favorable for the drying process. When the weather is hot, dry, and windy, however, hang burlap bags over the edges of the plywood protectors to avoid cracking caused by dry winds.

After four days set the bricks on one side to promote rapid, even drying. From this time on, the plywood protector will not be needed. Let the bricks dry in the sun for six weeks.

The molds, when not in use, should be kept in a container of water to prevent their drying out, warping, and separating at the joints.

External Treatment of Adobe Bricks

A good protective covering for adobe walls, both inside and out, is linseed oil. Apply three brush coats. These may be followed by two coats of household paint for interior walls.

Inside walls can also be treated by first applying waterproof glue. Make it of one part quicklime, six parts cottage cheese, and enough water to create a smooth-flowing mixture. Over this primer coat of glue, apply buttermilk paint: 1 gallon of buttermilk to 4½ pounds of white cement.

POTTERY

Clay Sources

The amateur potter may buy commercial clay directly from a pottery supplier. He will advise you on the clay best suited to your purpose. It will have proper consistency and texture and already have been subjected to necessary tests, particularly firing.

An alternative is to dig and prepare the clay yourself. Clay so obtained will be just as good as commercial clay, cost nothing, and provide you with adventure while seeking it plus satisfaction in literally creating your pottery from start to finish. Likely sources are pond or stream banks, road or railway cuttings, excavation sites, and brick or pottery works. If you fail to find clay through your own efforts, consult a surveyor or local builder. In most states a published geological survey is available that offers tips on locations of clays.

Preparation of Clay

Two kinds of commercial clay may be bought, either of dry body or plastic body. Clay of dry body comes in powder form and has to be mixed with water for a very considerable time. Clay of plastic body has already been prepared and is ready for use.

Clay you have dug yourself will probably require preparation, though some can be used as is. Others, being too soft, too hard, or full of vegetable matter, stones, and other impurities, will require special treatment:

* First, let the clay dry thoroughly.
* Then break it into walnut-sized pieces.
* Soak them in a pail of water.
* Let the clay soak for one to two days until it becomes a thick slop. The slop will remain as a sediment on the bottom of the pail, with the water on top.
* Blend the clay and water in the pail to make a thin slop. With your hands or a stiff brush, pass the material through a fine garden sieve into a second pail to eliminate undesirable impurities.
* Let the slop settle once more. During the settling, water can be poured off little by little, and the thickening clay will stay on the pail's bottom. If the clay is needed urgently, it can be spread on a cloth to dry more quickly outdoors. When clay is not needed immediately, however, the ideal way is to let it dry naturally through evaporation until the proper consistency for modeling is reached. This would require several weeks. If the clay lacks sufficient plasticity, combine it with some bought clay by making alternate layers of both and kneading them together.

Storing Clay

Clay of ideal consistency, neither so soft as to stick to the hands nor so hard as to be unyielding to the touch, should be stored to maintain it in this condition. Keep it in airtight containers. Plastic ones are preferable to those of metal, which develop rust, although the rust has no adverse effect on the clay. To insure that the clay is kept free from air, cover it with a plastic sheet or damp sack. Check it often for drying. If suitable containers are not available, closely wrap the clay in a plastic sheet. Unfinished clay work must also be kept free from air to prevent hardening. Wrap objects in plastic bags or sheets

Slip

Slip is clay thinned to the consistency of cream. It is used for binding sections or coils of clay together. Make it by soaking pieces of clay in water until they become refined slop. Sieve it through an 80- or 100-mesh sieve, obtainable from a pottery supplier or lumberyard.

Wedging and Kneading

To prevent the explosion of clay articles during firing, trapped air must be expelled from the clay. This is done through wedging and kneading home-prepared clay. Bought clay will not require such treatment.

Wedge the clay by cutting it into thick slices and forcefully slamming them down on your work table, one after the other. Form them into a mass again, and repeat the procedure ten to twenty times.

Knead the clay by pressing down on it with the base of your palms and pushing it from the body. Lifting the farthest edge of the clay, bring it over and toward you, and then press down again with the palms. The clay has been sufficiently kneaded when a cross section, cut by a wire, shows close, even texture without air pockets.

Clay that is to be fired in a primitive kiln must be strengthened with sand. Slice the clay, and make alternate layers of it and the sand. Then knead them together. Since sand tends to dry clay, you may need to put a thin layer of slop between each clay slice. Use one part sand to two or three of clay.

Techniques of Pottery Making

* *PINCH TECHNIQUE:* Shape a chunk of clay (the size of a small orange) in your hands as if shaping a snowball. When a smooth ball is formed, cup it in one hand while pressing the thumb of your other hand into its center, thus making a deep hole. Now you have the beginnings of a pot with thick walls. Still cupping the clay in your palm, pinch the wall between

thumb and fingers, with the thumb inside and the fingers outside. Slowly rotating the pot in your hand, very gradually pinch
out all sides of the pot and gently ease the clay. If cracks begin
to appear as you are working, smooth over them with a wet
finger.

* *COIL TECHNIQUE:* Roll clay backward and forward beneath your fingers to form long coils. A beginner should make
the coils somewhat thick—approximately the diameter of a
fountain pen. Although it is not essential, try to keep them
fairly uniform in length and thickness.

Flatten a sphere of clay into a disc roughly as thick as the
coils. This is the pot's base. Now start the coiling. Shape the first
coil around the inner edge of the disc, and press the coil's inner
edge down on the base. When the coil completes the circle,
guide it around on the top of the primary coil, pressing it firmly
in place by smearing the inner edge down on the coil under
it. Continue this procedure, coil upon coil, until the pot is
finished. Control its shape by the placement of the coils. If you
want the pot to swell out, place the coils on the outer edge of
the coil below. If the pot is to be narrower, place the coils on
the inner circumference. To join the ends of coils, simply
smear one against the other.

After a wall of seven to ten coils has been built up, permit
the clay to become a bit firm in order to prevent sagging when
the weight of more coils is added. Generally, one hour is
needed for the clay to firm up sufficiently. If the clay overhard-
ens, soften the top coil by scoring it and applying thick slip
until it acquires the same consistency as the new coils.

* *SLAB TECHNIQUE:* With the slab technique, the object
is constructed from sheets of clay. Using a rolling pin (or a
section of broom handle, a bottle, or a metal pipe), roll out a
lump of clay into a flat sheet or slab of the desired thickness.
Rolling should be done on a piece of cloth or paper to keep the
clay from sticking to the work surface. Clay for the slab technique should be just a bit firmer than that for pinch or coiling
work. If it is too soft, allow time for it to harden slightly.

Slabs can be cut into tiles with a knife and decorated with
pictures that are incised or impressed on their surfaces. Containers can also be made. For example, to make a round pot,
first cut out the base. Then mark it by outlining on the clay
some circular object of suitable size. Holding a table knife
vertically, cut around the outline. Then cut a long, narrow strip

to form the side. Score all edges to be joined with a matchstick or modeling tool. Paint the scored edges with thick slip. Very soft clay can be bonded together securely without scoring and slipping. Stand the narrow strip on its side around the inside circumference of the base; attach it by firmly pressing the pieces together and smoothing over the joinings with a tool. Clay slabs may be wrapped around cardboard tubes of various lengths. Remove the tube as soon as feasible. A disc of appropriate size cut from a slab forms the base. Make a simple dish by pinching up the edge of a circular slab. Any number of articles found about the house—plates, bowls, cardboard boxes, etc.—can be utilized as molds in slab work. Roll out a slab of clay a little larger than the selected mold. Using a damp sponge, gently press the clay, still on its cloth (to prevent sticking), into the mold. Cut away excess clay. Hold the clay down in the mold while cutting in case it should stick to the knife and be pulled out. With a damp sponge, smooth off the rim of the receptacle. Remove it when the clay is hard and pull away the cloth.

Decorating

While a finished clay article is yet in its soft, plastic stage, it can be decorated by impressing. Experiment by pressing small objects on the clay to make interesting patterns. In slab work, the design may be pressed on with the clay still in sheet form, prior to building up the final shape.

Relief decorations—small clay pieces applied to the object's surface—are pressed on while the clay is soft. If the clay is not soft enough, score and coat the surfaces to be bonded together with slip (a small brush is handy for this).

Clay surfaces can be decorated by incising. The clay should be almost completely dry. Experiment with simple tools to scratch, score, or carve.

Kilns and Firing

The beginner can fire his pots in a simple, homemade sawdust kiln. Select a kiln site where the ground is free of vegetation and well away from buildings. Collect dry fuel— wood shavings, twigs, wood—the amount depending on the kiln's size.

For the kiln floor, lay a groundwork of shavings and twigs. Cover this with a 3- to 4-inch layer of sawdust.

Fill the articles to be fired with sawdust. Place a layer of pots, 2 inches apart, in the bed of sawdust. Be sure the articles do not touch each other and are not too close to the edge of the foundation. Cover the pots with a layer of sawdust. Continue to build alternating layers of pots and sawdust.

The complete mound should then be thickly covered with sawdust, followed by shavings, twigs, and wood. The purpose of the foundation of shavings and twigs and the outer layer of the same materials is to ignite the sawdust. The firewood will burn strongly for about ten minutes and then die out. The sawdust, once lit, will smoulder for quite some time. Sudden changes in temperature would cause the pots to explode. However, the temperature within your kiln will rise gradually because of the slowly burning covering of sawdust.

As the sawdust is consumed, more can be added. Leave the kiln until thoroughly burnt out. Depending on the kiln's size, firing time will last anywhere from twelve to twenty-four hours.

When the pots are cool enough to be lifted from the kiln, wash or brush them clean.

Firing of clay articles can also be done in a metal drum with holes pierced around its sides. Fill it completely with dry sawdust. The articles should be dispersed throughout the sawdust. Light the fire from the top. It will slowly smoulder downward and require no additional attention.

There are small electric kilns on the market that have been designed for testing purposes. If firing out of doors is not feasible, small objects can be fired indoors in such a kiln.

Should these first attempts at pottery-making spur you to work on a larger scale, a more sophisticated kiln may be constructed.

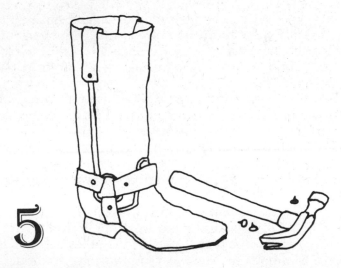

5

WAYS WITH LEATHER

TANNING HIDES AND FUR SKINS

Time and patience are the initial requirements for tanning hides and furs. Choose the hide and fur of deer and squirrel for your first attempts. They are more easily readied for tanning than those of some other animals having thin skins, which require greater skill in preparation to avoid damage.

For all soaking and tanning operations, use a wooden, earthenware, or plastic container. Metal containers react with the salt and tanning chemicals.

Preparations

After skinning the animal, flesh the hide; that is, remove all meat remaining on it. Be sure it is also free of blood and mud. Cutting from the skin side, trim any ragged edges.

The hide is now ready for the tanning process, unless you plan to tan a deerskin into buckskin. In that case, the hair must first be removed. In 5 gallons of water, mix 5 quarts of hydrated lime. Leave the hide in this solution until the hair is easily pushed from the skin with your hand, generally between six and ten days. Spread the hide on a board, and push off the remaining hair with the blunt side of a knife. Then work over both sides of the skin with the back edge of a knife. Hold it nearly flat to remove any fleshy material, grease, or lime. (This is known as *scudding.*)

The remains of the liming process—fleshings, limewater sludge, and lime—can be put to good use as fertilizer because they are particularly suitable for acid soil.

The hair, collected as it is removed from the hide and rinsed several times, can be utilized in plastering. After being washed thoroughly in repeated changes of water and dried completely, it is useful in padding, upholstery, and in the insulation of pipes. The body hair of deer is valuable for making the bodies of fishing flies. By adding a water-repellent dressing to the already naturally buoyant deer hair, dry flies can be fashioned that will remain afloat almost indefinitely. Without the protective dressing, a fly of deer hair will become soaked after a time and will serve only as a wet fly.

Now soak the hide in clean water for five hours. Scud again. Fill a 10-gallon container with water. Stir in 1 pint of vinegar with a wooden paddle. (You may substitute 1 ounce of lactic acid for the vinegar.) Leave the hide in this mixture for twenty-four hours to halt the action of the lime. Then proceed with tanning.

Tannage Procedures

* *SALT AND ALUM TANNAGE:* Prepare the salt–alum solution by dissolving 1 pound of ammonia alum (or potash alum) in 1 gallon of water. In another container, dissolve 8 ounces of salt and 4 ounces of washing soda in ½ gallon of water. Slowly empty the salt–soda solution into the alum solution, while stirring rapidly. Immerse a clean skin in this solution for two to five days—according to its thickness.

Due to the effect of alum on certain furs, it might be advisable, in general, to apply the tanning solution in paste form, and only on the flesh side. Gradually, add flour mixed with a little water to the tanning solution until a thin paste forms. Blend well to avoid lumps.

Spread the skin smoothly and tack it, flesh side out. Completely coat the skin with the paste to a thickness of approximately ⅛ inch. The following day, scrape off the paste. Apply a second coat. Thick skins will require an additional coating on the third day. The final coating should be left on for four days. Then scrape away the paste, wash the skin in 1 gallon of water with 1 ounce of borax, and rinse in fresh water.

Lay the skin out on the board and, using a dull edge, press out much of the water. Proceed with oiling and finishing.

* *ALCOHOL AND TURPENTINE TANNAGE:* Tannage with alcohol and turpentine is easiest for a small fur skin. Mix ½ pint each of wood alcohol and turpentine in a wide-mouthed gallon jar having a screw-on lid. Put in the small fur skin. Since alcohol and turpentine tend to separate, shake or stir the solution daily.

After a week to ten days, take out the skin. Wash it in detergent water, removing grease, alcohol, and turpentine. Rinse thoroughly several times to get rid of the detergent. Squeeze water from the skin without wringing. When it is partially dry, begin the oiling and finishing operation.

Oiling and Finishing

Allow the tanned, wet leather to dry somewhat. While it is yet fairly damp, apply a coat of sulfated neat's-foot oil. The amount of oil will vary according to the natural oiliness of the skin. For example, a racoon skin, being normally more fatty than a deerskin, would require less oil. For a 10-pound deer-hide, the following solution is recommended: In 3½ ounces of warm water, mix a like amount of sulfated neat's-foot oil with 1 ounce of ammonia.

Lay the skin, hair side down, on a smooth surface. Evenly spread one half of the mixture over the hide with your hand or a paint brush. Wait thirty minutes. Then apply the remainder in the same manner. Cover the hide with a plastic sheet. Keep it covered overnight. If several skins have been coated, stack them, flesh sides together, overnight.

The next morning hang the skin, fur side out, over a saw-horse to permit drying of the hair. Then nail the skin, hair side down, on a plywood board and stretch it slightly. Hammer the nails (no. 6 finish) ½ inch in from the edge, spaced about 6 inches apart. The flesh side should be dried at room temperature.

While the skin is still slightly damp, stretch it from corner to corner. Work the flesh side over some wooden edge, such as a chair back. Achieving a soft skin depends on repeatedly working it while it is in the process of drying.

When softening and drying are complete, give the skin a quick bath in unleaded or white gasoline to deodorize it and remove any excess grease. (Do this outdoors, away from flame or fire.)

Clean and brighten the pelt by tumbling it again and again in warm, dry, hardwood sawdust. Shaking, beating, and brushing will clean sawdust particles from the fur.

If need be, you may smooth the flesh side with a sandpaper block. Also, this will further soften the skin.

Preservation of Pelts

Unless tanning is to take place within twenty-four hours, hides or pelts should be treated or cured to avoid deterioration.

Preserve a small animal pelt by air-drying it. Tack it flat, hair side down, on a board.

A large pelt must be salted immediately. Place it, flesh side up, on a smooth surface. Sprinkle the hide thoroughly with salt and work it into wrinkles, neck, legs, and cut edges. For every pound of hide, use 1 pound of salt. If you are curing more than one hide, lay one on top of another, hair side down, and thoroughly salt the flesh side of each. The surface on which the pelts are stacked should have a slight incline to aid drainage of any liquid from the pile.

In two weeks you may hang the hides for complete drying. If salted a second time, they may be stored as late as May, but no longer.

A cured skin must be softened prior to tanning by soaking it several times in a 5- to 10-gallon container of cool water. Renew the water for each soaking. The soaking time is relative to the skin's condition. Some may require two hours; others, more.

As the skin starts to soften, spread it on a flat board. Begin scraping the flesh side with an old hacksaw blade to break up tissue and fat. To do a thorough job of removing the adhering tissue, you may need to alternately scrape and soak the hides. While scraping, take care not to damage the true skin.

Now mix a solution of 1 ounce of borax or soda to every gallon of lukewarm water. You may also add soap. Put in the skin when it is just short of being soft. Stir it about with a paddle. This procedure cleanses the skin, cuts grease, and induces the final softening.

Again place the skin on a board, and scud it. Then rinse it well in lukewarm water. Press out the water without wringing the skin. Unless you intend to dehair it, proceed with the tanning operation as previously described.

American Indians removed the hair from hides with wood ashes. Their tanning agent was deer's brains. To make buckskin soft, weary-jawed squaws laboriously chewed the hides. Though these methods are of interest, we feel sure you will prefer those already set forth.

MAKING RAWHIDE

Hide that has been taken as quickly as possible after the death of an animal is called "green hide"; from it the best rawhide is made.

First, stake out a green hide on the ground in some shaded spot for roughly two hours. To stake it properly, pull outward from the center before fastening it down.

After two hours Nature will have changed it from green hide to rawhide, which should be sufficiently stiff to work with. Cut off any bits of hanging flesh. Using heavy shears, cut the hide in an oval or round shape, and remove legs, neck, and other projecting portions.

Now cut the oval or disc into one continuous strip about 2½ inches in width by scissoring around the circle until you reach its center. In thinner areas (such as the belly), cut the strip a bit wider, for after it has thoroughly dried it will shrink to approximately two-thirds of its original width. When rawhide is neither too dry nor too damp, it can be cut with ease. If the strip becomes difficult to cut due to excess dryness, dampen the hide somewhat.

Attach one end of the long strip to a post, pull taut a section at a time, and grain off the hair with a keen-edged knife. Hold the blade almost flat. Guard against cutting the top skin (scarf skin), which gives strength to the rawhide string.

Once the hair has been removed, stretch the rawhide strip between posts or trees in complete shade. Leave it for five days to dry thoroughly. Then it will be ready for cutting into strings.

Bevel rawhide strings on the hair side to prevent the sharp edges from curling up. If the rawhide strip or strings are to be softened, rub them well with saddle soap (yellow laundry soap is also effective) and work them back and forth against a piece of wood, such as a post or sawhorse.

SEWING NEEDLE FOR LEATHER

Fabricate a needle for sewing leather articles from the "key" used to open sardine cans. Straighten the handle end, and hammer and file—or grind—it to a point. Thread sewing material through the slot at the opposite end.

PRESERVING AND MOUNTING SNAKESKINS

Carefully skin the snake by centrally slitting the underside of the skin from top to bottom. If the snake is a rattler, take care not to disjoin the rattles. Using steel wool and borax, scrub the skin to remove all meat.

Leave the skin overnight. The following day, paint both sides with a mixture of one-half wood alcohol and one-half glycerin. After twenty-four hours, paint on a second coat. The skin will now be pliable as well as durable.

Select a board of interesting grain, saw it to the correct length, and finish it. Fasten the snakeskin on the board with any good glue.

SHOE REPAIRS

In olden times the shoemaker was itinerant, as were tinkers and other tradesmen. His kit consisted of a leather apron, a lap stone on which to work, an awl, knives, pincers, hand-forged nails, a hammer, wax filched from beehives along the way, and sturdy, bark-tanned leather heavily impregnated with whale oil.

The shoemaker was welcome in every home not only for his craft, but also for the "news" he dispensed. Ensconced in a chimney corner with his last, he would fashion new boots and shoes or repair old ones.

However, a good many rural folks were often obliged to tan hides and make their own rough footwear, either for the sake of frugality or because the shoemaker's calls were too infrequent. Whether for purposes of economy or the pure satisfaction involved, you can repair your own boots and shoes by using these guidelines.

Ripped Seams

The repairing of ripped seams in shoe and boot uppers requires a very small outlay for tools and materials. You will need a kit of hand-sewing needles, which can be purchased inexpensively at any dime store or shop selling sewing supplies. The packet contains five different needles, each about 4 inches in length and designed for a specific purpose. You will also need extra-strong thread, either the kind used over the years for sewing carpets and buttons or the more recently manufactured polyester–cotton-wrapped thread.

Follow these steps to repair the seams in footwear:

* Pull apart the seam until you meet with resistance. Stop at this point. Remove all old stitching with the help of a penknife.
* Choose the proper needle from the kit. If your hand will fit behind the seam, a straight needle will be appropriate. If the seam is located close to the shoe's toe, select the curved needle.
* To sew a fine seam, use single thread. Use double or even triple strands of thread when the original holes in the leather are large enough. For a more water-resistant seam, first coat the thread with the wax from a beeswax candle. If beeswax is unavailable, ordinary candle wax will do.
* Close the seam by sewing through the original holes. Take care not to enlarge them. Make the stitching taut.
* Secure the finished seam by repeating the final stitch several times; a knot is unnecessary. To achieve a smooth finish, pound or rub the stitching into the leather.

Attaching Leather Half Soles

Sewing on new half soles will require a last, an item not as easily come by today as in the 1930's and 40's, but nonetheless available to the adventurous of spirit. Search secondhand stores and you may find one for a dollar or two. Antique shops are sometimes a source, but there a last would sell for considerably more. Made of metal, it resembles an inverted leg with a foot (for holding a shoe) and is attached to a wooden base.

In addition to a last, you will need clinching nails and an awl for making new holes in leather. Fashion one from a hardwood dowel of a size that fits comfortably in your grip. Drive a long, heavy nail perpendicularly through the center of the dowel, allowing a portion of the point to extend beyond the wood. Hammer this extension flat against the wood to secure the spike in the dowel. Flatten the nail head with a hammer, and grind it to a smooth point with a coarse file.

Follow this procedure for stitching on leather half soles:

* Buy precut half soles, or purchase leather and cut your own.
* Soak the half sole or leather piece for ten minutes in tepid water. This step will make cutting and sewing easier. Then wrap newspaper around the leather to absorb excess water.
* If you're making a sole, place the sole of the shoe on the new leather and trace around it. Carefully cut along the outline with a sharp knife.
* Place the shoe on the last. With a penknife or razor blade, cut the old threads on the original half sole. Lift the sole and separate it from the shoe with a somewhat diagonal cut at the arch.
* Bevel the half sole so that it slightly extends over what remains of the old sole.
* Clinching-shoe nails range from ⅜ inch to ⅞ inch in length. Choose one a half size longer than the total thickness of both new sole and shoe. Hammer in about nine nails along the juncture of the new and old half soles. Next nail down the tip and sides of the half sole.
* Using a sharp knife, trim the edge of the sole for neatness.
* Cut a shallow depression or trough on the sole's bottom where the stitching will be. Having the stitches slightly recessed protects them from wear.
* With the old holes of the shoe welt (a strip of leather sewn in the seam between the upper of a shoe and the sole to reinforce their joining) to guide you, use the awl to make holes from the topside in the half sole. Every other hole will be enough.
* Take a waxed strand of thread 3 feet long and thread two needles, one at each end of the thread. Begin at the first hole closest to the arch. Run the needles consecutively through the same opening, one needle in one direction and the second needle in the other direction. Sew such

opposing stitches all around the sole. To secure the final stitch, either sew the last stitch several times or make a knot. Snip off excess thread.

* Complete your work by pounding down the depression made for the stitches in the sole. Rub all the needle holes, stitches, and cracks with beeswax or shoe polish.

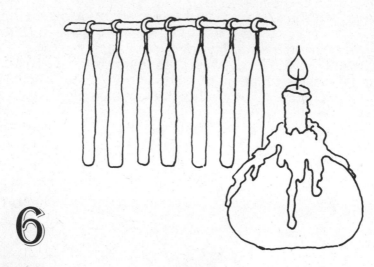

6

WAYS WITH WAX

CANDLES
Materials and Equipment

For simple candlemaking, assemble the following materials and equipment:

* **PARAFFIN FLAKES:** They can be bought in bags by the pound from a candlemakers' supply shop. Paraffin wax is quite hard and makes a smooth-burning candle.

* **BEESWAX:** When a small amount of beeswax is added to the paraffin, the candle has a smooth finish, gives off the aroma of honey while burning, and drips only minimally. Small beeswax discs can be purchased as an addition.

* **STEARIN** (sometimes known as sterene or stearic acid): This flaky white substance, when melted separately and added to the melted paraffin, facilitates the removal of the candle from the mold, gives it a harder finish, and prevents guttering. As a general rule, you should use 10% stearin to 90% paraffin–beeswax mixture. It can be bought by weight at a candlemakers' supply shop.

* *COMMON WHITE STRING:* Use ordinary white string to make your wicks. Closely braid it in two or more strands according to the thickness desired. To achieve a smoothly burning wick, it is necessary to correlate the wick size with the candle size, particularly with its diameter. The bigger the candle, the bigger the wick. Experience will teach you to gauge the wick size correctly.

Now make a solution of 8 ounces of water, 1 tablespoon of salt, and 2 tablespoons of borax. Soak the wicks in this mixture for about six hours. Then hang them up. Once they are completely dry, they will be ready for use. (You may purchase ready-made wicks very reasonably. Most have a label indicating the diameter of the candle for which they are suited.)

* *WAX-BASED DYE:* If you care to color your candles, use commercial wax dyes. Buy them in either powder or liquid form.

* *WAX PERFUME:* Scenting your candles is optional. Oil-based perfumes for wax are available at your supplier.

* *TWO OLD SAUCEPANS:* One pan should be small enough to fit into the other.

* *SUGAR THERMOMETER:* Measure the temperature of the wax with it.

* *SCISSORS:* You will need a pair of scissors to cut and trim wicks.

* *PLASTICINE:* Use this to keep melted wax from leaking through the wick hole in the bottom of the candle mold and to attach bases on bottomless molds.

* *KNIFE:* Have a sharp one handy for evening the bottoms of candles and doing other small jobs.

* *CANDLE MOLD:* Almost any container can serve as a candle mold as long as it has straight sides and a mouth with at least the same width as its base. You can probably find many appropriate containers in your kitchen—vases, cups, mugs, and jugs. By exploring secondhand stores, you can often turn up interesting and inexpensive containers to use as candle

molds, and various types can be bought at a candlemakers' supply shop.

Be sure that the molds will allow for easy removal of the finished candle. Check this by oiling their interior and compactly filling them with Plasticine. If the "candle" of Plasticine slips out easily, the chosen container is acceptable as a mold.

Copper and plastic piping provide excellent molds. Purchase off-cuts from a builders' supply center. Making certain that they are perfectly level when standing on end, saw them to the desired length. Smooth the edges with fine sandpaper. Make notches opposite one another on the rim of the top to hold a skewer or pencil from which to hang the wick. Find a jar lid the size of the mold's bottom (or cut one from cardboard, plastic, etc.). Make a central hole in it for the wick, and seal its edges to the bottom of the mold with Plasticine.

* *WICK RETAINERS:* These are metal discs for candle molds lacking wick holes. Fasten the wick to one and lower it into the bottom of the container. Wick retainers can be bought at a candlemakers' supply shop.

Procedure

Fill the larger of your saucepans one quarter full of water, and place it on a lighted stove burner. Bring the water to the boiling point. Put the required amount of paraffin wax in the smaller saucepan, and lower it into the hot water. Reduce the heat so that the water barely simmers, and let the wax melt.

Cut wicking to correct lengths, somewhat longer than the molds' height, and knot one end of each. Dip them in the melted wax and hang them until dry.

Make sure your molds are absolutely clean. Then insert wicks in their bases, pulling the unknotted ends through the holes until the knot is firmly against the bottom. Carefully seal the hole with Plasticine. For molds without wick holes, use a wick retainer by attaching the wick to it and lowering it into the middle of the bottom.

Now tie or tape the free end of a wick around a metal skewer or pencil placed horizontally and centrally across the opening of the mold. Be sure that the wick is taut and precisely centered.

If the base of the mold is not recessed, the wick knot will cause imbalance. Remedy this by placing your mold on an improvised platform made of two slightly spaced wood blocks, bricks, or any objects of exactly the same height.

When the paraffin has melted, add a small amount of the beeswax. Gently introduce it into the molten paraffin; let it melt. In a separate pan, melt stearin in an amount equaling 10% of the total of the paraffin wax plus beeswax. Add the dye immediately if you desire tinted candles. When melted simultaneously with the wax dye, stearin imparts a more vivid color to the finished product. Tint the mixture a slightly lighter shade than is desired, since the finished candle, being denser, will be darker in color. Carefully spoon the tinted stearin into the paraffin–beeswax mixture.

Insert the sugar thermometer into the saucepan of wax. Check for the temperature to reach 180° F. At this point, take the container from the stove.

Using a spoon or soup ladle (you may prefer to empty the wax mixture into a warm metal jug with a long spout), pour the wax very carefully into the candle mold at its center. Be sure to avoid wax drips on inner side surfaces. Then tap the mold to release air, thus preventing air bubbles from forming on the surface.

Now let your candle set. Depending upon its size, this may require as many as twenty-four hours. During the setting period, "top up" the candle. As the candle sets, the wax will contract and a depression will appear around the wick. Fill in this hollow with leftover wax from the batch made up for your candles. At the first appearance of the depressed area, make several holes in the surface of the wax. As the candle firms up, pierce more holes and pour in melted wax until level with the surface. You may need to repeat this procedure three times before the surface hardens without forming a hollow.

When your candle has shrunk from the mold's sides, it is set and ready for removal. First, free the wick from the skewer or pencil. Then, holding your hand over its mouth, invert the mold. Remove the Plasticine seal around the wicking knot. Cut off the knot with a sharp knife. Handling the candle delicately in order not to mar its surface, gently shake the candle from the mold. If the surface does not appear sufficiently smooth and shiny, hold on to the wick and dip the candle in boiling water and then ice water.

Stand your candle upright. You may need to trim the wick with scissors. It should be about ¼ inch in height.

Cure the finished candle in a cool, dry place for three days before using it.

Candle in a Glass

To make a candle that will remain in its glass container requires but one item in addition to the supplies already mentioned—glue.

Select some transparent glass container that is eye-catching. Make sure it is thoroughly clean.

Wax a wick somewhat beyond the usual size appropriate for the container's diameter. (The whole surface of a candle in a permanent holder becomes molten; therefore, a too-small wick would fall over and be extinguished.) Turn a short span of the wick at a right angle, and glue it in the middle of the container's bottom. Fasten it at the top in the customary way.

Pour in melted wax that does not exceed 180° F., or you will risk cracking the glass.

Let the candle set, and top up in the usual manner. Try to achieve as smooth a surface as possible. Trim the wick to ¼ inch.

Your dripless candle in glass will need no other holder.

Dipped Candles

Fill a vessel with a prepared candle–wax mixture. Choose one that is somewhat taller than the length of candle intended.

Cut a wick about 3 inches longer than necessary. Completely soak the wick in the melted wax, and hang it to dry, keeping it as straight as possible. Tie the dry wick on the horizontal bar of a wooden coat hanger.

Now add stearin to the wax—about 20% for dipped candles—along with dye (optional). When the temperature of the wax is 160° F., dip the suspended wick slowly into the wax. Be careful to hold the coat hanger as nearly on a level as possible. Leave the wick in the wax for approximately five seconds; then slowly lift it out. Suspend the hanger from a hook located away from a wall, and let the taper dry for roughly two minutes.

Continue dipping and drying until the taper reaches the desired thickness. Allow the candle to set hard, an hour or more, before cutting it from the hanger. Trim the base evenly with a sharp knife.

More than one taper can be made at a time by using a

vessel with a wider mouth to hold the wax and by hanging more wicks on a longer rod which, after the dipping process, can be suspended across the backs of spaced chairs. Remember to place newspapers beneath the tapers to catch drips.

7

OUTDOOR GEAR

HAMMOCK
You will need these materials to make an inexpensive hammock:
* 25 feet of strong rope, cut in 2 equal lengths
* 1 10-foot piece of lumber, 1 by 3 inches
* 12 1½-inch wood screws
* 1 piece of canvas, 2½ by 7 feet

Cut the wood into four 2½-foot sections. Place each canvas end between two of the boards. To secure the canvas, insert six screws in each set of boards. Drill holes through the wood 3 inches in from the ends to accommodate the rope. Run the equal lengths of rope through the holes at either end, and knot them on the underside of the fastened boards.

WALKING CANE
The first step in making a walking cane should be taken in the woods. Explore the ground for a fallen branch that approximates the diameter of cane you have in mind.

Make the next stop a junkyard. Buy a rod of lightweight steel to reinforce your walking stick.

Saw the chosen branch into cross sections about 1½ inches in thickness. Bore out their centers, and string them on the steel rod. Glue each addition to the one before.

When it comes to the cane head, let your imagination take over. Almost anything that strikes your fancy (the more unique the better) will serve, provided it fits comfortably in your grip.

GOLF TEES

Purchase a polyethylene rod, ³⁄₁₆ inch in diameter. Cut it in 2-inch segments. While holding one end of a segment with pliers, immerse the opposite end in boiling water. After a few seconds it will be soft. Press the softened end on a golf ball. It will expand slightly and become molded to the ball's curve. Keep it against the ball for several seconds until cooling and hardening take place. Sharpen the other end in a pencil sharpener.

TRUCKWAGON

Cut four wheels by sawing 2-inch-thick cross sections of logs. The wheels may be of any desired size as long as all four diameters are similar; a suggested satisfactory diameter is 12 inches. In the center of each wheel, bore a 2-inch hole to accommodate the axle hub. Make the axle from a hardwood pole, 30 inches long and 3 inches in diameter. If desired, the rear axle may be longer than the front axle. Carefully trim the ends of the hubs, and fit them in their holes so that they extend about 1 inch beyond the wheels. Bore a hole close to the end of each axle; insert a peg to keep the wheel on the hub.

Connect the axles with a narrow coupling board that runs from the center of the rear axle to the middle of the one in front. Bore a hole through the coupling board and front axle for a metal bolt, which will enable the front wheels and axle to rotate at almost 180 degrees. Bolt the rear axle in similar fashion, but do not allow it to rotate. Run short boards, as braces, at an angle from a position near the wheels on the rear axle to the coupling board. Secure the braces with bolts or pegs.

If your truckwagon is intended for the fun of racing down

a hillside, fasten a board seat to the back axle and braces. Control direction by foot pressure on either side of the front axle or by pulling pressure exerted on wires that have been attached to the axle close to the wheels. If hauling is your truckwagon's purpose, build a wagon bed at the rear instead of a seat, or nail on a good-sized wooden box.

BOW SAW

If you have an old bicycle-tire rim from a 26-inch wheel, a few scraps of wood, some nuts and bolts, and a metal rod on hand, you are well equipped for making a bow saw. The only expense involved—and that a small one—will be the purchase of a 24-inch steel saw blade.

Make two handles from wooden dowels of a circumference to fit within the tire rim's groove. One handle should be 16 inches long; the other, 22 inches in length. Fasten the saw blade, its cutting edge lowermost, at one end of the 16-inch handle with a nut and bolt; the free end of the dowel should project downward. Fasten the opposite blade end approximately at the 16-inch point on the other handle so that the lower ends of the dowels are on an even plane. Six inches of the longer handle should project above the back of the blade.

Cut the wheel rim in half. Using one of the pieces, fit its groove around the inner side of the dowels, close to the blade's cutting edge; the arch of the bow should face downward.

Run a metal rod along the groove of the arch and through holes bored in the handles. Secure the rod with nuts. It will create tension in the rim and pull the blade taut.

When preparing stove or fireplace wood with your bow saw, grip the extension of the 22-inch handle. The bowed rim will act like a pendulum weight, keeping the saw blade vertical. If you need to cut a log that is too large to fit within the saw's frame, the blade can easily be reversed.

BACKPACK

Make a roomy, serviceable backpack from an old pair of bib overalls. Simply knot each lower leg securely, and the pack is ready to be filled. Slip the suspenders over your shoulders.

OLD-FASHIONED LANTERN

An old-fashioned lantern can be completed in no time with a few discarded materials. Begin with a 1-pound can, preferably the old-style, squat variety of coffee can. If one is not at hand, almost any tin with a diameter of about 5 inches will serve as well—a 1-pound lard can, a large tobacco tin, etc.

From the bail of a paint can, a piece of coat hanger, or any stiff wire, fashion a handle shape. Lay the can sideways, and punch one hole in the front edge and two more holes straight across at the rear edge. Hook the handle ends into these holes.

Through the side directly opposite the handle, cut a criss-cross midway between the front and back of the can. Use a strong, sharply pointed knife to make each crosscut, which should be from 1½ to 2 inches in length. Gently push a utility candle, one that is thick and slow-burning, through the middle of the slits until it protrudes about 2 inches inside the container. The sharp metal points in the center of the slits will be forced inward and will secure the candle in place. As the wax is consumed in use, the candle can be shoved in further.

When the candle is lit, the can acts as a shield against wind, rain, or snow and as a reflector, spreading illumination over a wide area.

To store your candle lantern, hang it by the handle.

SNOWSHOES

If you need snowshoes, make a pair from string and saplings. They won't have much eye appeal, but they will serve their purpose well.

Cut four fairly straight saplings having a circumference approximating that of a man's thumb. Trim each to a length of 4 feet if the shoes are intended for a person of average height; for a taller person, make them 5 feet long. These sticks should be sufficiently supple to bend a little without breaking. They will serve as the frame of the snowshoes. Slice one side of their ends at an angle so that the resulting flat surfaces of each pair of sticks will fit together, forming a point. Bind together the ends of each pair in the following way: Tie string (heavy cotton string or nylon fishnet twine) around one of the sticks at a point several inches before the two saplings join. Next, encircle both sticks with the string, spiraling toward the pointed end and stopping a few inches short of the tip. Now reverse your direction. Wind backward and finish by securing the string on the other stick, opposite the starting point on the first one. While working, keep the string taut.

Make cross supports for the frame by cutting four 1- by 2-inch bars roughly 8 to 10 inches in length. Using your knife, carve a concave opening in the ends of these crossbars so that they will fit snugly around the contour of the long saplings. Insert each cross support between the vertical sticks of the frame at the point where they are no longer parallel but begin to taper toward the pointed ends.

Bind the frame and crossbars together with a webbing of string. Tie strings securely near the ends of the long vertical sticks, and crisscross them rather closely for the length of the frame. Now run strings vertically, weaving them in and out of the horizontal cords to minimize slippage. By keeping the string taut as you weave, the tension will be evenly distributed throughout the snowshoes.

Make a rope bridle across each snowshoe to fit around the toes of your boots. Bind the bridle in place just in front of the snowshoe's center of balance. The toe of the snowshoe will then be raised each time you lift your foot and move forward. Fasten on your new footgear by running a loop of rope around your ankle and hooking it into the bridle rope with a bent nail or some other workable contrivance.

Add extra strength to the areas where your boots will be resting; use a piece of rawhide, a sturdy fabric, or rope for reinforcement purposes. Binding short sticks on the inner sides of the long saplings, from one cross support to the other, will strengthen the main part of the frame, especially the boot area. Your homemade snowshoes are now ready to be strapped on for a long trek over the snow.

ICE CHOPPER

An ax may be used to chip holes in ice, but take the precaution of first warming the blade near a fire or, at least, of blowing on it. A cold blade, being very brittle, can easily break.

Avoid the risk of damaging ax blades by making an ice chopper for winter fishing. Assemble these materials:
* a chisel having a very wide blade (the kind used on brick or wood)
* a section of iron water pipe, 4 feet in length

* 1 bicycle handlebar grip
* 15 feet of rope

Drive the chisel into the pipe. In doing so, you may dull the cutting edge. Grind or file it sharp when your ice chopper is completed. Push the bicycle handlebar grip on the other end of the pipe to provide a comfortable handle. Tie the length of rope to the ice chopper so that you can retrieve it should the tool slip into the water.

NECKERCHIEF HOOD

Make a protective hood from a plain, 36-inch-square neckerchief. Spread it flat. Fold the two upper corners down to form contiguous right triangles. Now roll up the bottom of the neckerchief until the upper corners are included in the roll. Put your head in the gap between the two triangles. The ends of the roll can be carried forward to be knotted beneath the chin.

Since the hood covers the back of the neck, you have only to pull your coat collar close against it to keep out chill air and wind. It also protects the back of the neck from sunburn on hikes and fishing trips.

Cowpokes of the old days originated these useful hoods.

HOBNAILED BROGANS

Hobnailed wading brogans are a boon to the sportsman fishing in streams where slippery, moss-covered rocks abound. Those on the market are expensive.

It is a simple matter to make your own hobnails from ordinary work shoes that have leather soles. Depending on the soles' thickness, you will need wood screws about ½ to ¾ inches in length. Although brass screws don't rust, they wear down more quickly than steel ones. Don't drive in too many screws or place them too near each other, or else they will fail to make proper contact. Be careful not to insert them too deeply. Screw them into the heels and soles, and leave ¼ inch to function as hobs. You'll discover that the sharp screw edges do a better gripping job on slimy rocks than rounded hobnails.

TYING FISHING FLIES AND DEVISING LURES

You will need the following tools and materials for tying flies:

Required Tools and Materials

* *VISE:* You must have a steel vise with a clamp for fastening it securely to the work surface. The height should be adjustable for ease in working; the jaws should be adjustable to accommodate small and large hooks.

* *RUBBER BUMPER:* A bumper can be purchased at a hardware store. Attach this rubber button by its screw center to the edge of your work table some 8 inches on the right side of the vise. It will serve to grip the tying thread, maintaining the necessary tension on it. Drive a small nail into the work surface, several inches to the right of the button, as a spindle for the spool of thread.

* *SCISSORS:* You will need a pair of steel scissors, no more than 4 inches in overall length, with strong, straight blades that taper to a sharp point.

* *STYLET:* The stylet is used for many small jobs, such as the removal of hardened lacquer from the eyes of hooks. Make this handy tool by embedding a needle in a dowel of wood. A hat pin is a good substitute.

* *HOOK HONE:* Have a 4-inch hone at hand to keep sharp points on the hooks.

* *THREAD:* You will need a spool of white nylon thread.

* *WAX:* Wax for the tying thread can be made as follows: Fill a wide-mouthed jar (about 2½ to 2¾ inches wide and 3 or 4 inches high) with powdered rosin to a 1-inch depth. Add only enough turpentine to permeate the rosin. Put the open jar in hot water over low heat. When the contents become syrupy in consistency and clear amber in color, remove the jar from the stove, cover, and let cool. The cooled wax will be semifirm and will harden when used to bond materials. It will not dissolve in water.

* **WAX PAD:** A 2-inch square of oilcloth will serve to hold wax, making it accessible when you need to wax the tying thread. Simply pull the thread slowly through the wax.

* **LACQUER:** Coat the fly head and other areas wound in thread with waterproof varnish. Colorless nail polish is inexpensive and convenient to use. For ease of application, sharpen the small brush.

Attaching Thread to the Hook

The curve of the hook must be firmly clamped in the vise, with the barb below. Wax the thread by folding the wax pad over it and pulling it through the wax. Wax 6 inches at one time. The thread binds all parts of the fly to the hook in one continuous piece.

Slip the thread over the hook shank a short distance from the eye end. This spot will be designated as the wing site. Always keep the thread taut in your hands as you work. Bring the thread in your right hand down under the hook shank, up over the thread in your left hand, and over the shank. Follow this procedure three times. There should now be a spiral winding of thread, with the thread of the left hand bound firmly against the hook shank. Press the middle finger of your left hand against the wound thread to keep it from loosening. Slide your right hand down the thread, and wedge it behind the rubber button to hold it taut. With your free right hand, cut the thread's short end close to the hook.

Making Fly Bodies

Two simple fly bodies that can be fashioned successfully with little practice are made of flat tinsel and chenille.

* **FLAT TINSEL BODY:** After attaching the tying thread at the wing site, cut diagonally a 1-foot length of medium-width flat tinsel. Holding the strip between the left forefinger and thumb, press the thread windings against the hook shank with the middle finger. Free the thread from the button with your right hand. Lay the diagonally cut end of tinsel against

the hook's side at the wing site. Carry the thread up and over the tinsel. Bring the thread down under the hook shank, up, and across the tinsel again. The second turn of the tying thread should be on the right side of the preliminary one. As the thread is brought down behind the shank the last time, slide your thumb and forefinger down the thread; catch it in back of the rubber button. Using the right thumbnail, bend the tinsel point back over the windings of thread. Holding the thread windings in place with the left hand's middle finger, free the thread with your right hand. Wind a fourth turn of thread over the folded tinsel and secure it. Fasten the thread behind the button. Keeping it flat, carry the tinsel forward and beneath the hook. Hold it slanted in the direction of winding —in this case toward the hook's curve. Bring it over the hook shank and down behind. Take it with the left hand as the right is on the point of meeting the thread. Make each turn of tinsel contiguous to the preceding strip but not overlapping. Always keep the tinsel taut between the hands and the hook, changing hands when required. Continue wrapping the tinsel around the hook shank until it reaches a point parallel to the barb. Be careful not to snag the tinsel on the tip of the hook as you near the curve. The point on the shank parallel to the barb marks the end of the body of your fly. It is the tail site. At this point, reverse the direction in which the tinsel is held. Holding it taut and slanting forward, wrap it over itself toward the eye of the hook. Wind as previously described, with each turn flat and each edge touching the preceding one. Guard against overlapping. When the spot where the tinsel was tied to the hook is covered, press a left-hand finger on the tying thread, and free the thread from the button with your right hand. Wrap two turns of thread about the tinsel, winding in the direction of the hook eye. This will secure the tinsel. Catch the thread behind the button. Diagonally clip off the excess tinsel. Bend the tip of the tinsel over the thread with the left hand. After releasing the thread with your right hand, bind the folded tinsel with one turn of thread. The body is now finished.

* *CHENILLE BODY:* Clamp the curved end of the hook in the vise with the barb down. Wax about 6 inches of tying thread in the manner already described.

Fasten the thread at the tail site. Hold the short end in the left hand, and with the right hand, place the thread against the hook at the spot above and parallel to the hook's point. Bring the thread down and in back of the hook shank and then up in front, crossing over the piece held in the left hand. Repeat this procedure four times, spiraling toward the curve of the hook and ending the windings just in front of the spot above the barb. Catch the thread behind the button. Cut off the short end of the thread.

Pull fuzz from one end of a chenille strand, and expose ¼ inch of the thread's core. Place the core of thread directly over the spot above the barb. Have its end face in the direction of the hook eye. With the right hand, remove the thread from the rubber button and, spiraling toward the hook eye, wind it around the core. Continue winding an open spiral of thread; stop at the wing site. Catch the thread behind the button.

Now begin wrapping the chenille around the shank of the hook. Make close spirals to completely cover the hook and the tying thread. Release the thread from the button. Carry it over the end of the chenille body at the wing site, and bind it twice to the hook shank. Secure the thread at the button. Clip off excess chenille. Bind down any fibers of chenille or core visible in front of the windings of thread. The chenille body is finished.

Making Tails and Wings

The tail hair of a deer is good material for tails and wings of fishing flies, particularly when the hair is slightly wavy. Such hair undulates in water currents and attracts fish better than straight hair.

* *BUCKHAIR TAIL:* Put the hook in the vise; fasten on thread at the tail site.

Cut a small hair tuft from a buck's tail. Try to avoid trimming the edges to give a uniform appearance; take advantage of the naturally tapering hair ends. In order to even the tips, remove all short and long hairs. Longer hairs may sometimes be replaced lower in the wisp. Eliminate those with broken ends. The length of the tail should equal the length of the hook shank.

Grasp the hair tuft in the left hand just short of the middle, and put a dab of nail polish on its center where the thread will cross over it. Hold the tuft on the hook shank at the tail site. Free the thread with the right hand. Carrying it up and over the hook, slide it between the tuft and thumb and then between the tuft and forefinger on the farther side. Maintain the tuft on the top side of the shank, slightly in front of the spot above the barb. Bind it once more with thread. Raise the tuft, and bring the thread under and behind it to the other side. Encircle the tail's base with a complete turn of tying thread. Next, make two thread windings around both hair and hook shank. Have them spiral forward. The tail is now securely bound to the shank. Catch the thread at the rubber button. Clip away the hair projecting toward the hook eye at the spot just after the thread windings. Cut at an angle so that the ends will taper.

* *BUCKHAIR WING:* Fasten thread on the hook at the wing site. Cut a slender tuft of hair from a buck's tail. Make the ends uniform as you did for the fly tail. The wing length should extend just beyond the curve of the hook. Put a dab of nail polish on the tuft where the thread will cross over it. Make two complete windings of thread around the hair and hook shank to anchor the tuft. Now lift the wing; bring the thread around in back of it. Carry it forward on the farther side and above the hook. Repeat this procedure. Holding the hair close to the shank, make a turn of thread over the spot where the encircling thread meets on the top side of the hook. This will keep the wing down in the correct position. Wind the thread twice more around the hook and hair; again, it should spiral forward. Catch the thread at the button. Cut off the forward shaft of hair, tapering it at an angle. Wind one more turn of tying thread around the cut ends. The wing should recline along the hook shank.

Practice
Practice tying each part separately until you develop skill and speed. When you have thoroughly mastered these steps, make a fly from start to finish with one continuous thread, beginning with the tail and ending at the head—formed by the final knot—known as the wrap knot. As you add each material, it must conceal the thread already in place and the snipped ends of materials already used. Cover the tail stub with the body material, hide the snipped end of the body with the wing, and cover the ends of wing material with the head, composed of the wrap knot.

Making the Fly Head

Attach the tying thread at the wing site. The thread should enter the right hand beneath the fourth finger, across the underside of the fingertips, and should be held by the thumb and index finger. With the left hand, seize the thread coming from the right hand, and hold it against and in front of the hook shank by extending the middle and fourth fingers and catching the tying thread between them. It should be parallel with the hook shank and on the side nearer you. The thread now forms a large loop from hook to fingers. In your right hand, tautly grasp the thread descending from the hook. Carry it up and then across the parallel thread that is in front of the shank. With the taut thread holding the parallel thread against the hook shank, the left hand is free to aid in wrapping it about the hook, thus binding the parallel thread to the shank. Going up, over, and around the hook shank and parallel thread four times, wind the taut thread spiralling closely in the direction of the hook eye.

While gripping the taut thread in the right hand, begin pulling the long end of the parallel thread with the left hand. The loop of thread will start to diminish in size. As it grows smaller, press it from in back against the thread windings on the hook with your right middle finger. The loop will constantly diminish as you pull. Release your right hand's hold on the thread, but continue pressing on the threads with the middle finger until the loop completely disappears. Cut off the long end of the thread. The tying thread is now securely bound on the hook by the wrap knot, terminating your fishing fly. Several applications of nail polish or lacquer will completely cover the separate thread windings and give a finished appearance.

Fly Varieties

There are many types of flies and a variety of materials from which to create them. Fly bodies can be fashioned from rayon, silk, or synthetic floss, chenille, tinsel, wool, fur, and feathers. As much as possible, try to use recycled materials: scraps of fur that you can obtain free from furriers; local reed fibers; and discarded tinfoil. Let your dog donate a snip of hair!

After conquering the preliminaries, you may want to use a wider range of materials and progress to more complicated flies. You may also want to increase your supply of tools by adding fly-tying pliers with strongly gripping jaws and a hackle gauge to determine the correct hackle size for the different hook sizes.

RUBBER-BAND FLY: Here is a fly requiring no skill and only a few seconds to make. Take a handful of rubber bands, preferably green or white, and push them through the eye of a short-shanked hook. When they are centered in the eye, cut off the looped edges with scissors. Now encircle the rubber bands just below the eye with several windings of thread, and tie them to the shank. The rubber bands will quiver temptingly as they move through the water. For extra weight a small spinner may be added above the fly.

Nail Lure

An excellent and inexpensive homemade lure requires nothing more than a twenty-penny nail, two split rings, and a treble hook. Using a saw and file, remove both ends of the nail so that a 3½-inch length remains. Near each end drill a hole, and on either side of it file a bevel. Insert a ring in each hole. Fasten your fishing line to one ring; attach a treble hook to the other.

A nail lure can be cast to a surprising distance right on target. You will find it especially effective where fish are schooling.

Spinner-Blades and Spoons

From the shallows and shores of lake and stream, gather freshwater mussel shells. You may find some quickly and in one spot, thanks to raccoons. They know the location of mussel beds; shells will be left on the banks as evidence of their feasting. The mother-of-pearl interiors of the mollusks, shining with iridescence like darting, brightly scaled minnows, make fine lures.

Shape shell pieces into spinner-blades and spoons with a coarse hand file. Drill a hole at each end to accommodate split ring, swivel, and treble hook.

Make small pearl spoons for trout lures; fashion bigger ones to attract large pike and bass.

COLLAPSIBLE FISH LANDING NET

Make the handle for your landing net from a sturdy broomstick. A length of 18 inches is generally satisfactory, but this dimension may be adjusted to suit your preference. From an electrical supply shop, acquire a ¾-inch piece of brass tubing. Turn the cut end of the handle on a lathe or use a wood rasp to diminish its circumference so that the tubing will slip on to a depth of 3¼ inches.

Fashion the hoop for the net from a piece of telegraph wire with a ³⁄₁₆-inch diameter. To shape it smoothly and evenly, wrap it about a large crock or anything round of the proper circumference. Just short of closing the circle, bend the remaining two ends of wire (which should measure about 2 ½ inches) straight out from the hoop. Keep them parallel. The space between the parallel wires should be sufficient to accommodate the narrow end of the handle. Then bend the tips of the wires inward, forming small right angles, by holding them in a vise or the jaws of a monkey wrench and hammering them down. Bore a ³⁄₁₆-inch hole on either side of the handle for inserting the right angle hooks. From these holes, gouge a groove along the handle for the wire to fit in flush with the wood. If you lack a gouge, use a piece of red-hot wire to burn in the groove.

Buy an inexpensive net and attach it to the hoop. Slide the piece of brass tubing to the far end of the thinner portion of the handle. Fit the ends of the wire in the grooves, inserting the hooks in their holes. Now move the tubing forward and cover the wire. Your landing net is assembled.

Wind a good length of the handle with some old fish line to make it easy to grip. Putting a screw eye "g" in the end of the handle will enable you to hang the net from a hook in your belt. For storage or carrying, slip the tubing back and fold the net back over the handle.

CREEL

An excellent creel can be fashioned from the simplest of materials. Use shingles, preferably of cedar, for the sides and ends. Make the top and bottom of ¼- or ½-inch boards. These boards should be cut curved to fit the shingle sides of the creel, which will bend accommodatingly without splitting. Use small nails to tack the shingles to the top and bottom boards. Before nailing on the front, saw a generous notch in it for the insertion of fish. Make a cover for the opening, attaching it to the creel by a strap or a small pair of hinges. Tack a shoulder strap onto the back. The creel can be made in whatever size suits you.

A box of this kind will maintain your catch in a firm, fresh condition, especially if you layer leaves, moss, or green clover between the fish.

FISH SCALER

In no time at all, you can make an efficient little device for removing scales from fish. It requires a short piece of wood suitable for a handle and a bottle cap having sharp, scalloped edges. Tack the cap on one end of the handle, hammering the nail through the underside of the cap. Bend down any extension of the nail on top to attach the cap more securely. You will find this contrivance a very serviceable scaler.

SIMPLE SMOKER FOR FISH

Here is an easy way to make a cheap fish smoker: Take a good-sized, firm cardboard carton. Open one end, and tape or tie the flaps so that the box can be set upright on them. Pierce the carton, 6 inches below the other end, with metal coat hangers or skewers to form a level grillwork.

Add a little brown sugar to a brine solution so salty as to float a potato. Steep any fish of solid meat in this solution for a minimum of four hours, overnight being preferable.

Take out the fish, pat it with paper towels, and let dry completely in the air. When dry, it will exhibit a slight glaze.

Build a small charcoal fire. When the coals become white, add hardwood chips. Hickory or apple impart a distinctive flavor.

Lay the brined fish on the grill. Set the box on its flap legs over the smoldering chips. Close the flaps on top, and weight them shut with a rock. Fish about two inches thick will need to smoke approximately four hours. Less time is required for thinner pieces.

The wood chips should be hindered from flaring up by the lack of oxygen in the closed box. However, if the lower portions of the carton become hot to the touch, sprinkle them with water as a precautionary measure. If the lower edges of the box ignite, quickly dowse them with water.

FIRE RACK

To keep frying pans and coffee pots from tipping over into your campfire, make a fire rack from hinges. You will need a stove bolt and three 8-inch strap hinges.

Lay one segment of the three hinges on top of one another, and line up their middle holes. Put a stove bolt through them. Now you have the top of your fire rack; the remaining hinge segments will act as legs. When the rack is not in use, it can be conveniently folded for storage or for carrying in a pocket of your camping clothes.

CROW DECOYS

You will need one wire coat hanger for each crow decoy. Straighten the hook with pliers to make the feet for anchoring it in the ground. Bend the rest of the hanger in the outline of a crow. To achieve a realistic shape, compare it as you work with a picture of a crow in profile.

Cut newspaper in strips. Saturate them with a papier-mâché paste of flour and water. Vertically wrap the wire framework with the moist strips. Let dry overnight.

Fasten a wire hook on the bird's back if you plan to hang it in a tree. More papier-mâché may be added on the sides to give the crow a fuller body, if so desired. Finish by applying flat black paint to your decoy.

DECOY WEIGHTS

You can make excellent weights for floating decoys with small expenditure in money and effort. Purchase premixed concrete at a hardware store. Add water according to directions. Fill paper cups with the concrete, and insert spread cotter keys for a string eye. Twelve weights can be made from a 1½-pound bucket of cement.

DUCK RETRIEVER

To make a lightweight duck retriever that can be carried easily in your hunting coat, cut strong cord or a heavy fishing line to a length of 6 feet. At each end tie a loop. In the center of the cord (or fish line), tie another strong string, from 75 to 150 feet long.

Take a small scrap of wood about 2 by 4 inches in size, and wind the string around it. Start with the free end of the longer length, leaving the cord with the loops to be rolled on last. Tuck it in your pocket.

When the duck you have killed lies far out of reach in the water, look for a stick about 4 feet long. Slide a loop of your duck retriever over each end; draw it tight. Throw the stick out beyond the bird. Pull the triangle over your duck, and haul the fowl in to shore. Toss aside the stick. Roll up your string retriever as before, and put it in your hunting coat.

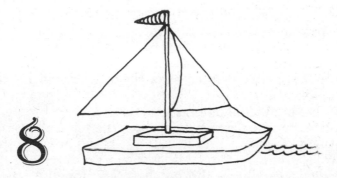

8

PLAYTHINGS

BEAN BAG

In times past, a bean bag was generally found in most every child's collection of toys. It was fun to throw back and forth and could be used for playing games of skill, such as tossing it into a receptacle placed at a distance. A bean bag had the advantage of staying put if it failed to be caught or missed its mark, not rolling out of reach like a ball.

Make your bean bag of some heavy material that will stand up well under hard use. Cut two 6-inch squares. With their right sides facing, sew them strongly together, allowing a seam depth of ½ inch. Leave a few inches open through which to fill your bag with dried navy or pinto beans. Turn it on the right side. If there is any chance that the bag might become wet, first heat the beans in a 200-degree oven for about one hour to keep them from germinating. Do not over-stuff the bag so that it is rigid. It should be somewhat limp and flexible, no more than 1½ inches in thickness. Turn in the raw edges of the gap, and stitch the bean bag closed.

CLOTH BALL

Ransack your rag bag for cloth scraps too small for patch-work. These odds and ends can be used to create a safe toy for babies and toddlers: a cloth ball.

The more variety in the color and texture of the fabrics, the more attractive the plaything. Suedes, sailcloth, and other such sturdy materials are especially suitable for cloth balls, but any fabric will do nicely.

You will need a cardboard pattern in the shape of an equilateral pentagon when cutting the cloth remnants. A size 3 inches across between the farthest points is about right; how-ever, you can alter this measurement to suit yourself. The more you increase the pattern size, the bigger will be the completed ball.

Cut twelve pentagons, allowing an extra ⅜ inch for seams as you scissor about the pattern. Sew down the seam allowance on all five sides of each piece. Iron the stitched areas so that the cloth will lie flat.

Now begin assembling the patches. Sew together three pentagons, which will form the top of the ball. First, put two patches together, and whipstitch their common seam line. After fitting the third piece against them, sew one of its sides to each patch. The three pieces will have formed a sort of dome. Fit the points of three more patches against the triangu-lar edges beneath the dome, and stitch them in place. You have finished the top half of the ball. To make the bottom half, repeat the same steps.

Complete the toy by matching up the jogs in the two halves and sewing the remaining seams. Leave an opening in one to insert stuffing. You can fill the ball with batting or old nylon stockings snipped in pieces. Sew the opening shut with the blind stitch.

Just before closing the last seam, tuck a big jingle bell in the center of the stuffing. It won't ring but will rattle as the toy is rolled or tossed.

DISC TOP

Cut the disc for your top from a 5-inch square of pine wood, 1 inch thick. In the center of the disc, make a hole having a 1-inch diameter. Saw 3 inches from the tip of an old broom handle. Push the flat end into the hole in the disc until it is flush with the wood's surface. Secure it with glue. Use a slender 5-inch-long dowel for the top's stem. Bore a hole in the middle of the flat end of the broom handle nub. Insert the stem, and reinforce it with glue. Into the rounded tip of the broom handle section, hammer a domed tack to facilitate the top's spinning smoothly. Paint the toy a bright color.

Drill a small hole about midway in the stem; run a cord or shoelace through it. Thread the other end of the cord through the width of a short dowel to use as a grip, and knot it on the far side of the hole. Make winding the cord or shoelace about the stem easier by placing the top's tip in a hole cut in a wooden block. After winding the cord around the stem, set the toy on the floor, give the cord a quick pull, and let your top spin.

SOCK DOLL

Use a boy's or man's sock to make a sock doll. Lay it flat, and cut off the upper half of the ankle section. Vertically cut through its double thickness in the center so that you have two folded portions for the arms. Turn the pieces on the wrong side, and sew seams ⅛ inch deep, except on one end. Fill the arms with stuffing through the open ends; then sew them closed.

Vertically cut open the remainder of the ankle section at each side to form the legs. With the heel of the sock at the rear of the body, sew the leg seams on the wrong side, ⅛ inch from the edge. Turn the material right side out again.

Cut off the toe. Through this opening you can stuff the legs, body, and head with cotton. Fill the doll until firm but not stiff. Sew the head closed and stitch on the arms.

To form the neck, tightly tie a piece of string around the doll just below the face area. Shoe buttons make good eyes. For a realistic touch, you might stick on two of the white circles used to reinforce the pages of looseleaf notebooks. Then sew small black shoe buttons in the center of each. Embroider the other features. Use yarn for hair, and dress the sock doll according to whim.

SOCK PUPPET I

To create a sock puppet, select a size of sock appropriate for the hand that will work it. Lay the sock flat, and cut a slit several inches deep for the mouth, starting from the middle of the toe end. (The length of this slit will depend upon how big or small you want the mouth to be.) For the interior of the mouth, cut a piece from felt to fit the opening, crease the fabric in half across its width, and sew it in place.

Complete the puppet with embroidered or button eyes, yarn hair, ears, and clothing. Let imagination be your guide.

Now put your hand in the sock, the thumb below and four fingers in the upper section above the mouth. By opening and closing your hand, the puppet will speak. The resiliency of the material allows you to make your creation smile, look grumpy, or move its head in any direction.

This type of puppet is particularly adaptable to animal characters.

SOCK PUPPET II

Turn the sock inside out. The closely knitted sole is just right for the puppet's face. Roll thin cardboard or heavy paper into a tube with a circumference to fit around the index finger and a length of about 5 inches. Glue or tape it together, and insert it in the foot of the sock. Stuff the part intended for the puppet's head with cotton, using enough to give it a round shape. Let the tube extend from the stuffed portion downward, forming a neck. At the point where you judge the head should end, tightly tie string or thread around the tube.

At appropriate places on each side of the body, cut slits for arm holes. Sew on simple arms shaped like glove fingers.

Embroider or paint on features (use poster paint). Add hair and clothing.

To work the puppet, put hand and arm into the sock leg, using thumb and center finger to manipulate the arms and the index finger in the tube to move the head.

HAND PUPPET

Design a cloth puppet according to the hand dimensions of the person who will use it. Place the hand flat on a piece of

paper with the three middle fingers together and the thumb
and little finger spread at a comfortable distance. Trace around
the hand, including several inches of the arm. Cut along the
outline.

Pin the paper pattern on some heavy cloth (wool, drapery
material, etc.), and cut two sides. With the right sides facing,
sew them together. Hem the edge of the "sleeve." Turn the
puppet back to the right side of the material. It should cover
the hand like a glove, but a glove with three fingers: a large
middle one for the head area, flanked by two smaller ones for
the arms.

You may transform the puppet into any character you
wish, human or animal, by adding yarn hair or ears, embroider-
ing facial features, and dressing it.

Insert your middle fingers in the head to move it, using the
thumb and little finger for arm actions.

TOY PARACHUTE

A square of lightweight scrap material or a man's old
handkerchief can act as the chute. To each corner tie a piece
of string 12 inches long. If you use a square of fabric larger than
handkerchief size, increase the string length proportionately.

Saw several inches off the rounded end of a discarded
broomstick. Line up three metal washers of about the same
circumference as the nub of the broom handle, and run a
screw eye through their centers and into the flat end of the
broomstick tip. Now you have a weight for the parachute.
Attach it by knotting the four strings to the eye of the screw.

MODELING CLAY

To make an excellent modeling clay for children, blend 1
cup of cornstarch with 2 cups of baking soda. Stir in 1½ cups
of cold water, and add food coloring, if desired. Heat the mixture over a medium flame. Stir constantly until it reaches a
doughlike consistency. Cool the clay, and cover it with a moist
cloth until ready for use.

Finished pieces can be preserved by coating them with
shellac.

WOODEN BLOCK PUZZLE

Cut cubes of white pine wood, 1½ by 1½ inches. Select six paper pictures, and cut precisely around each. Next, brush three sides of the cubes with several coats of lacquer. When the sides are dry, repeat the procedure with the remaining three sides.

The cubes, having six faces, will form six different puzzles when correctly assembled. Using wooden blocks to construct picture puzzles originated long ago in Germany.

RUBBER-BAND BOAT

Cut a piece of wood 8¼ inches long, 2⅝ inches wide, and 1 inch thick for the hull of your boat. Shape the front in a tapered curve for the bow. Cut out a rectangle at the stern, 2 inches deep and 1⅞ inches across, to accommodate the paddle wheel. Cut notches ⅛ inch deep on the outer edge of the resulting projections, ½ inch in from their ends, to hold a rubber band. Make the four-blade paddle wheel of two lap-joined pieces of thin board, fitted together as in egg-carton construction. Reinforce the joining with waterproof glue. If you like, you may make a cabin of a block of wood 3½ inches by 1¾ inches by 1 inch, fastening it in place with waterproof glue. Fit the rubber band into the notches in the stern. You may need to test different sizes of rubber bands to find a suitable one. Place the paddle wheel on the rubber band and wind.

SIMPLE SAILBOAT

Cut a hull about 8 inches long and 2½ inches wide from a sheet of cork. Taper the front of the boat to shape its bow. Sharpen a straight twig somewhat, and drive it into the cork for a mast. Make a sail from paper or thin cardboard. A hole at the bottom and top of the sail will allow you to slip it on the twig mast. If a strong gale is up, the owner of the craft may request that a small hole be punched in the stern for attaching a long string to keep his sailboat from being carried out of sight.

DIAMOND-SHAPED KITE

A diamond-shaped kite is the easiest of all kites to make. Essential materials are these:

* one straight strip of wood for the vertical piece, 3/16 by 3/8 by 36 inches in length
* one straight strip of wood for the cross piece, 3/16 by 3/8 by 30 inches in length
* tissue paper or lightweight cloth for the covering material, 30 by 36 inches
* whipcord string
* white glue

At the ends of both sticks, make a 1/4-inch deep cut with a saw. Center the cross strip perpendicularly on the vertical strip at a point 9 inches from one end. Bind the strips together using string. Glue the binding. Run a string around the edges of this framework through the slits at the ends of the strips, and tie it. Place the framework on top of the covering material, and cut it 1 inch larger than the kite's framework. Fold the extra 1 inch over the taut string. In the case of tissue paper, glue it down; if cloth is used, sew it. Bow the cross piece to a depth of 4 inches, with the convex curve away from the covering. Keep it in this bowed position by tying a piece of string from one end to the other. Fasten the bridle string to the vertical strip at the kite's top. Then punch a small hole in the paper 10 inches from the bottom, and again tie the string to the vertical piece. Flying conditions will dictate at what point to attach the main string to the bridle.

When the wind is blowing at 12 miles an hour or more, test your kite. If the kite has a tendency to dive downward, add a tail string with rags tied to it at intervals.

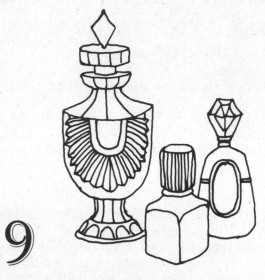

9

SCENTS, SALTS, AND SUCH

HAIR CARE
Shampoos and After-Shampoo Rinse
Old-time Shampoo
Prepare a shampoo by dissolving 1 ounce of salts of tartar in 2½ cups of soft water. To this add 4 ounces of bay rum and 1 ounce of castile soap shavings. The salts of tartar will remove dandruff; the bay rum will cut oil and act as a preservative for the shampoo; and the soap will cleanse scalp and hair.

Rosemary-Lavender Shampoo

1 cup rosemary leaves   *⅛ ounce Castile soap*
½ ounce lavender oil

Sprinkle 1 cup rosemary leaves into a vessel holding 4 cups of water; simmer for fifteen minutes. Strain the contents, returning the liquid to the vessel. Put in the soap; heat until dissolved. Take the pot from the stove, and add the lavender oil, beating it in until well blended. Bottle for use.

Natural Shampoo

Churn the following ingredients in a blender:

1 ounce olive oil	½ teaspoon apple cider
1 egg	vinegar
1 tablespoon lemon juice	

Wash your hair with this natural shampoo. Rinse.

After-Shampoo Rinse

Steep 2 teaspoons of dried nettles in boiling water. When the solution is lukewarm, strain it for use as the final rinse after shampooing your hair.

Natural Hair Dyes and Hair Spray

Blond

To lighten blond hair that has begun to darken, prepare a safe vegetable rinse. Put ½ cup of chopped rhubarb roots into 3 cups of water. Leave the saucepan uncovered, and simmer its contents for thirty minutes. Steep overnight; then strain the liquid.

Towel dry the freshly shampooed hair. Pour the plant bleach through it several times, and squeeze out the excess liquid. Drying your hair in the sun will heighten its color.

Light Brown

If gray or white hair doesn't become you, mix the following formula to achieve a light-brown color: In separate saucepans, boil onionskins and black walnut skins in enough water to cover them. Combine the resulting juices, using ¼ onion-skin juice to ¾ walnut-skin juice. When a deeper shade of brown is desired, use more walnut juice; for a redder color, add more onion juice.

An old-time treatment for coloring gray hair light shades of brown is tag alder bark. It can be purchased from botannical supply houses. Simmer 2 ounces of the chips in 1 quart of water for sixty minutes. When the liquid cools, strain it.

Use the whole quart to shampoo and rinse your hair. Usually, you will need to apply the coloring once a week for a few weeks before desired results are apparent.

Dark Brown

Gather black walnuts during the summer while the hulls are still soft and green. Pry the hulls from the nuts, and press their juice into a jar. Wear rubber gloves to prevent staining your hands. If a walnut tree doesn't grow close by, the hulls can be purchased at health food stores or herbalist shops.

Stir in a small amount of powdered cloves and a little purified alcohol. Close the jar, and let the mixture steep for a week. Occasionally shake it.

At the end of a week, pour the jar's contents through porous cloth to filter out any solid particles. Bottle the dye, and add a bit of salt as a preservative. Store it in a cool place.

Wear rubber gloves to avoid staining hands and scalp. Apply this harmless dye to the hair only.

Black

Blend the juice of green walnut hulls with neat's-foot oil. Add one part of oil to four parts of juice. For very oily hair, reduce the amount of oil a bit; for exceptionally dry hair, add a little more oil.

Natural Hair Spray

Chop a whole lemon. Put the pieces in a saucepan and cover them with hot water. Boil the mixture until the liquid is reduced to one half. Let it cool; then squeeze the lemon and liquid through cheesecloth. If the resulting lemon solution is too thick, mix in a little water. Preserve the hair spray by adding lavender water or cologne. You may prefer to prepare a smaller amount at one time, using half a lemon, and to eliminate the need for a preservative by storing the grooming aid in the refrigerator.

To use, lightly spray it on your hair from a pump-valve bottle.

SKIN CARE
Skin Lotions and Paste

Almond Milk

Shell enough sweet almonds to amount to an ounce. Put them in a strainer, and dip it first in boiling water, then in cold to blanch the nuts. Slip off their skins.

After drying the almonds, reduce them to a powder with mortar and pestle. (A bowl and old china doorknob can substitute for the mortar and pestle.) To achieve speedier results, first grind the nuts in your blender at its highest speed. Then pour the resultant coarse powder into your mortar to further refine the powder, or you can pour it on a piece of clean muslin, producing the desired fine powder with a rolling pin.

Return the powder to a bowl or mortar, and blend in, several drops at a time, 1 cup of distilled water. Grind the almond powder until a milky, smooth liquid forms. Strain it through cheesecloth to eliminate any coarse particles. Bottle for use.

Almond milk has been used for generations to smooth and protect the complexion.

Almond Complexion Paste

Crush 4 ounces of bleached sweet almonds with a rolling pin. Then pulverize them in a marble or earthenware mortar. Almonds may more easily be reduced to paste in a mortar by moistening them with rose water before grinding with a pestle. Or the almonds may be heated in a saucepan of water until they become a granular mass, similar to cooked oatmeal.

Now add one egg white and equal portions of alcohol and rose water to make a smooth paste.

Sweet almonds contain about 50% almond oil. The oil is a gentle emollient that softens and feeds the skin.

Cucumber Milk

Finely mince one cucumber. Cover it with ⅓ cup of boiling water in a saucepan. Put on the lid, and simmer the contents for thirty minutes, using minimal heat.

Strain the mixture into a bowl, and add tincture of benzoin in drops until the liquid takes on a milky appearance. Add ⅓ cup of boiling water. Put the lotion in a small jar. Close it securely, and shake the contents to blend them thoroughly.

Cucumber milk provides a cooling, soothing lotion for various skin conditions.

Honey-Whey Lotion

Beat ½ teaspoon of rose water into 1 teaspoon of whey. Continue beating until the whey dissolves into the rose water. Stir in 1 teaspoon of honey. Thoroughly blend the mixture.

Apply this soothing facial lotion to troubled skin, leaving it on for ½ hour. Then wash it off with tepid water followed by a cold rinse.

Watercress Lotion

Wash a handful of cress. Simmer it for ten minutes in 2 cups of water. Strain the solution into a bottle.

To smoothen rough skin, bathe the face with this soothing lotion. Allow it to dry; rinse with warm water followed by cool.

Lettuce Lotion

Remove the deep green outer leaves from a head of any type of lettuce but the iceberg variety. Wash them well. Put the leaves in a saucepan (do not use an aluminum one). Pour in enough boiling water to cover them. Then put on the lid, and let the contents simmer for about forty minutes.

Beat the leaves in the water, and strain the liquid into a jar. Add several drops of tincture of benzoin. After the addition of each drop, beat the liquid to blend it thoroughly. The lotion will now have a milky appearance.

Apply this cooling facial lotion to help your skin retain moisture.

Sesame Milk

Ladies of an earlier era found that sesame seed milk, applied externally, could soften, nourish, and cleanse their skin. Today, used as a substitute for commercial suntan oil, it can also help to protect the skin from burning or too rapid tanning.

Make this skin aid by grinding one handful of sesame seeds in your blender. Add sufficient water to cover them, and blend for about sixty seconds. Strain the resulting milk into an appropriate container.

Use it to revitalize your complexion or for overall body care. When you wish to remove the milk, rinse your skin with warm water, followed by cool. Blot dry.

Since a little of the sesame seed milk goes a long way, it is not an extravagance. Keep it in the refrigerator.

Sunburn Remedy and Suntan Lotion

Sunburn Remedy

Whip one egg white; then beat in 1 teaspoon of castor oil until the mixture is well blended.

Apply it to sunburned areas on face and body.

Suntan Lotion

Beat one egg yolk until it becomes lemon-colored. Gradually beat in 8 ounces of vegetable oil. Whip until thick. Add 1 tablespoon of vinegar and 1 tablespoon of wheat germ. Thoroughly beat the mixture.

Apply the preparation to all skin areas that will be exposed to sunshine. This speeds the tanning process, reducing the time necessary to acquire a tan and thus limiting exposure to ultraviolet rays.

MOUTH CARE
Preparation for Chapped Lips
Melt 1 ounce of spermeceti and 2 ounces of beeswax in a glass double boiler (a glass bowl set in a saucepan of hot water will also do). Keep the heat very low. Add ¼ cup of honey, and blend it in well. Slowly pour in ½ cup of sweet almond oil.

Take the upper part of the double boiler from the stove, and stir the contents until cool. Before the mixture solidifies, pour it into a small, shallow jar and put on the lid.

Use this preparation as a remedy for chapped lips.

Toothpowders and Paste
Charcoal-Sage Tooth Powder
Scrape the charcoal from burnt toast, and crush it to fine powder. Reduce an equal amount of dried sage leaves to a powder. Blend both ingredients well.

Dip a moistened toothbrush in the mixture to clean teeth.

Soda-Salt Tooth Powder
Make an effective tooth powder by mixing well baking soda and salt, in a proportion of three parts to one. If you prefer flavored tooth powder, add several drops of wintergreen or peppermint oil. Keep the compound in a small-mouthed container.

Toothpaste
To make toothpaste, add 3 teaspoons of glycerin and about 15 drops of some flavoring (cinnamon, peppermint, wintergreen, etc.) to each 4 ounces of homemade tooth powder. Blend the ingredients thoroughly in a bowl, and then add only enough water to turn the mixture into paste form. Spoon the toothpaste into a plastic squeeze bottle for use.

BATH ENHANCERS
Old-fashioned Beauty Bath

1 pound barley	½ pound bay leaves
1 pound bran	½ pound dried lavender
1 pound oatmeal	flowers
1 pound brown rice	

Boil all of these ingredients in 4 quarts of rainwater for sixty minutes. Then strain the mixture.

Use 2 quarts of the liquid for each tub of bath water. An extra rinse after this herbal bath is unnecessary and would deprive you of some of its benefits. Follow it with a vigorous towel drying.

Bubble Bath

Make effervescent salts for your bath by mixing well these materials: 4 tablespoons of cornstarch, 15 tablespoons of cream of tartar, and 18 tablespoons of bicarbonate of soda. You may want to add several drops of water-soluble perfume.

About 2 tablespoons of the mixture will give you a tub full of bubbles. Store it in a tightly closed glass or metal container.

Bath Vinegars

Put 1 cup of some fragrant plant material—lavender flowers, rose petals, violet leaves and blossoms, etc.—or a combination of your choice in a 1-pint jar. Heat 8 ounces of white vinegar until it just begins to boil. Pour it into the jar and put on the lid. Then let it stand for two weeks, shaking it several times each day. After two weeks, strain the contents and bottle in attractive containers.

For a spicy bath vinegar, try blending ½ cup of lavender, ½ cup of dried rosemary, a pinch of sage, and 3 teaspoons of bruised, whole cloves.

One cup of perfumed bath vinegar will scent your bath water and leave your body clean, refreshed, and free of soap film.

Afterbath Powder

You will need a shoe box, 2 ounces of orrisroot powder, and a 1-pound box of cornstarch. Mix the orrisroot and cornstarch. Line the box with aluminum foil. Put in the powdered mixture, and directly over it lay a section of cheesecloth somewhat bigger than the bottom of the box.

Collect fragrant, fresh materials: bark, blossoms, flower petals, leaves, roots, seeds, and stems. Shake them lightly to remove any moisture, and place them right on the piece of cheesecloth. Cover the box snugly. Every two or three days, examine the plants for mold. If any are so affected, discard them. Whenever you find new petals or other aromatic materials, put them in the mix. Continue adding to the box in this way, occasionally stirring its contents. The orrisroot will absorb and hold the combined fragrances.

When a pleasing scent is achieved, take out the plant material. Allow the powder to dry if it has soaked up any moisture. Then package it in attractive containers, and close them tightly.

HAND CARE

Fingernail Paste

1 ½ ounces spermaceti	12 ounces oil of sweet
¼ ounce white wax	almond
2 ounces alkanet root	½ teaspoon rose oil
(powdered)	

Melt the spermaceti and the wax in the top portion of a double boiler. Mix in the alkanet root and almond oil. Beat the ingredients until well blended. As the mixture is cooling, stir in the rose oil.

For best results, buff clean, unpolished nails with an old-fashioned chamois buffer before applying the rose paste. Then rub in the paste, and gently buff again to develop a rosy sheen. Daily treatment will increase the health, luster, and beauty of your nails.

Hand Paste

An easily prepared paste to soften hands requires these ingredients:

2 egg yolks	2 ounces blanched almond
¼ pound honey	meal
¼ pound sweet almond	
oil	

Beat together the egg yolks and honey until a smooth paste is formed. As you continue to beat the mixture, gradually add the sweet almond oil. Then slowly mix in the almond meal. Store the unused portion in the refrigerator.

Hand Lotion

Warm 4 ounces of honey in a double boiler. Thoroughly blend in 8 ounces of lanolin. Take the pot from the stove, and allow the contents to cool somewhat. Then beat in 4 ounces of sweet almond oil.

Bottle the preparation, and use it for good hand care.

SCENTS AND SALTS

Toilet Water

Long ago the famous mineral baths of Budapest found favor with the Queen of Hungary. The Queen herself was renowned for a perfumed toilet water she had concocted for use after bathing. This preparation, known as Hungary Water, has been passed down from mothers to daughters for generations.

To prepare old-fashioned Hungary Water, put 1 dram (¹⁄₁₆ ounce) of essence of ambergris and ½ ounce of oil of rosemary into a pint jar. Add 2 cups of deodorized 95% alcohol. Close the jar tightly and shake thoroughly. Open it and allow to stand for twenty-four hours. Again close the jar tightly and let stand for six weeks, shaking it every five days. Transfer the contents to a suitable tightly stoppered bottle for use.

Solid Perfume

Melt 2 ounces of beeswax chips in the top of a double boiler. Using a wire whisk, slowly blend in ¼ cup of sweet almond oil. As you continue stirring, add 2 tablespoons of distilled water. Take the pot from the stove. Add 8 dropperfuls of your favorite cologne, and blend thoroughly with the whisk.

Pour the mixture, while still warm, into 4-ounce pimento jars or other suitable small containers that can be closed tightly. You may divide this recipe in half, perfuming each portion with a different scent.

Pomanders

Scent your linen and clothes closets with pomanders. To make them you will need large, well-shaped oranges, a few boxes of whole cloves, ground cinnamon, a roll of ¼-inch-wide cellophane tape, colored ribbon, a nutpick, and some silver foil.

Let the fruit dry for several weeks. Then fasten a strip of cellophane tape around the center of each orange. With the nutpick, pierce holes in the skin about ¼ inch apart, avoiding the tape. (Since the oranges will shrink more as they continue to dry, a small space should remain between each hole.) Push a clove into each hole. Now dust the oranges lightly with powdered cinnamon. You may use ground allspice or orrisroot for dusting, if you prefer. Wrap them in silver foil, and store them in a dry spot for about seven weeks.

Take the pomanders from the foil, remove the tape, and substitute a length of bright ribbon, tied in a bow, for hanging them in your closets.

Spiced Potpourri

Mix ½ ounce of each of the following in a bowl: allspice, borax, ground cinnamon, whole cloves, ground nutmeg, and ground orrisroot. Blend a cupful of lemon, orange, or tangerine peel with the spices.

Put the spicy mixture into an open china jar, or one with holes in its lid to allow the scent to escape.

Rose Potpourri

On a fair morning, collect unblemished rose petals. Spread them in single layers on paper in a dry, cool spot. Turn them daily for about two weeks until dry.

Put some of the petals in a glass jar to a depth of two inches, covering them lightly with salt. Continue to alternate layers of petals and salt until the jar is full. Close it tightly. Put it in a dark, cool spot for seven days.

Blend these ingredients: ½ teaspoon of ground cinnamon, ½ teaspoon of ground cloves, ½ teaspoon of ground mace, 1 ounce of orrisroot, 10 drops of oil of bergamot, 20 drops of oil of eucalyptus, and 6 drops of oil of geranium. Mix the petals thoroughly into this blend, and put the mixture back into the jar, closing the lid tightly. After a period of two weeks, the potpourri is ready for use.

Smelling Salts

To make smelling salts, put 8 ounces of true carbonate of ammonia (a volatile salt of lasting pungency) and 1 ounce of oil of lavender (or any other essential oil) in a glass bottle. Close the bottle tightly.

10

SPICK-AND-SPAN

CLEANING AIDS

Homemade Lye

Here is how to make lye the old-fashioned way. Save fireplace ashes from hickory or oak logs. Find a fallen hardwood tree trunk, and burn it out hollow. Put in the ashes, and set it over an inclined wooden trough, with a bucket at its lower end. Due to the corrosive effect of lye, the bucket should be of enamel, pottery, or iron. Pour a considerable amount of water on the ashes. It will filter through them, run down the trough, and drip into the bucket as a lye solution.

Soap (yield: 9 pounds)

The making of soap is thought to have developed accidentally through early Roman sacrifices. After animals were burned to appease a god or win divine favor, ashes and a little fat remained. Rain added the final ingredient that produced suds.

Homemade soap is very inexpensive and will efficiently whiten your laundry. Here are the requirements:
* 6 pounds grease (drippings or drippings mixed with half suet for a whiter soap)

* 1 can lye (13 ounces)
* 5 cups cold water

Whenever you trim meat, save the fat. Keep bacon fat, beef fat, or pork fat in the refrigerator. After several cupfuls have accumulated, cook it slowly, rendering out the liquid fat. Strain the grease through cheesecloth. You will need 6 pounds of drippings to make a good batch of white soap.

If you failed to strain the drippings after rendering the fat, prepare the grease the day before making soap. Melt each 3 pounds of grease in 2 quarts of water. While it is heating, stir. Allow it to cool. The following day, remove the cold grease from the surface of the water. The salt and cracklings should remain at the bottom of the vessel.

Put a large stainless steel pan or glass jar in the sink. Fill it with 5 cups of water. Wearing rubber gloves (remember that lye is caustic), carefully and slowly stir in 1 can of lye with a steel or wooden spoon. Reheat the grease, and cool it until tepid (130° F.). Stir it into the lye and water. Continue stirring for twenty minutes, when the soap should have the consistency of honey. Pour it into a granite or heavy metal pan. Allow to set overnight.

The next day, cut the soap into large practical bars or small, personal-sized cakes. However, do not remove them from the pan for several more days. After that, let them season from six weeks to two months.

One-quart milk cartons provide good soap forms. After fourteen to eighteen hours, cut away the cardboard and slice the blocks. Allow the soap to dry further.

You may shave and melt down larger bars for such household tasks as washing woodwork.

If you like, scent the personal-sized soap by adding a few drops of any essential oils before it becomes cool enough to set. Should perfume be added while the soap is too hot, it will escape with the steam; if the soap is too cold, the fragrance cannot be easily incorporated. Try almond oil, attar of roses, lemon, wintergreen, or whatever you prefer. Another method is to wait until the soap hardens, run it through a meat grinder, and melt it in a double boiler with orange-flower water, rose water, or various other scented waters and common salt. Use 1 pint of scented water and 2 ounces of salt to each 6 pounds of soap. After boiling it, let the mixture cool. Cut it into small cakes with a wire, and dry them away from direct sunlight. Allow to season.

A small bottle of inexpensive hand lotion can be added to

hand or bath soap as both emollient and perfume. To make floating bath soap, fold in air (as you would eggs into batter) when the mixture thickens.

Glycerin soap can be made by adding 6 ounces of glycerin to the soap mixture after pouring in the lye solution. This is a good complexion soap.

For saddle soap, use 1 can of lye, 2¾ pints of water, and 6 pounds of tallow. It is excellent for cleaning and preserving leather.

To make tar soap, prepare tallow soap and let it stand, stirring now and then until thickening occurs. Then work in 8 ounces of wood tar. Stir the mixture thoroughly to prevent lumps. Use the soap for shampooing hair.

Water Softener

Thoroughly mix 4 cups of soda ash (found in hardware stores) with 8 cups of waterglass (sodium silicate, available in drugstores). Store the mixture in glass containers.

To soften 5 gallons of water, stir in approximately ½ teaspoon of the concentrate. This ratio is a general recommendation and subject to adjustment according to the water hardness in your particular locale.

Bluing

In 1 quart of soft water, dissolve 1 ounce of Prussian blue powder and ½ ounce of powdered oxalic acid to make a good bluing. It should be added to the last rinse water.

Cleaners for Carpets, Tile, Copper, Glass, and Leather

* CARPET CLEANER: Blend equal amounts of salt and baking soda. Add several drops of white vinegar to each 8 ounces of the dry mixture. Stir in sufficient water to form a paste.

Spread the paste on the soiled area, and let it dry completely. Then brush away the powdery cleanser along with the dirt. In the case of stubborn stains, gently scrub the rug when the cleanser is first applied.

* CERAMIC TILE CLEANER: An inexpensive cleaner for ceramic tile can be made by dissolving 1 tablespoon of trisodium phosphate (found in hardware stores) in ½ gallon of water. Store in a glass container.

To use, moisten a sponge with the cleaner. Always wear rubber gloves when preparing or applying the solution.

* *COPPER CLEANER:* Combine vinegar and salt. Apply the mixture to copper surfaces with a rag, and rub clean.

* *GLASS CLEANERS:* Mix a handful of cornstarch in a pail of lukewarm water. Wash windows and mirrors with the solution, and wipe them dry. They will be clean and shiny.

Or mix 1 cup of isopropyl alcohol in 2 cups of water. Add 5 drops of lactic acid (found in paint and hardware stores). Transfer the mixture to a spray bottle for cleaning glass and windows.

Another excellent window cleaner is made by stirring 2 tablespoons of ethylene glycol into 3 cups of water. (Ethylene glycol can be bought at service stations.) Put the solution in a spray bottle for use.

* *LEATHER CLEANER:* To maintain leather articles in a clean, supple condition, combine these ingredients: ¾ cup of isopropyl alcohol, ½ cup of white vinegar, and 1½ cups of water. Stir to blend. Keep the cleaner in a glass container. Rub it on leather with a damp sponge or cloth.

Air Deodorants

Air Deodorant Spray

Mix 4 teaspoons of baking soda in 4 cups of water. Fill a convenient-sized spray bottle. To dissipate offensive odors, spray the solution in a fine mist.

Herbal Deodorant Vinegar

Fill a 1-pint jar with an aromatic material (flower blossoms, leaves, dried herbs, etc.). Heat 2 cups of white vinegar. When it reaches the boiling point, add it to the jar. Put on the lid, and allow the mixture to stand for several weeks, shaking it daily.

After two weeks, check the scent. If it is satisfactory, strain the jar's contents into a decorative container. Set it wherever odors are a problem.

REFURBISHING AIDS

Creamy Furniture Polish

Grate 2½ ounces of beeswax into a tin can. Melt the wax by placing the can in a pan of preheated water. Blend 1 cup of turpentine with the melted wax. Using a separate vessel, dissolve 2 tablespoons of powdered rosin and 1 ounce of Castile soap in 2 cups of water. Add this to the turpentine mixture. Store the creamy polish in a glass jar.

For use, rub a little at a time on furniture and polish with a dry, soft cloth.

Lemon Oil Furniture Polish

In 1 quart of mineral oil, mix 1 tablespoon of lemon oil (available at drugstores). Use a spray bottle to apply the polish. Wipe clean.

Rust Preventive

Combine raw linseed oil and about 30% turpentine. Coat steel tools—spades, chisels, etc.—with the mixture. It will dry quickly, forming a longlasting, waterproof finish. When the coating eventually wears off, smear on another. Make sure that the steel is completely dry before applying the mixture, which should never be used on wood.

Whitewash

In 3 gallons of water, soak 25 pounds of slaked lime until a paste forms. You will have roughly 4 gallons of lime paste.

Dissolve 3 pounds of salt in 1½ gallons of boiling water. Allow the solution to cool. Then add it to the lime paste, and stir in 1½ pounds of white Portland cement.

Apply the whitewash to a slightly damp wall for best results.

Another good whitewash can be made by adding ½ pound of salt, dissolved in 3 gallons water, and 1 pound of sulphate of zinc to 8 quarts of slaked lime. This combination produces a firm, hard wash that will not crack. The salt makes the whitewash stick better. For a clearer white, add a little bluing.

PEST AND FIRE CONTROL

Ant Remedy

Save cucumber peelings and mix them with salt. Place the mixture wherever ants are a problem.

Flypaper

Mix equal amounts of castor oil and melted resin. Spread the gooey mixture on nonporous paper (for example, magazine and catalog covers) with a warm knife. Leave the edges clear so that you can fasten the paper down wherever flies are a nuisance.

Fly Remedy

To keep flies out of the house, mix equal amounts of bay leaf pieces, coarsely ground cloves, broken eucalyptus leaves, and clover blossoms.

Put this blend in small bags of mesh or some loosely woven material. Hang them just inside entrance doors to repel flies.

Roach Control

Place shallow pans or fruit jar lids containing powdered borax in dark corners of the house, especially around the kitchen sink and cabinets. Replace with fresh borax once a week. Do not allow any food waste or pet food to accumulate in infested areas.

Mice Control

Mix corn meal and cement, half-and-half. Place in shallow containers where mice run.

Fire-Extinguishing Powder

Make a low-cost, effective fire-extinguishing powder by combining 6 pounds of fine silica mason sand (available from a dealer in building supplies) and 2 pounds of sodium bicarbonate (available at grocery stores). Mix them thoroughly, and keep the powder in 1-pound glass or metal containers. Locate them in strategic places.

When extinguishing flames, scatter the mixture on the base of the fire.

ADHESIVES

Ordinary paste is made by mixing rice flour or wheat flour in water, with or without boiling. To improve it, various adhesives, such as glue, gum arabic, and rosin, may be added along with alum.

Simple Flour Paste

Make simple cold flour paste by mixing 1 tablespoon of flour with 1 cup of cold water. Add several drops of carbolic acid as a preservative.

Library Paste

Dissolve ½ ounce of alum in 2 cups of warm water. Stir in flour until the consistency of cream is reached. Break up all lumps. Add a few drops of oil of cloves and 1 teaspoon of powdered resin. Boil until thick. If the mixture becomes too thick, thin it with a small amount of hot water. Put it in a glass jar and close it tightly. Keep it in a cool place. When necessary, soften the paste with several drops of warm water, and melt it over very low heat.

Gum Arabic Paste

Dissolve 2 ounces of gum arabic in 2 cups of water in the top of a double boiler. Combine ½ ounce of white sugar and ½ ounce of laundry starch. Stir the mixture into a little cold water until it reaches the consistency of thick paste, free of lumps. Add this to the contents of the double boiler and boil until the starch is clear. Put in several whole cloves or a few drops of any essential oils, such as oil of cloves, lavender, etc., for a preservative. A little alcohol will also serve as a preservative.

Isinglass Glue

Isinglass—not to be confused with mica, which is often so named—is an animal tissue mainly derived from the air bladders of some fish. It dissolves easily in water and is a strong adhesive.

Dissolve 1 pound of isinglass in 2 cups of soft water in a double boiler. Slowly add ¼ cup of nitric acid, and stir continuously. Bottle the liquid glue and close tightly to prevent evaporation. It is excellent for paper, leather, wood, and many other materials.

11

ONE THING AND ANOTHER

BLACKBOARD

You can make a large blackboard in no time from a sheet of hardboard, which is a thin sheet composed of pressed fibers, one side being hard and glossy brown. One 4 by 8 feet would be a good size. Coat it with blackboard paint. When the paint is dry, nail up your homemade blackboard.

CORNCOB PIPE

Self-sufficient old-timers seldom spent money for things they could produce themselves. The corncob pipe is an example of such thrift.

To try your hand at making one, select a firm ear of corn having sufficient pith to be properly hollowed out. You will need to break several ears and examine their cross section. In addition, choose one with ends that fit comfortably in your hand. When you have found the right cob, dry it.

Now decide which of the ends better suits your hand.

Some people prefer the pointed end. Snap off an appropriate length for the size of bowl you favor. A bowl of 1¾ to 2 inches should be satisfactory. You may trim the break evenly, but this step is not essential.

Using the bigger blade of your pocketknife, dig out the pith to an approximate depth of 2 inches. The next layer will be woody and hard. Because it will give strength to your pipe, be careful not to remove too much of it. The completed hole should have a diameter of ½ to ¾ inch, depending on the cob's size.

Whether or not you believe the claim that a thicker bowl means a cooler smoking pipe, don't shave its outside walls. You'll like the rustic appearance and cushiony feel.

The pipestem can be made from the cornstalk by cutting the most slender part that's close to the top of the plant. An elder twig makes a good pipestem, too. Either can be hollowed out with a hot coat-hanger wire. After piercing the stems, below through them to force out any loose debris. A section of wild rice stalk, being naturally hollow, can provide a convenient stem. Cut the mouthpiece end directly above a joint in the reed. This strong area can be gripped between the teeth without concern about splitting the pipestem. Cut the opposite end directly above a joint in the stalk. The solid joint at the mouthpiece end is the only place you will need to ream out. Prepare the bowl end of the stem by cutting a flat slice, roughly ⅓ inch in length, from one side, forming a U-shaped opening.

Make a hole in the wall of the bowl just above the bottom of the hollowed-out area. This job can best be done with a twist drill having a diameter slightly smaller than that of the prepared pipestem. Maintain the bit at a right angle to the pipe bowl; bore a full twist in one direction followed by a half twist the opposite way. Work cautiously to keep the opening from becoming too large for the stem. After you have drilled clean through the bowl wall, insert the stem with the U-shaped opening uppermost. Firmly press in the pipestem for a snug fit.

Be patient with your pipe for the first few smokes. Any pith remaining in the bowl will have to burn away, and the woody part will need to season a little. Then, too, it's always difficult to keep a new pipe lit. After two or three smokes, however, you should be able to settle back and puff with satisfaction on your homemade corncob pipe.

CRYSTAL GARDEN

If the weather is too cold for outdoor gardening, make a garden indoors—of crystals.

A beautiful crystal garden can be created inexpensively and easily in any glass container, such as a jar or glass bowl. In addition, you will need enough coarse sand to layer the bottom of your container; some water glass, which is a stony powder that forms a colorless, syrupy liquid when dissolved in water (in times past, housewives preserved eggs by coating them with it); and packages of different crystals. The most satisfactory crystals to use are cadmium nitrate, cobalt nitrate, epsom salts, ferrous sulphate, manganese sulphate, and zinc sulphate. The water glass and crystals can be bought at most drugstores or hobby shops.

Before starting your crystal garden, place the container in its intended location; otherwise, the delicate growths might be damaged in moving. Layer the floor of the container with coarse sand, which can be obtained from a building supply company or from the beach. From Plasticine, available at craft shops, create miniature trees and shrubs, garden seats, and birds, positioning them in the sandy bottom. You might add a few small shells and pebbles. If you want the crystals to grow in specific areas only, put them in place now. For a beautiful effect, try slightly embedding some (not too deeply or they will not grow) in the branches of the Plasticine shrubs and trees.

Mix the water glass by dissolving 3 tablespoons of it in 2 cups of hot water. Prepare sufficient solution to fill the container. Pour it slowly into the glass receptacle until full. The crystals will immediately begin growing.

If you prefer a wild, unplanned garden, pour in the water glass and then drop in enough crystals to cover the bottom of the container.

The crystals will develop into beautiful plantlike forms within about ten minutes.

A crystal garden can also be made with some common household items, but it will require considerably more patience than the first one described.

Assemble these materials: ammonia, liquid bluing, food coloring, table salt (not iodized), water, a 6-inch container, and several lumps of soft coal or a brick.

Wrap the coal or brick in a rag, and pound it with a hammer into chunks about the size of a walnut. Arrange the pieces in the middle of the container.

Mix the following ingredients in the order in which they are mentioned: 4 tablespoons of salt (noniodized), 4 tablespoons of liquid bluing, 4 tablespoons of water, and 1 tablespoon of ammonia. Blend them until the salt liquefies.

Pour the mixture on the chunks of coal or brick. Using an eyedropper, spot the wet pieces with various shades of food coloring.

You will have to wait patiently for several hours before the interesting shapes of your crystal garden begin to sprout.

DRINKING GLASSES

The conversion of tall glass bottles into drinking tumblers requires a small amount of new, standard-weight motor oil, a ⅜-inch steel rod about 12 inches long, pliers, and a source of heat.

Decide at what level you want the bottle to break, and mark the spot. Pour in the oil to within ⅛ inch of that mark to allow for a slight rise in fluid when the rod is introduced. Before cutting the glass, let the liquid settle and be sure that none adheres to the bottle's sides above the intended cleavage line. The colder the container and oil, the more successful the operation. Fill bottles, and set them outdoors on a cool night. Complete the task the following morning.

Gripping the rod with pliers, heat the first 3 or 4 inches of the metal until they are visibly red hot. Immediately immerse it about 2 inches into the oil, keeping it there for at least thirty seconds. In approximately that amount of time, the majority of glass will snap off clean. If the method is unsuccessful, however, it may be that the glass is too thin. In that case, try a thicker-walled container, such as a wine or soda bottle.

Don't touch your newly created drinking tumbler until the oil has cooled. Empty it into a jar to keep for future use. Wash the glass in hot, soapy water. After rinsing and drying it, smooth the cut edges with sandpaper or emery cloth.

Another method for cutting glass containers involves wrapping ordinary cotton cord several times around a bottle at a slightly lower level than the planned severance line. Thoroughly saturate the string with alcohol; light it with a match. After the flame has subsided, pour ice-cold water over the jar or bottle. The glass will separate easily.

GOURD USES

Gourds, with their variety of colors, shapes, and textures, make an attractive table decoration; hollowed out, they become objects for daily use.

If you are raising your own gourds, train the vines on trellises or fences to prevent the fruit from growing lopsided or rotting on the bottom. Discourage bug attacks by sowing a few radish seeds among the plants.

Soft-shelled gourds serve for ornamentation; the more durable thick-shelled gourds are good for utilitarian purposes.

After harvesting, clean them in warm, soapy water containing a household disinfectant. Dry the gourds with a cloth, and spread them on newspaper in a warm, dry place. At the end of a week, wipe them with a cloth moistened only in disinfectant. Again spread the gourds to dry in a warm, dark, damp-free spot for about one month. Every other day, turn them. When seeds rattle about inside them, they are properly seasoned. Some thick-shelled gourds may require as much as a six-month drying period.

Now is the time to varnish or shellac thin-shelled gourds to prevent their fading and decaying. Waxing and polishing them will accentuate their lustrous hues.

Select large thick-shelled gourds for making containers. Using a sharp knife, cut the shell to suit its intended function as bottle, bowl, water dipper, etc. Smooth rough edges with sandpaper or a file. Remove seeds and fiber from the interior.

When creating a bottle, slice a nub from the narrow end of a gourd. In it, wedge a cork long enough to extend into the bottle's neck when stoppered. A bowl can be fashioned quickly from the bottom half of a gourd. You might like to glue on wooden feet. For a dipper, lay the gourd horizontally, and cut a slice from the top side, leaving the neck to serve as a handle.

If you want to attract birds to your yard, with the added advantage of keeping down the mosquito population, convert gourds into birdhouses. The purple martin likes both mosquitoes and a gourd home.

Choose large, round gourds having short necks. If you are growing your own, let them dry right on the vine until January. After picking them, cut a hole 2 inches in diameter on one side. Sand or file the doorway's edges smooth. Clean out the inside. To permit drainage, drill a few small holes in the gourd's bottom. Bore two more on opposite sides of the neck, and run a thong or nylon cord through them.

In February, suspend a number of gourd birdhouses 1 foot apart on wooden cross pieces fastened to a 20-foot pole. Locate the pole in an area no closer to trees or buildings than 15 feet. A teaspoon of sulfur in each residence will discourage mites and insure satisfied tenants.

Gourds can also be used for Christmas tree ornaments, flowerpots, napkin rings, toys—anything that your ingenuity might suggest.

Even the contents of a gourd are useful. They can provide you with a treatment that enhances well-being.

In Europe, dry bathing has long been famous for its favorable effect on one's skin. The bath, involving not water but a friction glove, stimulates blood circulation while removing any dead skin particles. The French claim that the dry bath is a remedy for insomnia.

The textured fabric of a friction glove is such that the slightest massaging movement tones the body. Friction gloves are fabricated from various materials: hemp, horsehair, wool, coarse cotton, plastic. You can produce one of the finest kinds of dry bath gloves in your garden by planting old-fashioned dishcloth gourds. Harvest them when they are ripe, and carefully cut the shell away, revealing the weblike interior. Lay it in the sun for seven days to eliminate all moisture. Once completely dry, the web will be stiff and just a few shakes will rid it of seeds. Your friction glove is now ready for use.

Gently massage your body in an upward movement with the glove. This type of bathing should be indulged in no more than once each week. If you find the dry bath a little too severe, accustom yourself to it gradually by using the glove in your water bath the first few times. Its effect will be softened by the water.

OATMEAL-BOX RADIO

Anyone can build a crystal set with a few simple components: headphones, a crystal, coil, a variable condenser, and a long wire for an antenna. Having no tubes, no transistors, and no amplification, a crystal set has almost no distortion; music and voices are pure in tone.

Cut a rectangle 14 inches long and 12 inches wide from a well-seasoned board to serve as a base for the crystal set.

Use a cylindrical oatmeal or salt box for the coil form. Cut off one end to a depth of 4 inches; immerse it in melted wax.

The wax coating will prevent it from absorbing moisture. The coil consists of about 150 feet of insulated copper wire (of a size ranging between numbers 22 and 28) or enameled wire (AWG number 24). Either fasten on the wire by running it in and out of three pinholes punctured about ¼ inch from one end of the cardboard cylinder, or secure the wire in place with cellophane tape. Wind on 166 turns. Every seventh turn, twist a small loop for a tap until you have a total of eight loops. Then wind forty turns with no taps. After that, make a loop on every tenth turn. Wind the coil tightly so that no space exists between turns. On each tap, scrape away any insulation to insure a good connection with the short wires leading to the switch points. When all the turns have been wound, attach the wire end with cellophane tape or thread it through pinholes in the cardboard. Bring down the various taps, and secure them beneath screws or brass-headed tacks on the baseboard. When the coil assembly is completed and working satisfactorily, you may give it a coat of varnish or paint it with melted candle wax.

Purchase a variable tuning condenser with the standard value of approximately 365 pF (picofarads). Position it on the board.

Headphones should be the high-impedance kind (at least 2000 ohms). Do not use hi-fi headphones.

In the old days the detector was an open crystal of galena (a lead-gray mineral), lightly touched by a delicate wire known as a "cat's whisker." Since such crystals are not easily found today, buy, instead, a germanium diode (for example, 1 N 34), costing about a quarter.

The longer the antenna the better. One about 200 feet long will give the best results. String it between trees or buildings, and bring a lead-in to your set. To be on the safe side, provide a lightning arrester. When the set is not in use, the lead-in wire can be ground to a water pipe.

A satisfactory ground connection is also necessary. Fasten the ground to a water pipe or radiator, making the lead as short as feasible.

The diagram will aid you in assembling the set properly.

Your crystal set uses no power and will cost nothing beyond the original small expense of constructing it.

SAWDUST STOVE

To make a cheap stove that burns either free or low-cost fuel, find a large empty paint can. Remove the top. In the center of the bottom, cut a hole 2 inches in diameter. Place the can on three improvised legs and your stove is finished.

For steady heat over a long period of time without refueling and without smoke, burn sawdust in your stove. Since powdered wood is generally discarded as a waste product, it can often be had for the asking at lumber yards and sawmills. When there is a charge, it is nominal.

Before loading your stove, be sure the sawdust is absolutely dry. To fuel the burner, you have a piece of water pipe or a smooth, round stick of sufficient length protrude above the can's rim when it has been inserted through the hole in the bottom and rests on the floor. After positioning the pipe or stick in the hole, keep it vertical while pouring sawdust around it. Every so often, press the fuel down firmly as you load the can. Make the sawdust as compact as possible. When the stove is just about full, spread a thin layer of ashes or sand over the sawdust. Then, carefully twisting the pipe and pulling upward, remove it from the packed sawdust. There will be a neat hole directly through the mass.

To light your stove, fold a piece of newspaper accordian style and gently push it through the hole until it appears underneath. Ignite the lower end with a match. The burner will need no further attention until all the fuel has been consumed. Because some fumes are given off by the stove, ventilate the room where it is used.

The rate of burning is approximately 1½ to 2 inches an hour. A sawdust stove 12 inches in diameter will burn for roughly six hours. The degree of heat generated is controlled by the can's depth. The longer the central hole, the greater the heat. A tall, narrow container will be very hot for a relatively short period of time; a squat, wide container produces gentler heat for longer time; a tall, broad drum burns hot and long. Select a container to meet your requirements.

A sawdust stove is an inexpensive, efficient means of both cooking and heating.

PET FOOD

Save all leftover food—meat, vegetables, etc.—and refrigerate it. When about 2 quarts have accumulated, put the scraps in a pot with enough water to cover them. Bring to a boil. Add 1 envelope of active dry yeast, 2 cups of dry beans (any kind), and 3 cups of oats. Cook the mixture over low heat for two hours. Refrigerate. Freeze the excess in containers.

QUILL PEN

The use of large, stiff, tail or wing feathers as pens was first recorded in the sixth century; however, quills may well have served as writing implements at a more remote time. They continued in use until the early nineteenth century, when steel pens were introduced.

Pens have been most commonly fashioned from goose feathers. Only the five outer wing feathers are utilized, the second and third being considered best; left-wing quills are more prized than those from the right because they curve outward, away from the writer.

Crow, eagle, hawk, owl, turkey, and swan have also contributed quills for writing instruments. A swan quill is ranked superior to that of a goose, and crow quills are favored when a fine line is required.

The choicest quills are obtained from live birds during the spring. To make a pen, clean an appropriate quill until it is free of fat and oil. Thoroughly dry it in a warm spot to induce brittleness. Then, using a keen-edged knife, slit the tip and sharpen it to a point.

CHRISTMAS WREATHS

The sight and scent of fresh Christmas wreaths add to holiday pleasures. Wreaths can be fashioned easily with little expense if you have access to fir trees of some type: balsam, Douglas, grand, red, silver, or white. Consult your local nursery or forester to learn what suitable trees grow in your area's woods.

When you know where trees are available, set out on a bough-collecting trip equipped with garden clippers and a carrier for the branches. Take a long strip of canvas several feet wide and deeply hem its lengths. Run one continuous piece of rope through the resulting tubes, letting it extend beyond both ends of the cloth to serve as handles. Knot the rope ends together, and cut off any excess. (This carrier is also handy for transporting firewood from chopping block to wood-pile and from woodpile to hearth. Use nylon rope. Not only is it strong and rotproof, but its elasticity will cushion the jolt when you lift a load of wood.)

Once you have found a good stand of firs, snip off branch ends to a depth of about 18 inches. Stack them on your canvas carrier. Trimming only the tips of boughs in this way will stimulate thicker, fuller growth; it will not damage the tree.

Transforming the greenery into wreaths will require a spool of thin wire (22–24 gauge) and the heavy wire hoops to which the evergreens are fastened. (Wreath frames range from 8 to 24 inches. You'll find a larger size easier to work with for your first attempt.) Both items can be bought at hardware stores.

Now follow these steps:
* Place a hoop on a flat work surface, and attach an end of the wire to it.
* Break a branch into three roughly equal pieces. Putting their thicker ends together, arrange them in a fan shape.
* Lay the fan horizontally along the hoop, right side up. Holding the twig ends together, bind the wire several times around them and the ring.
* Fashion a second fan.
* Turn the wire frame over. Lay the fan, right side uppermost, approximately 2 inches along the hoop from the first. Tightly attach it with a few turns of wire.
* Continue in this manner, shaping fans and fastening them on alternate sides of the frame. Try to keep all twig bunches the same size. Always attach them right side up and wind the wire tightly.
* Make the last two fans a little shorter than the others. Tuck them beneath the first fan to neatly complete the circle. Wrap them with wire, and tie it off. The knot will be invisible, covered by the twigs of the original fan.
* If your finished wreath is somewhat shaggy, use the clippers to even up the central hole and to trim away any pieces elsewhere that protrude too far.

Your fragrant holiday wreath is ready to hang. You might want to brighten it with a fat red bow.

CHRISTMAS-TREE ORNAMENTS

Use decorative odds and ends and your imagination to create beautiful Christmas ornaments.

Begin with plain silver glass balls. Glue on leftover ribbon scraps of colored grosgrain or velvet and lace ruffles made crisp with spray starch. Apply designs from discarded gift wrapping paper, cutouts from last year's Christmas cards, or appropriate decals. Before gluing paper decorations on the balls, glue them to a backing of thin, flexible cardboard.

Whenever you prepare a recipe calling for eggs, save the shells. Keep them whole by puncturing both ends with an ice pick and forcefully blowing out the contents. After a good number has accumulated, transform the pale shells into bright Christmas tree ornaments.

Lacquer them in brilliant hues or pastel shades. When they are dry, glue on sparkling sequins, small pearls, and colored beads from broken necklaces. Gold or silver cord can be glued on in a spiral pattern or used to outline four ovals of vivid velvet spaced around the shells' circumferences. Decorating possibilities are almost limitless.

Finish each ornament by fastening a bead to one end of a thin wire and running the other end through the bottom hole in the shell and out at the top. Fashion a loop in the wire for hanging your shell ornaments on Christmas tree boughs.

Make a whole collection of original Christmas ornaments to enjoy season after season.

CHRISTMAS-TREE PRESERVER AND FIRE PREVENTIVE

Dissolve the following ingredients in 1 gallon of hot water: 1 cup of ammonium sulfate (available at drugstores or chemical supply companies), ½ cup of boric acid (found in drugstores), 2 tablespoons of borax (found in hardware or grocery stores), and 8 tablespoons of 3% hydrogen peroxide (available in drugstores). If you like, add pine oil emulsion for an appropriate aroma. Store the mixture in a glass container.

For use, fill a spray bottle, and spray your Christmas tree with this fire-retarding solution. To prolong the life of your tree, keep the cup of its stand filled with the liquid. Help the tree absorb the solution by cutting the trunk anew at its base.

12

FROM THE SPRINGHOUSE

BUTTER

Back in the old days when butter was homemade, the process began with the care of cows. Some farmers, believing that a diet of corn fodder did not result in good butter, advocated a blend of half bran and half cornmeal. Others swore by a twice-daily feeding of early-cut hay and a mixture of scalded cornmeal and wheat bran, moistened with sweet skimmed milk.

The milk produced was strained through a cloth and "set" for cream. It was poured into deep tin pails either standing in vessels of ice or maintained at low temperature by cold spring water running through the milk house, if the building was so favorably situated. Cream setting lasted for a period of twenty-four hours or more, some dairymen claiming that a preliminary heating to a temperature of 130° F. would cause the cream to rise more quickly.

The temperature considered ideal for cream at churning time was 57° F. After being skimmed from the pails, the cream was put in a churn and worked for twelve to twenty minutes. The cylindrical dash churn, with a stick handle protruding through the top, was generally made of pottery or stripped cedar banded in brass hoops and powered by hand. Another old-time means of butter making was the dog churn. The sheep or cattle dog was recruited to run the equipment, freeing farm folks for other duties. Harnessed on a sort of treadmill, the animal set in motion an attached container for cream as it trotted in place. To each 20 pounds of butter, 3 ounces of white sugar and 6 ounces of salt were added.

In the absence of pasturage during the winter months, butter generally lacked sufficient yellow; so country housewives colored it with annatto, a dyeing material prepared from the seeds of a tropical tree. A lump about the size of a hickory nut was dissolved in 8 ounces of water. One tablespoon of the mixture was used to color 5 pounds of butter. Coloring the butter was also done with carrots. For each 3 gallons of cream, 6 large carrots were washed and coarsely grated. Boiling water was poured on them to extract their color. The carrot juice, allowed to cool, was then strained through coarse muslin into the cream prior to churning. Besides improving the appearance of the butter, the carrot juice gave it a sweet taste, similar to grass butter. Powdered turmeric, too, served as a yellow dye and was said to impart a richer flavor to sweet butter.

Tin pails and other dairy utensils were often scoured with the aid of nettles and plenty of suds from homemade lye soap.

Today, a simpler way of making butter is with your electric mixer. Attach the mixers, set the machine at its lowest speed, and slowly pour in all the cream while the mixer is running.

When pale butter grains appear, drain them in a muslin bag. Then put the substance in a bowl, and wash it thoroughly by spooning cold water over it until the water becomes clear. Finally, press the grains into one mass. If you wish to add salt, use about 1 teaspoon to the pound.

Perhaps the easiest means of making butter is provided by your blender. Put 4 cups of fresh cream into the machine. Let the cream reach close to room temperature (about 68° F.). Then run the blender at its slowest speed. After about three minutes, yellowish flecks should appear on the surface. Continue running the blender until the cream turns to butter, within eight minutes or so.

When butter has formed, drain off the buttermilk, reserving it for cooking purposes, and replace it with an equal amount of cold water. Cap the blender and churn the contents for ten seconds. Strain off the water. Repeat this cleaning method until the water is quite clear.

Drain the butter. Transfer it to a bowl, and press out excess moisture with a spoon. Add salt if desired.

CHEESES

Hard Cheese (yield: 1 ½ to 2 pounds)

If you have access to milk fresh from a farm, let 4 quarts of the evening's milk stand overnight in a cool place where the temperature ranges between 50° and 60° F. The next morning, mix in 4 quarts of fresh morning milk. Either cow's or goat's milk may be used. The best store-bought milk for cheese is fresh homogenized milk.

Be sure all utensils are completely clean. In a stainless steel pot or enameled or tin pail, heat the milk to 86° F. Use a dairy thermometer. You may add cheese coloring (optional) at this time by dissolving about one eighth of a cheese color tablet in 1 tablespoon of water and stirring it into the milk. In a glass of cold water, thoroughly dissolve one quarter of a cheese rennet tablet by stirring and crushing it with a spoon. Set the pail of milk in a larger container of warm (88°–90° F.) water, and place it in a warm spot protected from drafts. Thoroughly stir in the rennet solution for about one minute.

Leave the milk undisturbed for approximately forty minutes while a curd forms. Test the curd's firmness by inserting your finger at an angle and lifting. When it breaks clean over your finger, it is ready for cutting. With a knife long enough for the blade to reach the pail's bottom, cut the curd into small pieces. Cut in all directions so that the pieces will be quite small. Using your well-washed hand or a wooden spoon, gently stir the curd from around the sides and from the bottom upward. Carefully cut any large chunks that rise to the surface into smaller pieces; do not mash them. Try to make the curds of uniform size. To prevent their sticking together, continue the stirring for fifteen minutes.

Gradually raise the temperature of the pail's contents to 102° F. at the rate of 1½ degrees every five minutes. Stir frequently with a spoon to prevent the curds from sticking to each other. By this time, the curds should hold their shape and fall apart easily when they are held without being squeezed.

The next step in the process lasts one hour. Take the pail from the heat, and stir the contents often enough (about every five minutes) to prevent the curds from coagulating. Let the curds stay in the warm whey until sufficiently firm so as to shake apart after being pressed together in your hand. Turn the curds into a piece of cheesecloth 4 feet square, spread in a container. Gather up two corners of the cloth in each hand, and rock it gently for about three minutes so that the curds move about while the whey drains through. (When making cheese with cow's milk, don't discard the whey. It can be used to prepare butter that will taste like the salted variety, but with a delicate cheese flavor.)

Lay the cloth holding the curds in a clean pail. Sprinkle 1 tablespoon of salt over the contents and mix thoroughly. Add another tablespoon of salt and blend well.

Now tie the corners of the cloth together, forming a ball of the curd. Hang it so that it drips for a half hour or more.

Have your cheese press ready. Cheese-making kits are available in stores, complete with a cheese press, dairy thermometer, cheese coloring, and rennet tablets with directions for use. However, you can make your own cheese press by taking two pieces of wood, 8 by 12 inches, and putting a 1-inch dowel through both at either end. The dowels will keep the boards in place.

Take the cloth away from the sides of the curd ball. Fold a long cloth, such as a dish towel, into a 3-inch-wide strip, and wrap it tightly around the ball. Form the ball into a round, flat wheel. Smooth the surface of the cheese with your hands. Put several thicknesses of cheesecloth under and on top of the wrapped cheese. Set the cheese on the bottom board of your cheese press, and lower the top board to rest on the cheese. Place two bricks on top. That evening turn the cheese over, placing four bricks on top. Allow to stand until morning.

The next day remove the cloth from the cheese. Leave it on a board for half the day, turning it now and then to let the rind dry completely. Or put it on a wire rack; air will circulate around it, making turning unnecessary. Then paint on liquid paraffin with a brush. If you prefer, you can wrap the cheese tightly in plastic wrap. Store it in a clean and cool but frost-free place. Turn it over daily for the first few days and then several times weekly for four weeks. At the end of that time, your homemade cheese should be good to eat. However, you may leave it longer to develop a higher flavor if you like.

Cottage Cheese (yield: 1 cup)

2 quarts skim milk	1 ½ teaspoons vinegar
6 tablespoons	½ rennet tablet
homogenized	1 tablespoon cold water
milk	½ to 2 teaspoons salt

Combine milk and vinegar in the top half of a double boiler with water beneath. Gradually warm the milk to a temperature of about 70° F. (not more than 75°). Take the top of the double boiler from the heat. Blend into the milk one half of a rennet tablet that has been dissolved in 1 tablespoon of cold water. Cover the mixture, and set it in a warm spot (between 75° and 80° F.) for about fourteen hours. Leave it undisturbed.

After twelve hours, examine it. There should be whey on the milk's surface. Tilt the pan a little; the curd should separate. If these signs are not evident, allow it to stand several hours more.

Then place a colander, lined with a towel, in the sink. Pour the mixture into the colander, letting the whey drain off. Occasionally stir it lightly with a fork, and lift the towel, moving the curd about to further the drainage. Add salt to taste when the curd has thoroughly drained.

Creamed cottage cheese can be made by stirring in 1 or 2 tablespoons of cream or milk. Caraway seeds, chopped parsley, chopped olives, and pimentos may be used for flavoring, if desired.

Homemade Rennet

Here are ways to make rennet from four different sources:

* *RENNET FROM CALF STOMACH (dated 1887):* Ask the butcher for a calf's stomach. Scour it well with salt, both inside and out. Tack it to a wooden frame, and dry it in the sunshine for one or two days.

Cut the stomach into ½-inch squares. Put the pieces in a large jar; pack them in salt. Before using the rennet, soak it in water for thirty minutes and then wash it well. As an alternative to packing the pieces in salt, pour enough alcohol into the jar to cover them. With this method the rennet does not require soaking.

To easily remove the rennet from the curd when making

cheese, tie the rennet sections together with a string before immersing them.

* *RENNET FROM LAMB OR KID STOMACH:* Remove the stomach from a nursing lamb or kid that has eaten no solid food. Tie the opening securely; roll the organ in ashes until well coated. Hang it to dry out of direct sunlight in a warm, dry, well-ventilated spot. (Old-timers used to hang the stomachs in their grape arbors or from house rafters.) Once it is completely dry, the milk inside will have become brown powder.

When making cheese, pulverize a bit less than ¼ teaspoon of the powder in a mortar. (If you lack mortar and pestle, use a bowl and and old china doorknob instead.) Add enough water to form a paste. Then thin it, using a little more water. With the added water, the total liquid will equal about ¾ cup, enough rennet to help make twelve 2-pound cheeses, each made from 8 quarts of goat's milk plus 1 tablespoon of the solution.

* *WHEY RENNET:* Reserve 1 quart of whey for use as rennet. About ¼ cup cuts 5 gallons of milk. Replace the whey used each day; the quart of rennet will last two weeks before it is too weak to work as it should.

* *NETTLE RENNET:* It is said that a vegetable rennet for cheese making can be prepared from nettles. We haven't been able to learn the particulars concerning this method. You might like to experiment, however, with the idea on your own.

Goat's-milk Cheese (yield: 1 ½ pounds)

Pour 1½ gallons of raw goat's milk into an earthenware bowl. Leave it for seven days or until it becomes clabbered, when thick curds will rise to the surface. Heat the clabbered milk in a vessel until very hot but not boiling. Stir often to separate the curds and whey (the liquid). Continue to cook and stir for thirty minutes. When the curds are tough, drain them in a piece of cheesecloth. Remove as much of the whey as you can by squeezing and wringing. Put the cheese, still wrapped in the cloth, beneath a heavy weight in a pot. Leave it overnight to allow more whey to drain out.

The following morning, add 4 tablespoons of fresh sweet butter and ¾ teaspoon of soda. Mix the ingredients thoroughly, and chop the curd until very fine. Press the mixture flat on a board. Leave it in a warm spot for two hours.

Transfer the cheese to a double boiler over low heat. Put in ⅔ cup of very sour heavy cream and 1¼ teaspoons of salt. Stir until it starts to become a runny mass. Then empty the double boiler into a well-buttered bowl, and allow the cheese to cool. When solid, it is ready for serving.

To cure and store your goat's-milk cheese, take it from the bowl when cool and solid and coat the surface with melted paraffin, using a brush. Keep it in a cool place.

Clabbered Cheese

These are the necessary ingredients for clabbered cheese:

3 gallons clabbered, skimmed milk	¼ teaspoon dandelion-butter coloring
1½ teaspoons soda	
½ cup butter	2 teaspoons salt
1½ cups sour cream	

Heat the clabbered milk in a vessel until just bearable to the touch. Set the pot on the back of the stove; keep it hot for ½ hour.

Drain the curd through cheesecloth, thoroughly squeezing out the whey. Blend the soda and butter into the curd. Allow to stand for two hours.

Put the mixture in a double boiler, stir in 1 cup of sour cream, and melt it until smooth. In the meantime, blend the salt and dandelion-butter coloring into the remaining ½ cup of sour cream until the color is uniform. Add this to the contents of the double boiler.

Pour the mixture into a buttered pan, preferably one of stainless steel (do not use aluminum). Allow to stand uncovered for five days. Then coat the cheese with paraffin.

Cream Cheese

The best cream for making cream cheese is that skimmed from fresh whole milk. If you buy cream in a store, avoid the kind that has been treated for long shelf life. Allow the cream to sour at room temperature.

After two days put the sour cream into a cheesecloth bag. Suspend it over a bowl to let the whey drip through. Hang it from a cupboard door handle or the kitchen faucet.

A lump of cheese will remain in the bag. If desired, mix

in a little salt. Form the cream cheese into a cake; chill it. Should it be too soft to make into a cake, shape it after chilling.

Save the whey; it contains valuable nutrients. Use it as a substitute for water in baking. You'll find potato or spinach soup taking on a new, delicious flavor from its addition.

Ricotta-style Cheese

Slowly bring 2 quarts of milk to the boiling point, stirring it now and then. Turn off the heat, add 3 tablespoons of lemon juice, and stir twice. Set the vessel in a warm place for twenty-four hours.

Bring the mixture to a boil once more. Allow it to cool, and then strain it through cheesecloth.

If desired, the cheese may be seasoned with salt. To heighten its flavor, you may let it age in an uncovered dish for a few days.

YOGURT

Yogurt, a semisolid, cheeselike food that can be used in a variety of ways, is prepared from milk fermented by a particular bacterium.

All utensils used in making yogurt must be extremely clean. Wash them in hot soapsuds, followed by rinses first in hot and then in boiling water.

Assemble these ingredients:

1 quart skim milk
1 cup nonfat powdered milk

¼ cup plain, unflavored yogurt

Blend the skim milk and powdered milk in a saucepan. Put in a dairy thermometer and heat the liquid to about 180° F. over low heat. Be careful not to boil it. Take the pan from the stove, and cool its contents to somewhere between 100° and 115° F. Thoroughly blend in the yogurt.

Warm some containers by rinsing them in hot water. Fill them with the milk mixture and cover tightly. Put the containers in an incubator. You can purchase an electric yogurt maker or improvise one by placing the containers on a heating pad set on *low* and inverting a cardboard box over all. Maintain the incubator at 90° F. for three hours, undisturbed. For a stronger flavor, you may incubate the yogurt longer, checking its taste every thirty minutes.

Put it in the refrigerator. As the yogurt cools, it will thicken. Save ¼ cup of your homemade yogurt to start the next supply. Use yogurt that is no more than five days old for the starter.

Yogurt Dressing (yield: 1 serving)

3 tablespoons yogurt
1 tablespoon homemade
   mayonnaise

1 teaspoon Dijon mustard
dash garlic powder
salt and pepper to taste

Combine yogurt and mayonnaise. Blend in well the mustard and garlic powder. Chill.

On a bed of chopped lettuce moistened with basic dressing (oil and vinegar), arrange a double row of alternating slices of beets and hard-cooked eggs, slightly overlapping. Spoon yogurt dressing over the beets and eggs; sprinkle lightly with paprika.

This dressing is also excellent on crisp, shredded cabbage. Or fold diced beets into the yogurt dressing, and fill the hollow of half an avocado with the mixture.

Strawberry Yogurt Mold

1 cup homemade yogurt
4 tablespoons homemade
   strawberry jam
   (more or less to
   taste)

1 cup orange juice
1 envelope unflavored
   gelatin
¼ cup sugar

Thoroughly blend the strawberry jam with the yogurt. Pour ½ cup of orange juice into a small saucepan, and sprinkle it with the gelatin. Put the pan over low heat, stirring its contents until the gelatin dissolves. Remove the pan from the heat; stir in sugar. Add the remainder of the orange juice. Using a wire whisk beat in the yogurt.

Pour the mixture into four dessert dishes. Chill until firm.

Yogurt Topping (yield: 1 cup)

¼ cup light corn syrup
¼ cup mayonnaise

½ cup plain yogurt

Stir together the corn syrup and mayonnaise. Fold in the yogurt. Serve over unfrosted cake.

Honey Mayonnaise (yield: about 1 cup)

Put the following ingredients into a blender: 1 egg, 1 teaspoon of honey, 2 tablespoons of vinegar, 2 tablespoons of lemon juice, ½ teaspoon of dry mustard, ½ teaspoon of salt, and ½ cup of safflower or peanut oil. Churn them until smooth. Now blend in an additional cup of salad oil, pouring it into the center of the mayonnaise. Transfer it to a jar and refrigerate.

Wine Mayonnaise (yield: about 1 ¼ cups)

2 egg yolks	½ teaspoon lemon juice
1 tablespoon red wine	¾ teaspoon dry mustard
1 tablespoon white-wine	½ teaspoon salt
vinegar	½ cup salad oil
1 tablespoon	½ cup olive oil
herb-flavored	
vinegar	

Put the egg yolks in an electric blender; run it on high speed until they are frothy (about ten seconds). Blend in vinegar, wine, lemon juice, mustard, and salt at medium speed for slightly longer than one minute, very gradually adding oil in a thin constant stream while the blender is running.

Transfer the mayonnaise to a container, and remove every last bit from the blender with a rubber spatula. Store it in the refrigerator, where it will keep for two weeks. Before blending, you may add various fresh or dried herbs to the egg yolks.

Potato Mayonnaise

3 egg yolks	salt to taste
¾ cup olive oil	1 small potato, boiled
1 lemon	and mashed

Beat the egg yolks until they are thick. While continuing to beat them, add oil in drops. Slowly pour in the juice of one lemon. Put in the mashed potato and salt, beating until the blend is very smooth.

Store in a tightly closed jar in the refrigerator. When cooked vegetables and fish are garnished with this mayonnaise, their flavor is enhanced.

Country housewives of bygone days maintained that mayonnaise prepared when a thunderstorm was in the offing wouldn't thicken and emulsify. Whether or not the claim is valid, if your mayonnaise fails to thicken, be the weather foul or fair, remedy the matter by constantly beating one egg yolk while very, very gradually (drop by drop at the start) adding the unsuccessful, thin mayonnaise.

Vanilla Ice Cream (yield: 1 gallon)

2 quarts light cream (Half-and-Half)	2 tablespoons pure vanilla extract
1 quart milk	1 teaspoon salt
3 cups sugar	

Mix all ingredients until the sugar dissolves. Thoroughly chill, overnight if possible.

Wash the dasher, can, and cover of the ice cream freezer in hot, sudsy water. Rinse well in hot, clear water. Dry. Chill them in your freezer or refrigerator. Crush from 20 to 25 pounds of ice in an ice crusher. Return the can and dasher to the freezer bucket. Fill the can from one half to two thirds full with the ice-cream mixture. Cover the can. Follow manufacturer's directions for fitting the crank assembly or motor into the cover and securing it to the bucket. Place the freezer on several layers of newspapers. Allow the motor to warm up for about sixty seconds. During this time, add ice and salt.

Be guided by the instructions accompanying your ice-cream freezer. Freezers vary in their required proportions of salt and ice. Put in about 2 inches (6 cups) of crushed ice. Spread ¼ cup of rock salt over the ice. Continue these layers until they surround and cover the can. Keep the hole in the upper side of the bucket free to permit drainage of the brine. Place a plastic container beneath the hole to receive any drips.

A hand freezer should be cranked rapidly and steadily, with an increase in speed as the mixture thickens so as to whip air into it. Beating air into the ice cream gives it a smooth texture. Stop when the mixture becomes so thick that cranking is nearly impossible. When using an electric mixer, disconnect the freezer at once when the motor stops or runs sluggishly. Carefully tip the freezer to drain off the brine. Take out the ice and salt to a depth of two inches below the cover. Remove the cranking assembly or motor. Wipe away ice and salt from the cover, and take out the dasher. Scrape ice cream from the dasher into the can and from the upper sides of the can, using a rubber spatula. Blend it for a few minutes.

Next comes the ripening stage. Place several layers of waxed paper, plastic wrap, or foil over the mouth of the can, and then put on the cover. Fill the hole in the cover with some sort of plug; use wadded foil or paper towels. Add more ice and salt layers, using ½ cup of salt to each 6 cups of crushed ice. Cover the can completely with the layers. Wrap thicknesses of newspaper about the freezer, enclose it with a heavy cloth (an old blanket will do), and set it in a cool spot for three hours. (There are other ways of ripening ice cream. After the machine has been turned off, the can of ice cream can be transferred to your food freezer for ripening. Or you can immediately pack the ice cream in plastic containers and put them in the food freezer for the ripening process.)

Drain away the brine, and remove the ice and salt. Take the can from the freezer. If not eaten immediately, ice cream can be stored in plastic containers in the food freezer.

For a variation of flavor, you may add almost anything to the mixture just prior to freezing.

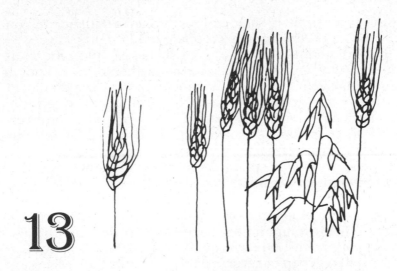

13

GRAINS AND SPROUTS

GRAINS
Grinding Grain

Whole grains, high in vitamin E, iron, and the B vitamins, are a nearly perfect food. To be eaten at their most nutritious, flavorful stage, they should be ground immediately prior to cooking; vitamins and flavor start to diminish with each hour that grains are exposed to air after grinding. However, if you prefer preparing a larger amount at one time, avoid grinding more grain than will be used within a period of three to four weeks. Store it in clean, airtight containers. Unground grain will keep almost indefinitely in closed containers stored in a dry, cool place.

Unless you are raising your own grain, purchase it (clean or uncleaned) from feed and grain stores, health food stores, or farms. Buy fresh grain that is untreated by chemicals.

You will need to winnow uncleaned grain. Make a frame of convenient holding size, using 1- by 2-inch lumber, and cover it with window screening. Pour uncleaned grain on the winnowing screen. Remove chaff and dust by shaking it. Most of the chaff will be blown away if you winnow on a windy day. Pick out any foreign material, such as heavy grit. To clean grain indoors, pour it back and forth from container to container in the breeze from an electric fan.

Barley, millet, oats, rice, rye, soybeans, and wheat are grain that can be ground successfully at home in a hand (or electric) mill, coffee grinder, or some blenders. Depending on its intended use, grain may be roughly ground or converted to very fine flour. About four grindings will produce fine flour.

Whole or ground grains can be used for all baking purposes and cereals. Cracked wheat imparts a nutlike flavor to breads and waffles. A combination of grains provides a delicious and unusual breakfast cereal.

To prepare a hot cereal, put cleaned, unground wheat in an iron skillet, which will not heat up too quickly and will maintain steady temperature. Spread the grain in a thin layer and stir continuously. It will double in size and turn brown. The kernels will pop but won't burst open. Grind your toasted wheat, and then cook it as you would regular wheat breakfast cereal.

Granola

Mix the following ingredients:

4 cups rolled oats (or rolled wheat)	1 cup sunflower seeds, hulled
1 ½ cups unsweetened coconut, shredded	1 cup sesame seeds
	½ cup bran
1 cup wheat germ	1 cup soybeans, ground and toasted
1 cup chopped nuts	

Heat these ingredients:

½ cup oil	1 to 2 teaspoons vanilla
½ cup honey	

Add the honey-oil-vanilla mixture to the dry ingredients; blend well. Spread on oiled cookie sheets. Bake for twenty to thirty minutes in a 375° F. oven. Stir occasionally.

If you would like to prepare freshly shredded coconut but avoid doing so because of the difficulty in opening the coconut shell, here are two tips to make the task an easy one: Either heat the coconut in a 350° F. oven or freeze it for about two hours. A blow from a hammer will then quickly crack it.

This recipe may be changed according to your taste. Substitute any suitable, wholesome ingredients that you prefer, but always maintain the same ratio of seven parts dry ingredients to one part wet ingredients for successful granola.

Hominy

To make hominy, first shuck ears of firm, dried corn. (*Hominy* comes from an Indian word meaning "parched corn.") Take off the underdeveloped kernels from either end of the cob. Then shell the corn by hand.

Put the kernels into an iron vessel. Cover it with cold water. Add 1½ tablespoons of lye to every gallon of corn. Boil until the husks start to separate from the kernels.

Transfer the corn to another vessel, and wash it seven or eight times in clear, cold water. Rinse out the first pot to prevent sticking when the hominy is boiled again later.

To completely remove the husks, put the kernels in a coarse-meshed sieve. Wearing rubber gloves as protection against the lye, run a forceful stream of water on the corn, at the same time rubbing it over the mesh. The water will carry away the unwanted husks. After husking, return the corn to the iron vessel and boil in fresh water until tender.

Hominy may be canned for future consumption. But if its golden goodness sets you to craving some immediately, try frying it in bacon drippings for a real treat. It can also be eaten just salted, rather like boiled peanuts.

In the old days, hominy was chiefly made during the winter months when country folks had fewer farm chores.

Southern Fried Corn

4 ears corn
¼ cup all-purpose flour
⅛ cup fine bread crumbs
½ teaspoon salt

½ teaspoon paprika
⅛ teaspoon black pepper
1 egg
cooking oil

Husk the corn and remove the silk. In a shallow dish, blend flour, bread crumbs, salt, paprika, and pepper. Lightly beat the egg in another shallow plate. Heat oil in a skillet. Dip the ears of corn in the egg. Drain slightly. Roll them in the flour mixture. Shake off any excess and fry in the hot oil for about four minutes. Turn occasionally. When golden brown, serve with meat, poultry, or seafood.

SPROUTS

Essentials for Producing Sprouts

Produce inexpensive, unprocessed fresh food in all seasons by growing seed sprouts. Besides seeds you will need water, air, a few readily available containers, and—in certain cases— some sunlight.

Just about any legume, grain, or seed can be sprouted for nutritious food (potato sprouts should never be eaten): garbanzos, kidney beans, lima beans, mung beans, pinto beans, soybeans, chick-peas, peas, corn, alfalfa, barley, oats, rye, wheat, unhulled sunflower and sesame seeds, the seeds of cress, parsley, radishes, and many more.

Choosing Seeds

Choose whole seeds that have not been treated chemically. They can be purchased from health food stores or through mail-order sources. Wash them thoroughly. Discard seeds that float; they are probably sterile.

Yield

A fairly small amount of seeds yields a considerable quantity of sprouts: 1 tablespoon of alfalfa seeds produces about 30 square inches of sprouts; 3 tablespoons of beans or peas produce a similar quantity. As a general rule, ½ cupful of seeds swells to 1½ cups when soaked, making a quart or more of sprouts.

Put the seeds in a vessel containing three times their volume in warm (70°–80° F.) water to soak overnight in some dark, warm spot, such as a kitchen cabinet. The following morning, drain off the water. Reserve this vitamin- and mineral-rich liquid for cooking rice, potatoes, and vegetables, or for adding to soups and fruit or vegetable juice drinks. Rinse the seeds, now double in size, to prevent mold. Put them in a moist (not wet) container. Keep it in a dark place where the temperature ranges between 80° and 90° F. If you prefer, instead of putting the container in a cupboard, you can invert a paper bag over it to keep out light. Rinse the seeds twice a day (three times daily in warm weather) to cleanse them and provide sufficient moisture for their growth. After each cleansing, drain them well to avoid rotting. Utilize the rinse water to feed your plants; they will thrive on it.

Begin a new batch of seeds each night to have a continuously fresh supply on hand. For variety in your menu, have about three containers of different sprouts developing at one time: a grain, a bean, and a seed. Don't crowd larger beans like blackeyed peas, kidney beans, and soybeans. Some folks maintain that garbanzos, lentils, mung beans, and soybeans grow better in the same container than when sprouted separately.

Procedure for Germination

Sprouts can be grown successfully in common kitchen containers: colanders, the strainers of coffee percolators, flour sifters, sink strainers, vegetable steamers, and tea strainers. A wide-mouthed jar can be used by stretching cheesecloth over the opening and fastening it on with a rubber band. A circle of wire mesh secured with a screw-on canning ring can substitute for the cloth. Put the jar in a bowl, top down, at a 45-degree angle to facilitate drainage. An unglazed earthenware flowerpot can serve as a sprout garden. It will absorb moisture, maintaining the sprouts in a moist, not wet, condition. Plug the drain hole with cotton or cheesecloth. Place a saucer on top, and set the pot in a shallow container of water. Regularly rinse the sprouts, as with those in other types of sprouters, to prevent mold from developing. Yet another way to germinate legumes, grains, or seeds is to place a rustproof metal rack in a glass baking pan. Put warm water in the container, but not enough to reach the rack. Spread a wet terry cloth towel (or several thicknesses of cheesecloth) on the rack, letting an end hang into the water beneath. This arrangement will provide the seeds with moisture without wetness.

Harvesting Sprouts

Within three to six days, depending on the type of seed, the sprouts will have greatly increased in volume and be ready for harvesting. If you like, during the last few hours of development, you can place them in indirect sunlight to generate healthful chlorophyl. Be sure to limit the exposure, however, since too much chlorophyl will toughen the shoots.

Seeds	Proper Size of Sprouts for Harvesting
Alfalfa	
Peas	Two to three inches long
Soybeans	
Grain	No longer than the length of the kernel
Sunflower	No longer than the seed length
Lentils	One inch
Mung Beans	Three to four inches

Most shoots are at their peak from sixty to eighty hours after germination, but you may wish to use personal preference in taste and texture as a guide for determining the harvest time.

The nutritional value of sprouts produced by the water method is high, but higher still when they are raised by the earth method. Eliminating the necessity to periodically rinse them is an additional benefit.

Soak beans or seeds for twelve hours. Then scatter them evenly on a layer of good soil in a wooden box or large flowerpot. Sprinkle on enough earth to cover them, water lightly, and spread a cloth over the container to retain moisture and exclude light. Several days later, pull out the entire sprout, wash away the soil, and enjoy this extra nutritious harvest in your favorite recipes.

If the sprouts develop before you are ready to use them, put them into a colander and steam them for several minutes. Then immerse them in cold water. Drain and refrigerate the sprouts until they are needed. To preserve them for an extended time, freeze or dry them; their nutritional value will not be diminished.

Sprout Uses

It is unnecessary to remove the seed hulls from sprouts before serving them. Use sprouts as meat loaf filler, as steamed vegetables, in stews, sprinkled on soups, mixed into beverages (with a blender), and raw in salads.

14

BREADS, BREAD SPREADS, PRETZELS,AND CRACKERS

DOUGH STARTERS

Some dough starters, kept active for more than 100 years, have been handed down from one generation to the next like family heirlooms.

Buttermilk Yeast Starter

   1 quart buttermilk
   flour
½ cup sugar

1 cup yeast
3 pints water

At midday, heat the buttermilk until it commences to boil. Put in the yeast and sugar. Stir, adding sufficient flour to form a stiff batter. Allow to stand in a warm spot until nightfall. Then add 2½ cups of water and allow to stand until the following morning.

Add the rest of the water. Your buttermilk yeast is ready for bread baking.

Peach-Leaf Yeast Starter

Steep 1 quart of fresh, well-washed peach leaves in 3 cups of boiling water for fifteen minutes. Drain, adding enough water, if necessary, to make 3 cups. The water will have a greenish hue, but this will disappear during fermentation. Bake three medium-sized potatoes. Peel them, and put them through a sieve or food mill. Scald ½ cup of cornmeal in 1 cup of water until it boils and thickens. Stir to prevent lumps from forming.

Put all these ingredients in a bowl with 2 teaspoons of salt and 3 tablespoons of sugar. Cover and allow to ferment in a warm place for twenty-four hours, stirring well every two or three hours.

Pour it into a glass jar, and keep it in the refrigerator. Stir it down several times until foaming ceases. When approximately ½ inch of clear liquid rises to the surface, it will be ready for use. Stir thoroughly each time you use it.

When the starter is reduced to 1 cup, add 3 cups of water, three baked potatoes, the scalded cornmeal, salt, and sugar as you did the first time. Leave it in a warm spot. In about seven hours it should become active.

Peach-leaf starter improves with age. It is advisable to use it about twice each week. If not, stir it every couple of days, adding 1 teaspoon of sugar.

You can make this starter into a dry yeast. Begin by sterilizing 2 quarts of cornmeal for one hour in a low oven. Mix it into the starter. Spread it in flat pans to a thickness of ½ inch. When it is set, cut it into 1½-inch squares. Move them apart to dry and harden. Wrap the cakes. Store them in the refrigerator; they will keep a year or more.

A starter can be made from the dry yeast in this way. In a bowl, mix 1 cake of yeast, ½ cup of warm water, ½ teaspoon of ginger, and 1 teaspoon of sugar. Keep it covered until you see white foam on top. Then stir in ½ cup of water, ½ cup of flour, and 1 teaspoon of sugar. After it foams again, add 1 cup of water, 1 cup of flour, and 1 teaspoon of sugar. Allow to foam, stirring often. Pour it into a jar and refrigerate. Put the lid on loosely until the foaming stops. When ½ inch of clear liquid has risen to the surface, the starter is ready to use.

Potato Yeast Starter

Cook three potatoes, peeled and cubed, until tender. Mash them, blending in the pot liquor, and add sufficient cold water to equal 3 cups. Put in ¼ cup of honey. Cool the mixture to lukewarm. Soak one package of dried yeast in 1 cup of lukewarm water. Add it to the mixture. Allow to stand in a warm spot overnight.

The following day, store 1 cup of the starter in the refrigerator; use the rest to bake four loaves of any recipe.

Sourdough Starter

2 cups all-purpose flour	2 cups warm water
1 package dry yeast	

Thoroughly blend all ingredients in a large bowl. Leave it uncovered in a warm spot for forty-eight hours. Stir occasionally.

Just before using the starter, stir it well. Take out the amount needed; replenish the remainder by blending in 1 cup of flour and 1 cup of warm water.

Leave the starter uncovered in a warm spot for several hours. When it bubbles once more, put it into a nonmetal container, cover loosely, and store in the refrigerator until needed.

The night before you plan to make sourdough bread, remove the starter from the refrigerator so that it can warm and commence working. The starter must be used at least once in a two-week period and be replenished each time. Using it daily is even better.

SOURDOUGH BREADS

The oldest of breads may well be sourdough bread. It dates back to 4000 B.C.

Sourdough Bread

3 cups all-purpose or whole wheat flour	1 teaspoon baking soda
1 cup sourdough starter	3½ cups (about) unbleached all-purpose flour
2 cups warm water	
2 tablespoons sugar	cornmeal
1 teaspoon salt	melted butter

Put the first six ingredients into a large bowl; beat until smooth. Cover the dough with waxed paper. Allow to stand in a warm spot (80° to 85° F.) for a minimum of eighteen hours.

Stir it down. Blend in the remainder of the flour, making moderately stiff dough. On a lightly floured board, knead the dough until satiny smooth for eight to ten minutes. Divide it in two. Form each equal portion into a ball. Roll them beneath your hands to make long thick ropes, more or less 12 inches in length.

Grease cookie sheets, and sprinkle them with cornmeal. Place the loaves on the cookie sheets; slash the top of each with a sharp knife and brush with butter. Cover them with transparent wrap. Allow to rise where it is warm for approximately one and a half hours until doubled. Bake from forty to fifty minutes in a preheated 400°F. oven.

Remove them from the oven, and brush the tops with melted butter. Place on a rack to cool.

Onion Sourdough Bread *(yield: 2 large, long loaves or 4 small, round loaves)*

1 ½ cups sourdough starter	1 cup milk 2 tablespoons margarine
3 ¾ cups (approximately) unsifted all-purpose flour	cornmeal egg white, beaten
3 tablespoons sugar	1 tablespoon water
2 teaspoons salt	⅔ cup finely chopped
1 package active dry yeast	onion caraway seed

Measure out the sourdough starter, and set it aside. In a large bowl, combine 1 cup of flour, the sugar, salt, and undissolved active dry yeast. Put the milk and margarine in a saucepan and heat over low heat. When the milk is very warm, somewhere around 125° F., slowly add it to the dry ingredients. Beat in a mixer at medium speed for two minutes, scraping the bowl now and then. Add ¼ cup of flour and 1½ cups of starter, beating for two minutes at high speed and scraping the bowl from time to time. Blend in additional flour to make a soft dough. Knead it until elastic and smooth on a lightly floured board for about nine minutes. Put it in a greased bowl. Then turn it over to grease the top. Cover it, and allow it to rise for one hour in a warm spot, away from drafts, until doubled.

Punch down the dough. Turn it out on a lightly floured board, and divide it in two. Cover and allow to stand for fifteen minutes. Shape as preferred. Form large, long loaves by rolling each section of dough into an oblong—8 by 12 inches. Roll the dough tightly from the 12-inch side, pinching the seam. Then pinch the ends and fold them underneath. To form small, round loaves, divide the dough in two again. Shape each into a round ball, and flatten slightly.

Sprinkle cornmeal on greased baking sheets. Place the loaves on them and cover. Allow to rise for one hour in a warm spot, away from drafts, until doubled.

Combine water and egg white. Brush this mixture on the loaves. Sprinkle them with chopped onion and caraway seed.

Bake in a 400°F. oven for twenty-five minutes or until done. Take from the baking sheets and let cool on wire racks.

Sourdough Rolls

1 ½ cups warm water	2 tablespoons sugar
1 package active	2 teaspoons salt
dry yeast	½ teaspoon baking
1–1 ½ cups sourdough	soda
starter	1 cup flour
2 tablespoons salad	
oil	

Into a large mixing bowl, measure 1½ cups of warm water. Blend in one package of active dry yeast. Add the sourdough starter, salad oil, sugar, and salt, stirring vigorously with a wooden spoon for approximately three minutes. Put in a large greased bowl, cover with a towel, and allow to rise for one and a half to two hours in some warm spot until doubled in bulk.

Blend ½ teaspoon of baking soda into 1 cup of flour and stir in, making the dough stiff. Knead it on a floured board, and add 1 cup of flour or an amount needed to control the stickiness. After eight minutes or more, it should be satiny smooth. Separate the dough into two sections. Shape into rolls by rolling the dough between your hands. Place them on a greased pan, cover, and leave in a warm spot. Leave for one to one and a half hours to rise and almost double in bulk.

For a crusty top, brush with water just before baking. If a softer crust is desired, brush with melted butter. Bake for seventeen to twenty minutes in a 400°F. oven.

CORN BREAD VARIATIONS

When preparing your favorite corn bread recipe, try using 8 ounces of cracklings in place of the shortening.

Basic Corn Bread

1 cup flour
1 cup cornmeal
4 tablespoons baking
    powder
2 eggs

1 ½ cups sweet milk
1 tablespoon cooking
    oil
1 teaspoon salt

Blend these ingredients thoroughly. Bake in a greased pan at 400° F. for thirty minutes or until crusty and brown.

Buttermilk Corn Bread

1 cup cornmeal
1 cup unbleached white
    flour
⅓ cup sugar
¼ teaspoon baking
    powder

¾ teaspoon salt
1 cup buttermilk
2 eggs, well beaten
2 tablespoons oil
1 ½ teaspoons baking
    powder

Sift all the dry ingredients into a bowl. Mix in the milk, eggs, and oil. Stir only enough to blend. Empty the batter into a greased cake pan (8 inches square).

Bake it for approximately twenty minutes at 425° F. When the top is nicely browned, take the bread from the oven.

Clabber Corn Bread

1 cup cornmeal
1 cup sifted flour
¼ cup sugar
4 teaspoons baking
    powder

½ teaspoon salt
1 egg
1 cup curd
1 tablespoon oil

Sift the dry ingredients into a bowl. Put in the eggs, curd, and oil; beat the mixture until smooth. Empty the batter into a greased pan (9 inches square).

Bake for about twenty-five minutes in a 425° F. oven. When a knife inserted in the center of the bread comes out clean, remove your clabber corn bread from the oven.

Honey Corn Bread

Thoroughly mix these ingredients:

1 ¾ cups yellow cornmeal	¾ teaspoon salt
½ cup wheat flour, plus 2 tablespoons	3 teaspoons baking powder

Beat well the following ingredients:

2 eggs	2 tablespoons butter (or margarine)
2 tablespoons honey	

Stir in 1 cup of milk.

Combine the liquid mixture with the dry mixture. Gently blend until the whole is moistened. Spread the batter in a greased 9-inch pan. Bake for twenty-five to thirty minutes in a preheated 400° F. oven.

Johnnycake

2 cups cornmeal	2 cups sour milk
1 ½ teaspoons salt	2 eggs, beaten
1 teaspoon baking soda	2 tablespoons shortening, melted
2 tablespoons sugar	

Sift together the dry ingredients. Add milk, eggs, and shortening. Blend thoroughly.

Pour the batter into a greased 8- by 10-inch-loaf pan and bake in a 400° F. oven for thirty minutes.

Molasses Corn Bread

Mix together these dry ingredients:

3 cups yellow cornmeal	1 teaspoon salt
1 cup whole wheat flour	
2 tablespoons baking powder	

Mix together the following wet ingredients:

3 eggs	½ cup sorghum molasses
½ cup butter	2 cups buttermilk

Blend the two mixtures until the dry ingredients become moist.

Bake the batter in a greased 12-inch pan for approximately thirty-five minutes in a 350° F. oven.

Southern-style Corn Bread

1 cup yellow cornmeal	1 ½ teaspoons salt
1 cup flour (whole wheat or white)	1 cup milk (or buttermilk)
2 to 3 tablespoons powdered milk	1 egg
	2 tablespoons vegetable oil
4 teaspoons baking powder	2 to 3 tablespoons wheat germ

Sift all the dry items, except the wheat germ, into a bowl. Mix in the remaining ingredients, making a uniformly moist batter. Put it in a well-greased 8-inch-square pan and bake for twenty to twenty-five minutes in a preheated 425° F. oven until golden brown.

Spoon Bread

2 cups boiling water	1 tablespoon shortening
1 cup white cornmeal	1 cup milk
1 teaspoon salt	2 eggs, separated

Blend water, cornmeal, salt, and shortening. Cool. Thoroughly mix in the milk and beaten egg yolks. Then fold in stiffly beaten egg whites.

Pour the batter into a greased baking dish. Bake for thirty to forty minutes in a 400° F. oven. Serve the spoon bread directly from its baking dish.

BREADS WITH HONEY

To cut easily through freshly baked bread, use a heated knife.

Granola-Yogurt Bread (yield: 2 loaves)

2 envelopes dry yeast
1 ½ cups very warm
    water
1 teaspoon honey
8 ounces homemade
    yogurt

5 cups unbleached
    flour, sifted
3 teaspoons salt
2 cups homemade
    granola

Sprinkle the yeast into a 1-cup measure holding ½ cup of the warm water. Add the honey and stir until the yeast dissolves. Let stand for ten minutes, more or less, until it is bubbly and the volume doubles.

Combine the rest of the water, yogurt, and salt in a big bowl. Stir in the yeast mixture. Beat in 4 cups of the flour for two minutes, setting your mixer at medium speed. Mix in the granola. Slowly blend in the remaining flour to form a stiff dough.

Put the dough on a lightly floured board, and knead it for about ten minutes until it is smooth and elastic. Use only enough flour to prevent the dough from adhering to the work surface.

Place it in a large buttered bowl; turn it to bring up the buttered side. Cover with a clean towel. Let rise in a warm, draft-free place for one hour or until double in bulk.

Punch down the dough. Put it on a lightly floured board and knead several times. Invert the bowl over the dough, and let it rest for ten minutes. Divide the dough in two equal portions; knead each half a few times. Shape them into two round loaves. Lay them on a greased baking sheet, about 5 inches apart. Allow them to rise in a warm spot, free from drafts, for forty minutes or until double in volume.

Using a sharp knife, cut a ½-inch-deep cross in the top of each loaf. Bake them in a 375° F. oven for thirty-five minutes or until they are golden brown and have a hollow sound when tapped. Cool them completely on wire racks.

Honey-Oatmeal Bread

1 ½ cups milk	½ cup honey
1 cup oatmeal (quick cooking)	2 yeast cakes
2 tablespoons butter	2 cups flour, unbleached
1 ¼ cups light cream	3 cups whole wheat flour
½ teaspoon salt	

Scald the milk, and put in the oatmeal, cooking it for three minutes. Add the butter. After it melts, put in cream, salt, and honey. Let cool. Add the yeast and the flour and beat well.

Mix in the whole wheat flour to make a soft dough. Knead it until smooth. Allow it to rise until double in volume. Shape the dough into three loaves. Let them rise until double in bulk.

Bake for fifty minutes at 375° F.

Peanut Butter Loaf

2 cups flour	¼ cup honey
4 teaspoons baking powder	⅔ cup homemade peanut butter
1 teaspoon salt	1 ¼ cups milk
¼ teaspoon baking soda	

Sift together the first four ingredients. Thoroughly mix the milk into the peanut butter; blend in the honey. Add the peanut butter mixture to the dry ingredients and beat well.

Turn into a buttered loaf pan. Bake in a 350° F. oven for forty-five minutes. Peanut butter bread is even tastier on the second day.

Whole Wheat Honey Bread

Mix the following dry ingredients:

12 cups whole wheat flour	1 tablespoon salt
1 ¾ cups instant dry milk	2 tablespoons yeast

Mix the following wet ingredients:

½ cup oil	½ cup honey
2 beaten eggs	(Dissolve it
3 cups warm (110°– 115° F.) water	thoroughly.)

Add the wet mixture to the dry, stirring with a wooden spoon. When the dough is well blended, stir it a little about every ten minutes for an hour.

Now knead the dough slightly until it becomes elastic. Form two large loaves and one small one. Put them in greased bread pans. Allow to rise for one hour.

Bake at 370° F. for ten minutes. Reduce the heat to 350° and bake thirty minutes longer.

UNUSUAL BREADS

Harvest Bread

1 ½ cups sugar
½ cup vegetable oil
2 eggs, beaten
1 cup canned pumpkin
   (or fresh)
1 cup oats
1 cup flour
1 ¼ teaspoons baking
   powder

1 teaspoon salt
½ teaspoon allspice
½ teaspoon cinnamon
½ teaspoon ground cloves
½ teaspoon nutmeg
½ cup chopped pecans

Combine sugar, oil, eggs, pumpkin, and oats. Beat well. Sift the dry ingredients, and add them to the pumpkin mixture.

Pour the batter into a greased 9- by 5-inch-loaf pan. Bake at 350° F. for an hour and fifteen minutes.

Tomato Bread (yield: 1 good-sized loaf)

2 teaspoons dry yeast
¼ cup warm water
1 ½ cups tomato juice
1 tablespoon sugar
½ teaspoon salt
1 tablespoon cooking
   oil

½ teaspoon powdered
   basil
4 ½ to 5 cups whole
   wheat flour

Grease a 9- by 5-inch bread pan.

Put the yeast in a big mixing bowl; pour the water on it. Let the yeast dissolve (about five minutes). Then mix in the tomato juice, sugar, salt, oil, and basil. Gradually add the flour until a stiff dough is formed that no longer adheres to the bowl's sides.

Place the dough on a floured board; knead it until smooth and elastic, about six minutes. Shape the dough, and put it in the loaf pan. Cover it with a clean dish towel. Let it rise until about double in volume.

Preheat the oven to 350° F. Bake the tomato bread for about fifty-five minutes or until done.

Zucchini Bread *(yield: 2 loaves)*

3 eggs	3 teaspoons cinnamon
2 cups sugar	3 teaspoons vanilla
1 cup oil	2 cups raw, unpeeled,
¼ teaspoon baking	shredded and
powder	packed zucchini
2 teaspoons baking soda	3 cups flour
1 teaspoon salt	

Beat the eggs until light and fluffy. Add sugar, oil, and vanilla. Blend well. Stir in the zucchini. Add the dry ingredients to the creamed mixture.

Pour the batter into two well-greased 9- by 5-inch-loaf pans. Bake at 350° F. for one hour.

UNLEAVENED BREAD
Hardtack

Make a stiff mixture of the following ingredients:

1 ½ cups graham flour	½ cup shortening
3 cups unbleached	1 ½ cups milk
white flour	1 teaspoon sugar
½ cup cornmeal	1 tablespoon salt

Lightly grease several cookie sheets, and sprinkle them with flour. Dust a chunk of dough (about the size of an egg) with flour, place it in the middle of the cookie sheet, and slightly flatten it with your hand. Now roll the dough out to cover the surface of the baking sheet, making it as thin as possible. Dust with flour when necessary to prevent sticking. You may want to use a flour sock on your rolling pin. Trim off any excess dough, and return it to the mixing bowl.

Bake the unleavened bread in a 400° F. oven. When the edges brown, turn it over; continue baking until the flat bread is almost as stiff as cardboard. Turn it once more, and when the hardtack actually is cardboard-stiff, remove it from the oven.

It may be eaten when freshly baked and hot but will last indefinitely if kept dry. Break it in pieces, and store them in an airtight container.

BREAD SPREADS

Apple Butter
Fill a kettle with cider, and boil it down to two-thirds of the quantity. Pare, core, and slice sweet apples. Add as many to the cider as the vessel will hold without boiling over. Allow to boil slowly; stir frequently to prevent burning. When the apple butter is smooth and thick, add cinnamon and sugar to taste.

Let cool. Keep it in the refrigerator in tightly closed jars.

Cherry Butter
Boil cherries until soft. Rub them through a sieve. Add 2 cups of sugar to each pint of pulp. Boil gently until a butterlike consistency is reached.

Store the spread in tightly covered jars.

Green Butter
Mash in a mortar two small green onions, one-half clove of garlic, some watercress, six sprigs of parsley, and salt and pepper. Blend these ingredients into softened butter.

Green butter is delicious when spread on toasted bread, fish, or bland vegetables.

Honey Butter

1 cup butter   *½ cup honey*

Cream the butter. Beat in the honey until uniformly blended. Honey butter is excellent on freshly baked breads.

Keep it in the refrigerator. Store any excess in an airtight container in the freezer.

Lemon Butter
Beat the yolk of one egg; mix it with the whites of three eggs. Stir in 1½ cups of sugar, ½ cup of butter, and the grated rind and juice of two medium-sized lemons. Set the vessel

containing the mixture in a pan of water and cook for twenty minutes.

Let cool to serve or store.

Peach Butter

Pare ripe peaches. Boil them in a kettle of enough grape juice to cook them until soft. Then rub the fruit through a colander to remove the stones.

Add 1½ pounds of sugar to each quart of peach pulp. Boil slowly for sixty minutes. Stir often to avoid burning.

When the peach butter is smooth and thick, season it with cinnamon or other ground spices to suit your taste.

Peanut Butter

Two tablespoons of peanut butter contain an amount of protein at least equal to that found in 6 ounces of milk or a medium-sized egg. This nourishing food may be prepared in a variety of ways, depending on your preference, all with good results.

Peanuts can be ground raw or given a slightly roasted flavor by first putting them, unshelled, in a 300° F. oven for thirty minutes. For a full-roasted taste, leave them in for sixty minutes. Allow them to cool; then remove the shells and skins, or leave the skins on for their nutritional value.

Put 1 cup of peanuts and 1 tablespoon of peanut oil (the amount of oil may be increased for a creamier spread) into a blender. Grind them, periodically turning off the machine to scrape the sides. Add salt to taste.

Refrigerate your homemade peanut butter in clean, tightly closed jars. After some while, the oil may begin to separate out from the peanut butter; stir a few times to blend it in again.

Make other delicious nut butters by the same method. Some nuts—for example, cashews and almonds—require little or no additional oil, having sufficient natural oils of their own.

Pumpkin Butter

8 cups pureed pumpkin	¼ teaspoon ground cloves
4 cups sugar	¼ teaspoon ground
1½ teaspoons cinnamon	nutmeg
1 teaspoon ground	4 lemons
ginger	

Pare and cube a pumpkin. Steam the pieces in a kettle until they are soft. Drain the pumpkin, and rub it through a sieve to produce 8 cups of pumpkin puree.

Squeeze the lemons. Add their juice and the spices to the puree. Cook the mixture in a 300° F. oven until it becomes thick and smooth.

Put your golden pumpkin butter into jars, and allow it to cool. Seal the jars.

Rhubarb Bread Spread

2 cups rhubarb, cut in pieces	1 teaspoon cinnamon
⅔ cup brown sugar	1 tablespoon butter (or margarine)
1 cup molasses	

Combine the ingredients in a pan. Cook over moderate heat, stirring continuously until well blended. Boil for ten minutes.

Transfer the pan to the oven. Cook its contents at low temperature until the rhubarb spread reaches the consistency of apple butter.

Tomato Butter

2 pounds tart red apples	3 cups white sugar
5 pounds ripe tomatoes	2 blades mace
juice of 1 small lemon	2 cinnamon sticks
1 cup cider vinegar	2 slices ginger root
3 cups brown sugar	½ teaspoon cloves

Put chopped apples, vinegar, and sugar into a big kettle. Blanch, skin, and chop the tomatoes. Add them to the kettle. Tie the spices in a cheesecloth bag, and place it in the pot. Slowly simmer for three hours or until the mixture is thick and smooth, stirring continuously.

Then take out the spice bag. Cool the tomato butter, and fill wide-mouthed jars with it. Store them in a cool place.

CRACKERS AND PRETZELS
Graham Crackers

⅔ cup graham flour   3 tablespoons shortening
⅓ cup white flour   2 tablespoons milk
½ teaspoon soda   ¼ cup honey
¼ teaspoon salt

Blend the dry ingredients; cut in the shortening. Thoroughly mix in the milk and honey.

Make a ball of the dough, and roll it out very thin. (Be sure to flour the board.) Cut the dough into squares. Put them on an ungreased cookie sheet and bake at 325° F.

Remove the crackers from the oven when they are crisp and golden brown.

Soda Crackers

4 cups flour   1 teaspoon vinegar
1 cup butter (or   ½ teaspoon baking soda
    margarine)   ½ teaspoon salt
¾ cup milk

Work the butter into the flour with a pastry cutter or forks. Stir the vinegar, baking soda, and salt into the milk; add this to the butter-flour mixture.

Form the dough into a ball. Then roll it out to a thickness of about ⅕ inch. Lightly score the dough in the size of cracker desired, and perforate the lines with a fork. Bake at 375° F. for twenty minutes or until crisp.

Pretzels

Make dough as for white bread with the following ingredients:

¼ cup shortening   1 ½ cups milk
¼ cup sugar   4 ½ cups flour
1 yeast cake   ¾ tablespoons salt

Scald the milk, shortening, sugar, and salt. Cool the mixture to lukewarm (80° F.). Crumble the yeast into a little milk, and dissolve it. Then blend it with the rest of the milk and 1½ cups of flour. Beat until smooth.

Cover the sponge, and set it in a warm, draft-free place.

Let it rise for one and a half to two hours until it is full of bubbles.

Slowly add the remaining flour and blend until the dough is elastic and smooth. Put it on a lightly floured bread board, and pound it with a rolling pin to develop a velvety texture. Turn the dough over frequently while beating it.

Lay it in a greased bowl, brush with melted butter, and cover with a clean dish towel. Allow the dough to rise for about one hour until it is double in bulk.

Roll the dough in strips about 3 inches long and the thickness of a pencil. Tie the strips in knots, lapping the ends over each other. Place them on a lightly floured board; cover them with a towel and allow to rise until light.

Fill a large kettle with boiling water. Cook each pretzel in the water, turning it over to cook the other side.

Take the pretzels from the water, and drain them. Lay them on a well-greased, lightly floured baking pan; sprinkle with salt. Bake in a 400° F. oven until brown and crisp.

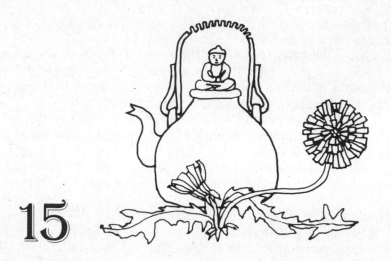

15

Raccoonberry Wine and Other Potables

ECONOMY COFFEES

Around A.D. 1000, Arab merchants carried home the coffee berry from Abyssinia. Not long after, coffee became the national drink of Arabia.

When Mohammedans were forbidden to use wine, a brew of coffee soon became a substitute. The drug properties of the beverage were recognized when people found themselves remaining alert in the evenings after drinking it. Probably because of this drug effect, it was given the name *kahweh* (from which our word *coffee* stems), meaning "wine and other intoxicating beverages."

In the sixteenth century the Arabs brought coffee to Europe, whence it spread to the New World.

Chicory Coffee

Coffee should have aroma, flavor, clarity, and strength. When chicory is blended with it, these characteristics are developed. The first mention of chicory occurred in an ancient papyrus roll dating about 4000 B.C. In the ninth century, monks of Holland cultivated chicory and found that its ground, roasted root enhanced the flavor of their coffee.

The addition of chicory not only results in a more aromatic, richer-tasting coffee; it also cuts by one half the standard measure of coffee required. Besides its use as a coffee adulterant, chicory can serve as a substitute for that beverage.

The plant grows most anywhere—along country roadsides and in city vacant lots. You will know it by the leaves sprouting from its tall, jointed stalk, which resemble dandelion leaves but are somewhat wider and darker green. If ragged blue flowers bloom at the stem joints, you can be fairly certain that you have found chicory.

Dig up the plants; remove the leaves. Peel the roots, and cut them in narrow strips. Roast the root slices for four hours in a 250° F. oven. Then grind them.

To prepare chicory coffee, use 1 teaspoon of the ground root for each cup of water. Boil for three minutes.

Barley Coffee

You can brew a delicious coffee drink, while using less of the product, by blending barley grains and coffee beans. First, roast the barley for forty-five minutes in a 400° F. oven. Occasionally stir the grains to avoid scorching. Remove the barley when it is a deep brown.

Grind it in a blender or coffee mill. Then mix it with your usual coffee to taste, and brew the blend as you would regular coffee.

A decoction of barley alone makes a pleasing, caffein-free beverage.

Chick-pea Coffee

Chick-pea (garbanzo) coffee can be prepared with an economical amount of coffee. Roast garbanzos in a 500° F. oven for ½ hour or until they are very dark brown and very dry. Grind them coarsely (like coffee) in your grinder.

Use 1 tablespoon of the ground peas to 6 cups of boiling water. Continue boiling for three minutes, and then put in 2 tablespoons of coffee (regular grind). Let the mixture cool a few minutes before serving. Sweeten with honey or sugar.

A caffein-free beverage can be made from chick-peas by roasting them in a 300° F. oven until dark brown and then grinding them in a coffee mill.

Use 1 teaspoon of ground chick-peas per cup of water. Prepare the drink in a percolator, or boil it in a saucepan for five to ten minutes and strain.

Sunflower seed hulls, dandelion roots, bran combined with other ingredients, and almonds—all provide good coffee substitutes.

Sunflower Seed Coffee

Shell sunflower seeds easily by first crushing them with a rolling pin. Then drop them into a vessel of water. Kernels will sink; hulls will float.

Reserve the seeds for wholesome eating. Heat the empty sunflower seed hulls in a skillet until just brown. Put them through your grain mill.

Use 1 teaspoon (this amount may be adjusted to suit individual taste) of ground hulls to each cup of water. Steep for three minutes. If desired, sweeten with honey.

Dandelion Root Coffee

Wash dandelion roots thoroughly. Peel off the brown skin. Roast them in a low oven (300° F.) for about four hours or until they are brittle and stiff. Then reduce them to a powder in your food grinder.

Use 1 heaping teaspoon of the powder for each cup of water. Boil for three minutes.

Bran-Cornmeal Coffee

Thoroughly mix 1 pint of yellow cornmeal with 2 quarts of wheat bran. Stir in three well-beaten eggs and 1 cup of sorghum molasses. Beat the mixture well, and spread it on a flat pan. Dry it in a 300° F. oven, stirring it often during browning.

Use the concoction as a coffee substitute, a handful being the right amount for two persons.

Bran-Molasses Coffee

Bran with molasses also makes a delicious caffein-free drink. Combine 1 cup of bran with 4 tablespoons of unsulphured molasses. Mix the ingredients with your hands.

Spread the mixture in a shallow pan, and put it in a 300° F. oven. Stir it now and then until browning takes place, usually in about ½ hour. Then remove it from the oven. Break up any lumps. The toasted granules will resemble freeze-dried coffee. Store bran coffee in an airtight container.

Pour boiling water on a heaping tablespoon of the granules to make each cup of beverage. Honey and cream or milk may be added.

Almond Coffee

Spread almonds on a flat pan, and roast them at 300° until they are dark brown. Grind them in your coffee mill, and then reduce the ground nuts to a fine meal with mortar and pestle.

To serve, stir the resulting powder—in an amount to suit personal taste—into a cup of hot milk. Almond coffee is a delicious and nourishing drink.

TEAS
Black Birch Tea

The black birch is a medium-sized tree, seldom exceeding 2 feet in diameter. Its bark is dark red to black, and the tree's twigs have a strong wintergreen flavor.

To brew a delicious, hearty tea, first gather 1 quart of twigs, and cut them into 1-inch pieces. Put them in a vessel; pour in hot (not boiling) water. Allow to steep until cool.

Remove twigs and impurities by straining the tea. Heat once more. Serve with milk and a little honey.

Hemlock Tea

The hemlock tree is often found in the company of black birches. Chop its needles into lengths of 1 inch. Pour boiling water on them. Allow to steep for a few minutes.

Strain your hemlock tea to remove the needles. Drink it warm.

Mint Tea

Mint is easily identified by its four-sided stalk and the minty aroma of its crushed leaves. Look for it in fields, along streams, or in sunny marshes. Bring home some of the plants, and spread them to dry on newspaper in some warm place away from the sun. The leaves, when thoroughly dry, can be quickly stripped from the stems. Stored in a tightly closed glass or tin container, they provide fragrant tea throughout cold winter months.

Brew the tea by using 1 teaspoon of dried leaves to each cup of boiling water. Allow to steep for a few minutes. You can make mint tea from the plant's green leaves as well; use 2 teaspoons of fresh leaves to 1 cup of boiling water.

Strawberry Tea

If you know the location of a wild strawberry patch, you can prepare a good tea to combat winter's chill by digging beneath the snow and collecting ·tender green strawberry leaves. After they thaw, put two handfuls of them into a teapot; add boiling water. Sweeten with honey to serve.

JUICES

Grape Juice

A glimpse of smoky blue amid vines twining through overhead tree branches probably means you've discovered wild grapes. Pick some of the fruit to make juice.

Crush the grapes, and simmer them for twenty minutes. Keep the water well below the boiling point. Put the fruit in a jelly bag, letting the juice drip into a container overnight.

To store, freeze the juice or warm it to just short of boiling, and transfer it to sterilized jars, closing them tightly.

Because the grape juice tends to be concentrated, you may need to add water before drinking it. Sweeten to taste.

Tomato Juice

Select juicy, ripe tomatoes; wash them thoroughly. After removing the stem ends, chop them into pieces. Simmer the tomato chunks in a pot until soft, stirring frequently. Then strain the vessel's contents.

To each 1 quart of juice, add 1 teaspoon of salt. Serve chilled.

Preserve any excess by reheating the juice to the boiling point immediately after preparation. Pour it into sterilized jars to within ¼ inch of the rim. Adjust the lids, and process for fifteen minutes.

NONCARBONATED DRINKS

Unique Eggnog (yield: 4 ½ quarts)

¼ teaspoon cinnamon
¼ teaspoon cloves
¼ teaspoon ginger
¼ cup sugar
6 eggs, well beaten
2 quarts orange juice, chilled

1 quart vanilla ice cream, soft
1 quart ginger ale, chilled
dash nutmeg

Beat the dry ingredients into the eggs. Blend in the orange juice and homemade ice cream. Just before serving, pour in the ginger ale and sprinkle with nutmeg. For extra zest, rum may be added.

Wassail Bowl

The word *wassail* was originally used as a salutation when offering a cup of wine to a guest or toasting the health of someone. It generally meant, "Be in good health." The word applied as well to the liquor in which healths were drunk. Long ago it was the custom to drink to cattle and fruit trees in wassail to insure that they would thrive.

Today, any festive occasion will thrive when the following drink is served:

2 pounds sugar
6 cardamom berries
6 whole cloves

½ teaspoon mace
1 stick cinnamon
1 nutmeg, cracked

1 teaspoon coriander   12 eggs
2 pieces candied ginger   ½ bottle brandy
1 cup water   6 baked apples
4 bottles Madeira or
    sherry

Mix the dry ingredients in 1 cup of water. Add the wine and simmer. Separate the eggs, beating whites and yolks apart. Now combine the eggs, and slowly add them to the hot mixture. Just before serving, blend in ½ bottle of brandy and six baked apples. Put in a stone crock. Keep it hot in front of a glowing hearth.

CORDIALS

First make a sugar syrup. The recipe you choose may require a sweet or medium strength syrup. To make a sweet syrup, combine 2 cups of white sugar with 1 cup of water, and bring it to the boiling point. To make a medium syrup, combine 1 cup of sugar with ½ cup of water, and bring it to the boiling point. Let it cool for several minutes. Pour the specified amount of syrup into a clean bottle, and add the indicated amount of extract. Fill the bottle with the required spirits. Close it, and shake the contents until all are thoroughly blended. Allow the cordial to cool before serving.

Apricot Brandy

1 bottle apricot brandy   1 fifth (or 1 quart)
    extract   brandy

This recipe needs no sugar. Follow the steps as already described, omitting the syrup.

Cherry Brandy

1 bottle cherry brandy   1 fifth (or 1 quart)
    extract   brandy
1 cup medium sugar
    syrup

The amount of spirits you use depends upon the size of the bottle that will hold the cordial. Follow the steps as previously outlined.

WINES

Blackberry Bramble Wine

Gather 4 pounds of blackberry brambles, cut them into small pieces, and put them in a large crock. Using the bottom of a quart bottle or a mallet, mash them to a pulp. Add 2 quarts of boiling water, and cover the crock. Allow to stand for seven days; stir twice each day.

Strain the contents of the crock to remove the pulp. Pour in an additional quart of boiling water and 12 cups of sugar. Blend thoroughly. When the mixture is lukewarm, sprinkle one package of yeast on it. Cover the vessel, and place it in a warm spot for two weeks.

Strain the mixture into a 1-gallon jug so that the sediment is left behind. Seal the jug by slipping a large balloon over its mouth. This will prevent air from entering while allowing the escape of gases. Occasionally you will need to bleed off the gas that accumulates in the balloon. After ninety days in this container, the wine will be clear and ready to serve. However, it will be even better if strained, poured into bottles, and permitted to age for several months.

Carrot Wine

4 pounds carrots	8 cups sugar
4 lemons	12 peppercorns
4 oranges, sliced in	1 ounce yeast, moistened
¼-inch pieces	1 slice whole wheat toast
2 cups raisins, chopped	

Thoroughly scrub the carrots; chop them fine. Boil for forty-five minutes in 4 quarts of water. When lukewarm, strain. Return the liquid to the vessel. Mix in the sugar, and add the fruit and peppercorns. Spread the toast with the moistened yeast. Let the toast float on the liquid. Place the container in a warm spot for fourteen days to ferment. Stir each day.

At the end of two weeks, strain the wine. Allow it to settle, then syphon your carrot wine into bottles.

Honey-Dandelion Wine

Put 4 quarts of water and 4 quarts of dandelion heads into a crock. Cover it. Allow to stand for eight to ten days.

Strain the dandelion heads, squeezing out the liquid. Add 3 pounds of honey, three sliced lemons, and one cake of wine yeast to the liquid. Let stand for nine days.

Strain the mixture into a jug. When the wine has ceased working, cork the jug.

Country Dandelion Wine

Pick 1 gallon of dandelion heads in the early morning while they are still fresh from dew. Put them in a 2-gallon crock; pour in boiling water. Spread a piece of cheesecloth over the mouth of the crock, and leave it for three days at room temperature.

Squeeze the juice from the flower blossoms, and discard them, reserving the liquid. Pour it into a large vessel. Add 3 pounds of sugar, three whole lemons, chopped, and four whole oranges, chopped. Cover the pot and boil for ½ hour. Let cool to lukewarm. Empty it into a crock; add 2 tablespoons of yeast. Cover with cheesecloth and allow to stand for two or three weeks.

When the bubbling stops, filter your dandelion wine through cheesecloth to remove the chunks. Bottle.

Honey Wine: Mead

Into a 1-gallon glass jug, put 1½ to 2 pints of honey. The amount depends on individual preference; the greater the quantity of honey, the stronger the wine. Fill the jug with warm water. Shake it vigorously.

Add one cake of yeast. Let the uncapped jug stand in the kitchen sink overnight, where it will foam. When the foaming largely subsides, slip a balloon over the jug's mouth to prevent air from entering and allow the escape of gases. Let sit for two weeks.

After bubbles no longer rise to the top, transfer the honey wine to bottles, and seal them with corks so that small amounts of gas can escape.

May Wine

Essential for making May wine is the perennial herb sweet woodruff. It grows in areas of filtered shade and is hardy in every zone. Once planted, it will spread as a ground cover, seeding itself. Sweet woodruff gets along well in the company of other plants, making its appearance in spring. Its dried stems and leaves help to make May wine.

Pick six sprigs of sweet woodruff. Let them dry for several days in a light and airy spot, but away from direct sunlight.

Put them in a punch bowl. Pour two bottles of well-chilled dry white wine over them. Cover the bowl. Allow the herb to steep for two hours. Take out the woodruff. Pour in another bottle of chilled wine. Blend in 2 cups of crushed, sugared strawberries and 2 tablespoons of simple syrup (one part water to two parts sugar, boiled for five minutes). Put your May wine in the refrigerator to chill.

At serving time you may garnish the wine with mint sprigs and float a few whole strawberries in it.

Rose Hip Wine

Collect 4 pounds of rose hips, those orange-colored fruits that grow behind wild or cultivated rose blossoms. They begin to form in July. Green at first, rose hips become orange by September, developing a red color with the approach of autumn.

When setting out to gather hips from thorny wild rosebushes, wear old clothes. It is advisable, also, to don an old pair of gloves for protection against briars. Snipping off their fingertips will allow you to work with freedom. To remove hips easily, use a twisting motion. Drop them into a bag suspended from your belt to free your hands for picking.

Put the fruits in a crock, pulverize them, and pour 2 quarts of boiling water over the pulp. Allow the mixture to sit for four days, stirring each day.

Strain the liquid to remove the pulp. Thoroughly mix in 2½ pounds of sugar, 6 ounces of orange juice (unsweetened), and 1½ quarts of warm water. Sprinkle in one package of yeast. Put the crock in a warm spot for two weeks.

Strain the wine into a 1-gallon jug. Plug the mouth with a wad of cloth. A seal of this kind allows extra air to enter, giving the wine a flavor somewhat similar to sherry. In ninety days it will be suitable for bottling and ready for drinking.

Raccoonberry Wine

During late summer, mayapples—lemon-shaped fruits— hang half hidden beneath their plant's large, shieldlike leaves. You may know them as mandrake apples, raccoonberries, or hog apples. No matter the name, these yellow fruits can be converted into a delicious golden wine. Search for them in lush woodlands.

Crush the fruit in a good-sized crock. Cover the vessel and let stand for seven days. Strain the contents, squeezing all juice from the pulp. Measure the juice; add water in equal measure. Stir 2½ pounds of sugar into each gallon of the liquid. Sprinkle it with yeast. Cover the crock, and set it in a warm place for ten days.

Strain the contents into 1-gallon jugs. Seal them with a piece of plastic wrap secured by a rubber band. Let stand for four months to clarify. Then strain and bottle your golden raccoonberry wine.

Clarifying Wine

When homemade wine is not clear, the best remedy is time. However, if your patience wanes before this cure is effective, try these methods for clarifying wine:

* Beechwood chips or shavings can be used to settle the haze in wine without affecting taste. Add several tablespoons per gallon; leave them until clearing takes place.
* Boil oak shavings for several minutes, drain them, and put 2 tablespoons of the wood bits into a gallon jug of wine. They will hasten clearing of the beverage and add a pleasant oak flavor; check the taste every few weeks to be sure the oak flavor doesn't become too strong.
* An old-time remedy for clarifying wine is egg white. Add one whipped egg white to each gallon of wine. Gently shake the container once a day for seven days or until the beverage has cleared.
* As a last resort, filter the wine through cloth.

Remember that haze in no way affects the taste of wine, only its eye appeal.

CARBONATED DRINKS
Applejack

5 pounds sugar
1½ gallons cider (fresh
  from your local
  cider mill)

5 pounds raisins,
  crushed

Put the sugar in a vessel; add sufficient water to dissolve it. Boil the solution for one minute. When the sugar water is lukewarm, mix it thoroughly with the cider in a jug. Add the crushed raisins.

Close the container tightly. Run a narrow hose from a hole in the cap to a pan of water below in order to free the gas during fermentation. Keep the jug where the temperature is maintained at 70° F.

When a few bubbles per minute agitate the water in the pan, the beverage is ready for drinking. Serve your applejack chilled on warm days and piping hot when the weather turns cold.

Birch Beer

Gather 4 quarts of black birch twigs, cut them into short lengths, and put them in a 5-gallon crock. In a large vessel containing 4 gallons of water, stir 8 pounds of brown sugar until dissolved. Heat to the boiling point and continue boiling for ten minutes. Immediately pour the bubbling liquid over the birch twig pieces in the crock.

Dissolve one yeast cake in 4 ounces of warm water. Stir this into the contents of the crock. Cover and allow to work for ten days or until clear. Ladle into bottles and cap tightly. Birch beer is best when served chilled.

Simple Root Beer (yield: twelve 1-quart bottles)

⅓ ounce root beer extract
4 ½ cups sugar

3 gallons lukewarm water
½ teaspoon wine yeast

Thoroughly wash and rinse all equipment, bottles, and caps. Dry them.

Shake the bottled extract well. Mix the sugar and extract in the water, blending until the sugar dissolves. Blend the yeast in well until it dissolves. Fill the bottles to within 1 inch of their rim. Close with plastic or crown lids.

When using plastic lids, stand the bottles up in a box. If using crown tops, lay the bottles in the box on their sides. Cover against drafts. Put the box in a warm spot. Where the temperature is approximately 70° F., the root beer will carbonate within one to five days; carbonation will usually take place in one day where the temperature is above 80° F. To check for carbonation, refrigerate a bottle after one day. When it is chilled, slowly open it over the sink. Inspecting and tasting it will tell you whether the root beer is sufficiently carbonated. If it seems a little flat, allow it to stand another day or longer.

Old-fashioned Root Beer

If certain roots and barks are available to you, make root beer the old-fashioned way from natural ingredients. Here is a good basic recipe:
* Mix 1½ gallons of molasses into 5 gallons of boiling water. Let stand for three hours.
* Put in ¼ pound each of wintergreen birch bark, sarsaparilla root, and bruised sassafras bark.
* Add 1 cup of fresh yeast, and increase the water content of the vessel to a total of about 16 gallons.
* Set the mixture in a spot where the temperature is kept at 65° to 75° F. Leave it for twelve hours to ferment.
* Draw off the root beer, using flexible tubing, and bottle it. Secondary carbonation will now take place; maintain the same temperature as before throughout the process.

The percentage of alcohol in the drink depends upon the length of time it ferments before bottling and the depth to which the containers are filled. The lower the level to which the bottles are filled, the longer the period of fermentation and the greater the alcoholic content. By experimenting, you can develop the taste you prefer.

Other ingredients that can be used for flavoring are the bark or root of the following: anise, boxberry, cinnamon, clove, deerberry, spiceberry, teaberry, and vanilla. If they are not available to you, their oils are commercially produced.

Granddad's Home Brew

Home-brewed beer requires these ingredients:

3 pounds malt extract (light or dark)	*1 package brewer's yeast*
3½ pounds corn sugar (You may substitute 1 or 2 pounds of honey for part of the sugar.)	*½ teaspoon powdered gelatin (in case the beer is cloudy)* *2 cups corn sugar*

To brew beer, follow these steps:
* Dissolve the malt extract in 2 gallons of boiling water. Continue rapid boiling for 1½ hours. Stir frequently to prevent sticking and burning.
* Put the corn sugar into a large crock. Pour the malt liquid

on it. Add enough water to make 5 gallons of liquid. Allow to cool.

* When the liquid is comfortable to the touch, thoroughly stir in one package of brewer's yeast (found at wine supply shops). Place cheesecloth over the mouth of the crock.
* After the foam has begun to subside, usually within two or three days, syphon the beer into a 5-gallon glass jug with the aid of a rubber hose. Fill it to within 6 inches from the rim to leave space for gas.
* Set the container on a table, and attach a gas lock. One can be purchased in a hardware store, or you can improvise your own. Run the rubber hose through a hole punched in the jug's cap. Do not let the end of the flexible tubing come in contact with the liquid. The other end should hang into a pan of water placed either on the floor or at least several feet below the level of the table. Rising gas from fermentation will be conducted through the tubing and will bubble in the water. When the action has subsided to about three bubbles each minute, the fermentation process is all but complete. The length of time to reach this stage varies with temperature. In a warm area, fermentation takes place in four to six days; where it is cold, the process takes twice as long.
* When bubbling has almost subsided, check for clarity. If the brew is not clear, dissolve ½ teaspoon of powdered gelatin in 8 ounces of water. Add it to the beer.
* Return the flat beer to the crock. Insure carbonation and a good head by stirring in 2 cups of corn sugar.
* Syphon the beer into bottles. Let your home brew sit for seven to fourteen days before drinking it.

Beer

Put ¼ ounce (one packet) of dry yeast in a cup; add warm water and 1 teaspoon of sugar. Stir.

Heat 2 gallons of water to just short of boiling. Dissolve 3 pounds of malt extract and 5 pounds of sugar in it. Empty the mixture into a 5-gallon jug. Add 1 gallon of cold water. Gently shake the jug. Now put in the yeast mixture. Then fill the jug to within 6 inches of the rim with cold water, and set it on a table or counter top. The 6 inches of space will allow for bubbles and froth as the brew works.

Attach a gas lock—a thin hose running from the air space in the container—through a hole in its cap, and into a vessel of water below. Let stand for four to six days or until only about three bubbles a minute disturb the water in the pan. The beer is then ready for bottling.

If the bottle caps you will use are cork lined, soak them in water on bottling day and they will seal much better.

Utilize your hose to syphon the brew into bottles. Add ¼ teaspoon of sugar to each bottle before capping it to insure a frothy head and proper carbonation.

Store the beverage in a dark, cool place for at least seven days before serving it.

Potato Beer

5 gallon container
6 good-sized potatoes
1 cup of sugar

3 packages active dry
    yeast
1 can malt syrup

Chop the potatoes. Put them in a 5-gallon container; a lard bucket will do nicely. Add the yeast, malt syrup, and sugar. Fill the bucket with water, and stir the contents thoroughly. Allow the mixture to ferment for five days. Do not cover the container.

At the end of five days, stir the brew until no sediment remains on the bottom. Then strain it through cloth. The beverage can be drunk now but will improve with time.

Different vegetables may be substituted for the potatoes to achieve a variety of flavors.

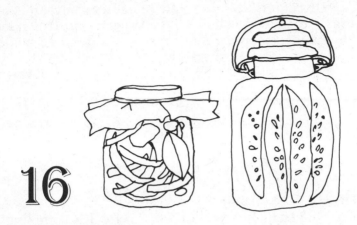

16

GARDEN TO PANTRY SHELF

CANNING FRUITS AND VEGETABLES

When I was a boy, canning season in the heat of a West Texas summer was a time to dread. It completely disrupted the rhythm of homelife. Mother, weary from long hours in a steaming kitchen, set out only hastily prepared meals at irregular times.

Every member of the family participated in the chores. I was obliged to forego fishing along shady river banks. Endless bushel baskets, filled to brimming with garden and orchard produce, had to be lugged into the scorching kitchen, the twang and sharp slap of the screen door marking each delivered load. Here peaches were peeled, peas shelled, and other work doggedly pursued to keep pace with the maturing fruits and vegetables. No sooner was one crop safely sealed in its glass containers than another reached peak ripeness, necessitating immediate preserving.

With the waning day, and strength and spirits flagging, my only thought was to swim or shoot marbles with my friends. At this moment Mother always seemed to say, "Well, let's do just one more batch."

By summer's end, canning was over at last. Memories of hard work faded at the satisfying sight of pantry shelves gleaming with jar after jar of colorful, mouth-watering fruits and vegetables. As the incomparable taste of wholesome, home-grown foods continued to spark midwinter meals, we were convinced that our canning efforts had been more than worthwhile.

Assembled here are the basic methods for preserving fruits and vegetables as used by home canners for several generations.

Canning Methods

* **OPEN KETTLE:** In this method the food is completely cooked, put into sterilized jars, and sealed. Since the jars are not sterilized after sealing, spoilage is possible. However, the open-kettle method may be safely used for canning preserves in thick syrup and tomatoes.

* **OVEN STEAMING:** To preserve food by oven steaming, seal jars completely. Then loosen the lids by turning them back ¼ inch. Self-sealing lids must be totally sealed. Space jars 2 inches apart in a shallow container of warm water placed on the middle rack of your oven. Preheat the oven to 275° F. Maintain steady temperature. Seal jars tightly right after their removal from the oven. Tighten the jar tops again during cooling, the exception being self-sealing tops; do not touch them. Set the jars on folded toweling or several thicknesses of cloth. Cool them rapidly and keep them out of drafts. When the jars are cold, test them for leakage.

* **COLD PACK:** The cold-pack method is used for food that must be arranged in the jars and is put into them when cold. By heating the jars in steam or boiling water, the food is cooked and sterilized at the same time. Caution must be taken to seal containers only partially before processing. Expansion of the food during heating may crack the jars if they have been sealed too tightly.

* **HOT PACK:** The hot-pack method involves filling the jars with boiling hot food and processing in steam or boiling water.

When processing is done in water, the jars can be tightly sealed. This method is generally preferred.

Equipment

Either tin cans or glass jars can be used as containers for preserving food.

Tin cans are available plain or lined with enamel. There are two kinds of lined cans: R enamel cans with shiny gold linings are suitable for very acidic foods and those of red color; the C type, having a dull gold lining, is used for vegetables of high protein content. Use plain cans for preserving meat. Lids for tin cans must be replaced each year. The cans themselves can be used three times by reflanging them.

Glass jars may be purchased with a variety of lids—zinc tops lined with porcelain or glass; metal ones with gaskets that melt during processing, automatically sealing the container; and glass lids. All tops, with the exception of those equipped with automatic seals, require rubber rings. Rubber rings and automatic seal lids must be replaced each year.

You can either buy a water-bath canner or substitute a large kettle for it. Use one deep enough for the boiling water to reach at least 1 inch above the jar tops. To keep jars from bumping and to allow water to circulate under them during processing, place a rack in the bottom.

Process nonacidic vegetables and meats in a pressure canner to kill bacteria that form spores. The pressure canner should be equipped with a safety valve, pet cock, and pressure indicator. Use one of sturdy construction.

Preliminary Procedures

To insure safe, high-quality results, you must check and clean all equipment. Carefully inspect lids for bent, uneven edges and jars for nicks and cracks. If none are apparent, put a new ring on the jar, fill it partway with water, and seal. Turn the jar upside down, and check for leaks or for tiny bubbles rising as the water cools. An imperfect seal on jars with a wire bail can be remedied by taking off the top bail, bending it in at the ends and down in the center, and replacing it. Check rings by folding them in two. Those that develop cracks should be discarded.

Give cans and jars a thorough washing in hot, soapy water, followed by a rinse in hot water. Fill them with water, and set them upright or sideways, with space between each, in a deep vessel of cold water. Gradually bring the water to a boil, and continue boiling for fifteen minutes. Leave the jars in the hot water until needed; let tin cans drain on a clean cloth.

Wash all tops in soapy water. Leave glass and zinc lids in very hot, clear water for five minutes. Keep them hot until used. Turn them upside down to drain. Pour hot water over lids with a sealing composition. Let them stand until wanted for use. Scald rubber rings quickly; never boil them. Sterilize knives, spoons, funnels, and other utensils by putting them in boiling water after a preliminary washing.

When tin cans are used, a mechanical sealer is a necessity. Test its adjustment each time you employ it by putting 2 tablespoons of water in the can, adjusting the lid, and sealing it. Put it in boiling water, keeping it beneath the surface until steam forms in the can and expands the ends. Air bubbles escaping from the can are evidence of improper adjustment of the sealer. Readjust it, and repeat the test.

Clean the removable safety valves and pet cocks on your pressure canner. Vinegar will remove any corrosion. Clean all openings in the canner lid. A toothpick or pipe cleaner is handy for the job. Be sure the gasket is free of dirt and grease, and examine it for a tight fit. If steam escapes or you have difficulty in removing it, grease with salt-free fat the closing surface of the canner cover that seals metal to metal. Tighten screws on the handle. Eliminate stains and odors with 2 tablespoons of vinegar in 2 quarts of water, processing for five minutes at 5 pounds pressure. With a master gauge tester or a maximum thermometer, check the dial gauge. A weight gauge should be cleaned according to the manufacturer's directions.

Preparation of Food

Select vegetables that are young and tender. Clean them thoroughly, and prepare them as for table use. Do not work with too great a quantity of vegetables at one time, particularly in hot weather. The various canning procedures must be accomplished rapidly to avoid flavor loss, called "flat sour." Large amounts of vegetables cannot be handled quickly enough. Can vegetables immediately after picking them. This applies especially to asparagus, beans, corn, and peas. To thoroughly heat nonacid vegetables, precook them, using the pot liquor to fill the jars. Pack vegetables evenly; do not crowd them. For a good pack, shake the jars. Because shell beans, corn, and peas are likely to swell, leave 1 inch of space between the liquid and the rim. Since spinach and other kinds of greens tend to shrink, pack them down lightly, cutting through them with a knife several times.

Approximate Vegetable Yield		
Vegetable	Weight	Yield
Asparagus	3 pounds	1 quart
Beans, Lima	2 pounds	1 quart
Beans, String	1¾ pounds	1 quart
Beets, Baby	2½ to 3 pounds	1 quart
Corn on the Cob	7 small ears	1 quart
Greens	2¾ to 3 pounds	1 quart
Peas, Green, Shelled	4 pounds	1 quart
Tomatoes	3 pounds	1 quart

Choose firm, well-developed fruit that is not overly ripe. Try to can it soon after it has been picked. Prick unseeded plums and cherries a few times with a big pin. When canning fruit without sugar, use fruit juice or boiling water in place of syrup, filling the containers to within ½ inch of their rim. Before serving the fruit, drain it, add sweetening to the liquid, and bring to a brisk boil. Pour it on the fruit and allow to cool. Then chill it. You may wish to cook berries and fruits in syrup for several minutes to achieve a full pack. Prepare syrups according to the fruit's acidity and the taste preference of those for whom the food is canned. One cup of sugar to 3 cups of fruit juice or water will yield 3½ cups of thin syrup. One cup of sugar to 2 cups of water or fruit juice will yield 2½ cups of medium syrup. One cup of sugar added to 1 cup of fruit juice or water will result in 1½ cups of thick syrup. Blend the sugar and liquid, stirring over heat until the sugar dissolves. Bring the syrup to a boil. Use approximately 2 cupfuls of syrup to each quart of large fruit, such as peaches, pears, and plums. Use 1 cupful of syrup to each quart of small fruit, such as berries and cherries.

To avoid dark fruit, take these precautions:

* Process fruit for the correct amount of time; too-short processing results in dark fruit.
* Maintain sufficiently high temperature. Water should be boiling at the start of processing time and remain at a boil throughout.
* Accurately count the time of processing. Start counting time when a rolling boil commences. Check the timetable, making any adjustments that might be required for altitude.
* The level of boiling water should be between 1 and 2 inches above the lids of the jars during the complete processing time.
* Before packing large raw fruits, such as pears or peaches, treat them with an antioxidant. Put them in a solution of 2 teaspoons of salt to 1 quart of water.

To keep fruit from floating, follow these tips:

* Do not use overripe fruits; use those in their prime.
* Pack fruit closely.
* Don't allow the syrup to get too thick.
* Process for exactly the right length of time.
* Be sure the temperature is not too high.

Approximate Fruit Yield					
Fruit	*Weight*	*Units*	*Yield*	*Bushels*	*Yield*
Apples	2½ pounds	7–8	1 quart	1	28 quarts
Berries	1¼–1½ pounds	5 cups	1 quart	1	24 quarts
Cherries	1¼–1½ pounds	6 cups	1 quart	1	20 quarts
Peaches	2–2½ pounds	8–10	1 quart	1	21 quarts
Pears	2–2½ pounds	5–6	1 quart	1	30 quarts
Pineapples		15			15 quarts
Plums	1½–2½ pounds	24–32	1 quart	1	28 quarts
Tomatoes	2½–3½ pounds	8–10	1 quart		18 quarts

Sort vegetables and fruits as to size so that each jar's contents will be approximately uniform. To peel foods like tomatoes and peaches, dip them in boiling water, until the skins loosen, and then in cold water for a moment. Once the vegetables and fruits have been heated, work quickly, filling only the number of jars that your canner accommodates. Don't allow the hot foods to stand prior to processing, for harmful bacteria develop between 105° and 150° F. Fill the containers to ½ inch from the top. For vegetables, use boiling water; for fruits, use boiling syrup. To help air bubbles rise to the surface and break, insert a spatula along the sides of the jar. If the contents of the jar are hot and processing is to take place in a water bath, seal the containers completely. Otherwise, seal them partially. If the food in tin cans is not hot at sealing time, rid the containers of air by boiling them for five minutes in 1 inch of water. After adjusting the lids, seal them immediately.

Processing

* *HOT WATER BATH:* Put hot, filled cans or jars on the rack in the canner. Cover them with boiling water to a depth of 1 inch above their tops. Heat rapidly to boiling. When bubbles commence breaking over the containers, begin the timing. Make sure that water covers the jars throughout the processing period. When necessary, add boiling water. Take the canner from the heat upon completion of processing.

* *PRESSURE COOKER:* There should be sufficient boiling water in the cooker to reach the bottom of the rack. Put packed cans or jars on the rack, adjust the cooker lid, and clamp it down firmly. Have the pet cock open. After permitting steam to escape for seven minutes, close the pet cock, and watch for the pressure to reach the required point. From that moment count to *nine.* Regulate the heat to maintain steady pressure. Changes in pressure generally cause liquid loss in the containers, especially if the pressure builds to the extent of releasing the safety valve, causing an abrupt fall in pressure. Immediately upon termination of processing time, take the canner from the heat. When sufficient cooling has reduced the pressure to zero, slowly open the petcock. Wait until pressure is completely released before opening the canner. When using number 2 cans, open the petcock just as quickly as processing is completed, permitting the pressure to drop rapidly. Open the canner and take out the cans. Submerge them immediately in cold water to avoid overcooking.

Cooling Containers

Take jars out of the canner. If they are partially sealed, complete the seal. Put them on folded towels. Invert those that do not have an automatic seal. From time to time, examine the jars. Rising bubbles or leakage indicates that the food should be used or immediately recanned. Never invert jars with self-sealing tops. Test them by tapping with a spoon. If the sound is dull instead of a clear-ringing note, the jar is not well sealed. After submerging tin cans in water, check for bubbles escaping from ends or seams. When containers are cold, wash and label them. Store them in a cool, dry spot.

Spoilage

If you detect any evidence of spoilage, dispose of the food. An odor that is not characteristic of the product is an indication of spoilage. There should be no signs of leakage, bulging of the rubber, spurting of liquid, or expulsions of air with glass jars. Never taste-test a questionable food; destroy it immediately. Always boil all canned vegetables for ten minutes before serving or tasting.

Canning Recipes for Vegetables, Fruits, and Fruit Juices

Vegetables

When seasoning vegetables for canning, use 1 teaspoon of salt for 1 quart of vegetables; for 1 pint, use ½ teaspoonful.

* ASPARAGUS: Carefully wash asparagus. Cut it in 1-inch pieces or lengths to fit the containers. Put them into boiling water and boil for five minutes, keeping the tips above water. Pack immediately in hot jars, stem ends down. Pour in seasoned cooking liquid to within ½ inch of the rim. Partially seal jars. Process at once at ten pounds pressure for forty minutes (for pint jars, five minutes less).

* BEANS, STRING: Wash beans and remove ends. Cut them into uniform lengths. Cover with boiling water. When the water commences boiling again, pack loosely in hot jars, adding salt and boiling cooking water to within ½ inch of their rim. Season, partially seal, and process immediately at ten pounds pressure for forty-five minutes (for pint jars, five minutes less).

* **BEANS, LIMA:** Select small green beans. Wash well, shell, and precook for four minutes. Pack loosely in clean, hot jars to within 1 inch of the rim. Add boiling cooking liquid to the same level. Season, partially seal, and process at ten pounds pressure for sixty minutes (for pint jars, five minutes less).

* **BEETS:** Choose very small beets. Wash carefully. Cut off tops. Leave 1 inch of root and stem. Scald until skins slip. Remove skins, and pack the beets in jars at once. Fill with liquid to within ½ inch of the rim. Season. Partially seal jars. Process immediately at ten pounds pressure for forty minutes (for pint jars, five minutes less).

* **BROCCOLI, BRUSSELS SPROUTS, CABBAGE, CAULIFLOWER:** Wash vegetables and remove stems. Discard coarse leaves. Precook for three minutes. Pack in hot jars. Fill them with fresh boiling water up to ½ inch from the rim. Season. Seal, and process immediately at ten pounds pressure for forty minutes.

* **CARROTS:** Wash young carrots. Precook for five minutes. Skin. Pack at once in hot jars. Fill jars with boiling liquid up to 1 inch from the rim. Season. Partially seal jars. Process immediately at ten pounds pressure for forty minutes (for pint jars, five minutes less).

* **CORN, WHOLE KERNEL:** Cut corn from the cob. Weigh. Add one-half the weight in boiling water. Season each quart with 2 teaspoons of sugar and 1 teaspoon of salt. Heat to a boil. Pack in hot jars, adding boiling liquid to 1 inch from the top. Partially seal jars. Process immediately at ten pounds pressure for seventy-five minutes (for pint jars, ten minutes less).

* **CORN, CREAM STYLE:** Remove uncooked corn from the cob with a shallow cut. Using the back of a knife, scrape the cobs. Follow directions for whole kernel corn. Process immediately at ten pounds pressure for eighty minutes (for pint jars, the same time).

* **GREENS:** Discard imperfect leaves and stems. Wash well. Add water and simmer until thoroughly wilted. Drain, saving liquid. Pack the greens in jars. Cut through their centers several times with a knife. Add boiling cooking liquid up to ½ inch from rim. Season with salt. Partially seal jars. Process

immediately at fifteen pounds pressure for sixty-five minutes (for pint jars, five minutes less).

* **MUSHROOMS:** Wash well. Skin mature mushrooms. Put them in boiling water with 1 teaspoon of salt and 1 tablespoon of vinegar per quart. Drain. Pack in hot jars. Pour in fresh boiling water to within ½ inch of the rim. Partially seal the jars. Process immediately at ten pounds pressure for thirty-five minutes (for pint jars, ten minutes less).

* **OKRA:** Thoroughly wash the okra. Discard the stem ends. Precook for five minutes. Pack hot into hot, clean jars. Pour in boiling cooking water to within ½ inch of the rim. Season. Partially seal and process immediately at ten pounds pressure for forty minutes (for pint jars, five minutes less).

* **PEAS:** Shell tender young peas. Precook for four minutes. Pack the hot peas loosely in hot, clean jars. Pour in boiling cooking water to within 1 inch of the rim. Season, and partially seal jars. Process immediately at ten pounds pressure for one hour (for pint jars, ten minutes less).

* **POTATOES, NEW WHITE:** Wash well. Cook for five minutes. Remove eyes and skin. Pack while hot, adding boiling cooking liquid to within ½ inch of the rim. Season. Partially seal the jars, and process immediately at fifteen pounds pressure for seventy minutes.

Fruits
Rules for processing in boiling water are for an altitude of 1000 feet or less. Increase processing time by 20% for each additional 1000 feet.

To use the cold-pack, hot-pack, and open-kettle methods, see the procedures under those headings.

These recipes are for quart and pint jars. Consult the directions already given for packing and sealing jars to be processed by the following methods.

MAKING PRESERVES

When fruits become plump from absorbing thick sugar syrup and appear bright and clear in color, you have successful preserves. Stew hard fruits before putting them in syrup.

Fruit	Hot Water Bath	Oven	Pressure Canner
Apples: Peel, core, and quarter. Precook or steam for five minutes in thin boiling syrup. Process immediately for	20 minutes	75 minutes at 250° F.	10 minutes at 5 pounds
Apricots: Wash. Leave apricots whole, pit them, or halve them. Pack in jars. Pour in thin boiling syrup to cover. Process immediately for	20 minutes	68 minutes at 250° F.	10 minutes at 5 pounds
Berries: Pick over berries. Wash and hull them. Fill sterilized jars. Pour in boiling syrup to cover. Process immediately for	20 minutes	68 minutes at 250° F.	10 minutes at 5 pounds
Cherries: Wash and stem. Prick with a large pin if unseeded. Fill jars. Cover with thick or medium boiling syrup. Process immediately for	25 minutes	68 minutes at 250° F.	10 minutes at 5 pounds

Fruit Juices: Crush ripe fruit. (Remove seeds from cherries.) Gradually bring to the simmering point. Strain. Add water and sugar to taste. Heat the juice, and pour it into hot jars. Seal and process at once for	30 minutes		
Peaches: Skin, halve, and pack in jars. Pour in boiling medium syrup to cover. Process immediately for	25 minutes	1 hour at 275° F.	10 minutes at 5 pounds
Pears: Remove skins, halve, and core. Boil 1 quart of pears at a time in thin syrup for about six minutes. Pack in hot jars, adding syrup. Process immediately for	30 minutes	1 hour at 275° F.	10 minutes at 5 pounds
Pineapple: Peel and remove eyes. Cube the pineapple and pack it in jars, pouring in boiling thin syrup to cover. Process at once for	30 minutes	1 hour at 275° F.	10 minutes at 5 pounds

Plums: Wash plums. Prick them with a large pin. Pack jars and cover the contents with boiling medium syrup. Process immediately for	20 minutes	1 hour at 275° F.	10 minutes at 5 pounds
Rhubarb: Wash. Cut into pieces. Pack in jars, pouring in boiling thin syrup to cover. Process at once for	16 minutes	50 minutes at 275° F.	10 minutes at 5 pounds
Strawberries: Wash and stem. Add 1 cup of sugar to each quart. Allow to stand for two hours. Simmer for five minutes. Fill the jars. Seal and process immediately for	20 minutes	68 minutes at 250° F.	10 minutes at 5 pounds

Sweet apples, citrons, hard pears, pineapples, underripe peaches, quinces, and watermelon rinds must be cooked until soft enough to absorb the syrup. Foods that have had this preliminary stewing should be thoroughly drained before being added to the syrup. Use this cooking water to make the syrup. Berries, cherries, ripe peaches, and other tender fruits can be put directly into heavy syrup. Don't cook fruits too long in the syrup, just long enough for them to become filled with it; otherwise a dark, stiff product will result. Bring it quickly to a boil, and continue the rapid cooking until the fruits are shiny and sparkling, indicating that they are saturated with syrup.

For extra-fine preserves, place the fruit in the heavy syrup, and heat it until bubbling begins. Remove from the stove and let stand in a covered enamel preserving pot for a few hours or overnight. Then commence the cooking again. In this manner the fruit absorbs more syrup. For an extra fine quality product, repeat the plumping process of heating and cooling a few times. Particularly suited to plumping are citrons, crab apples, green tomatoes, whole tomatoes, peaches, pears, and melon rinds. Always plump fruits that are to be candied.

Seal your preserves in hot, clean jars. Sterilize in boiling water all utensils used in filling the jars with preserves. As a precaution against mold, place the packed jars in boiling water or steam for ten minutes.

MAKING JAM

Making jam requires mashing or cooking to a pulp small whole fruits with sugar. Ideally, its texture should be tender and soft, its color sparkling bright, and the mixture's consistency uniform.

A jellying substance, pectin, is a necessity for good jam. Broken fruit or pieces remaining from canning may be used for jam making, but part of the fruit must be underripe because pectin is absent in overripe fruit. To develop the pectin, cook the fruit several minutes before adding sugar. When fruit lacks enough juice, add a little water to prevent burning, and cook it in a covered vessel. Porcelain or enamel cooking utensils are best. Use ¾ pound of sugar to 1 pound of fruit. After putting in sugar, cook rapidly until the jam takes on a jellylike appearance. To check whether it's done, test it by dropping a bit on a cool dish. If it sets quickly or hangs from the spoon in sheets, it is ready. Keep in mind that upon cooling, jam thickens. Make allowance for this so that the product will not become tough and thick from overcooking. Cooking for too long also darkens the jam.

Because jam is a highly concentrated substance, it will burn easily. To avoid this, always stir from the bottom with a wooden spoon, lifting the jam from the bottom of the kettle. Cook jam rapidly, watching it closely for twenty to thirty minutes.

To protect jams from mold, seal them in hot, clean jars.

Fig Jam (yield: 3 pints)

4 pounds fresh figs	*1 cup water*
1 lemon	*4 cups sugar*

Wash figs; peel them. Slice the lemon. Cook water and sugar together for five minutes. Add lemon and figs. Cook briskly until clear.

Seal in hot clean jars.

Grape Jam (yield: 2 pints)

4 pounds Concord grapes	1 ½ cups water
	3 cups sugar

Wash grapes. Remove the skins and seeds. Combine water and sugar; boil for five minutes. Add grape pulp and continue cooking until thick and clear.

Pour into hot, clean jars. Seal immediately.

Peach Jam (yield: eight ½-pint jars)

4 ¼ cups crushed peaches (about 3 ½ pounds of the fruit)	¼ cup lemon juice
	7 cups sugar
	½ bottle liquid pectin

Wash ripe peaches. Remove their stems, skins, and pits. Crush the fruit.

Put the peach pulp in a kettle, and mix in the lemon juice and sugar. Set over high heat, stirring continuously. Quickly bring to a rolling boil and boil hard for one minute, stirring all the while.

Take from the fire, and stir in the pectin. Skim. Fill and seal jars.

MAKING MARMALADE

Generally, marmalades are made from fruits containing both acid and pectin. The fruits are thinly sliced and suspended in a clear jelly. If fruit is used in which the jellying properties of pectin and acid are absent, tart apple juice or slices of lemon or orange can be added to supply them.

The preparation of marmalade is the same as for jams, except that the fruit is in cut pieces or slices, not mashed. Successful marmalade should be of sparkling clarity.

Grapefruit Marmalade

Cut the sections from three grapefruit. Discard seeds and white fiber. Grind the well-washed yellow rind (without the white) of one grapefruit in a food grinder. To the grapefruit sections, add the ground grapefruit peel and the grated rind and strained juice of three lemons. Cover with 6 cups of water; allow to stand overnight.

The following morning, boil the mixture for forty minutes. Repeat for two days more.

Then put in 1 cup of crushed pineapple. Measure the mixture, and add 1½ cups of sugar for each cup of fruit and juice. Cook for thirty minutes or until jellylike.

Seal in sterilized jars.

Tomato-Apple-Ginger Marmalade

Skin enough ripe tomatoes to make 2 cupfuls. Drain. Peel and core enough apples to make 2 cupfuls. Chop. Mince one lemon.

Mix these ingredients, and cook them for fifteen minutes. Add 3 cups of sugar, and cook until the mixture reaches the consistency of marmalade. For the last ten minutes of cooking, add 4 tablespoons of chopped preserved ginger.

Seal in sterilized jars.

MAKING JELLIES

To make jelly, sugar and fruit juice are combined in proper proportions and cooked until the mixture jells when cool. Jelly of good quality has the natural flavor and color of the fresh fruit, its clarity unmarred by crystals or sediment. It retains its shape when emptied from the jar but is supple enough to quiver. When cut, the jelly does not stick to the knife.

Fruit for jelly must be high in acid and pectin. When fruit is not rich in both of these, it must be combined with a fruit containing whichever substance is absent. The following fruits have pectin and acid in sufficient quantity: crab apples, tart apples, blackberries, gooseberries, loganberries, raspberries, currants, grapes, plums, and quinces. Those with insufficient pectin are as follows: cherries, peaches, pineapples, rhubarb, and strawberries. Fruits lacking enough acid are sweet apples, blueberries, huckleberries, and pears.

Although the flavor isn't as good, fruit that is a bit underripe generally has more pectin and acid than completely ripe fruit. A correct proportion is one-quarter underripe fruit to three-quarters ripe fruit. If either acid or pectin is lacking in a fruit, it can be combined nicely with tart apples, because apple juice has the most minimal affect on the flavor and color of the jelly.

When using commercial pectin, follow exactly the directions accompanying it. The juice from almost any kind of fruit can be used by adding a large quantity of sugar and the commercial pectin. Jelly is made in less time, but due to the shorter cooking period, the flavor is less rich and full than fruit juice boiled over a longer period. However, success is usually assured with the use of commercial pectin.

Extraction of Fruit Juice

Carefully inspect the fruit, and remove stems and areas of decay. Cut large fruits into pieces. Crush juicy fruits, adding little or no water. Fruits with less juice require adding just enough water until it is visible among the pieces, but not so much that they float. Cook the fruit in a covered vessel until tender and the juice flows liberally. Do not overcook. Apples need approximately fifteen minutes, berries from one to three minutes, and citrus fruits one hour.

Empty the contents into a jelly bag. Use a clean flour sack, or make one of heavy muslin, flannel, or four layers of cheesecloth. Suspend it on a strainer above a bowl to allow the juice to drip through. More juice is extracted by squeezing the bag, but the jelly will not be clear. The first time, let the juice simply drip through; the resulting jelly will be clear and appropriate for special occasions. Squeeze the bag with the second extraction; jelly from this juice will be cloudy, but acceptable for general use. Pulp for a second extraction can be prepared by putting it in a pot, adding water almost to cover, and simmering for about twenty-five minutes. If only one extraction is made, you can press the pulp that remains through a sieve and use it for preparing fruit butter or jam.

Pectin Test

The amount of pectin in a particular fruit juice can be ascertained by combining 1 tablespoon of the juice, 1½ teaspoons of Epsom salts, and 1 teaspoon of sugar. Blend the mixture. When the salts have dissolved, allow to stand for twenty minutes. The formation of large flaky particles or a solid mass means that sufficient pectin is present in the juice to make a good jelly.

Sugar Content

Too much sugar results in weak, syrupy jelly; too small an amount of sugar produces a too-solid jelly. As a general rule, the right proportion is a quantity of sugar equaling two-thirds of the amount of fruit juice. When in doubt, use less sugar instead of more. It is not necessary to heat the sugar.

Cooking Jelly

To produce jelly with the best texture, flavor, and color, cook no more than 2 quarts of juice at one time. Use a 10-quart vessel of large diameter to permit rapid evaporation. When the juice begins to boil, gradually add sugar, stirring slowly. Boil briskly until the jellying point, which can be determined by letting a little juice drip from the spoon. The running together in a continuous strand of the last few drops indicates the jellying stage. Immediately remove the jelly from the heat. Skim and pour into hot, clean glasses. Fill them to within ⅜ inch of their rims. Seal with paraffin either by pouring melted paraffin on the jelly at once or by covering the jelly with hot paraffin after it has cooled. Put metal covers on the jelly jars after the paraffin cools. Store them in a cool, dry place.

Butter Bean Hull Jelly

5 cups butter bean hull juice
7 cups sugar

2 packages (1 ¾ ounces each) powdered fruit pectin

Boil butter bean hulls for one hour. Strain them through cheesecloth. Add the pectin to 5 cups of strained juice. Bring the mixture to a boil, and stir in the sugar.

Allow to jell. Pour into clean jars and seal.

Amounts of Sugar and Fruit Juice for Jelly

Fruit	Juice	Sugar
Apple	1 cup	⅔ cup
Blueberry (with lemon juice)	1 cup	⅔ cup
Crab Apple	1 cup	⅔ cup
Currant	1 cup	¾ to 1 cup
Gooseberry (green)	1 cup	1 cup
Grape (underripe)	1 cup	¾ to 1 cup

Fruit Juice Combinations	Juice	Sugar
Apple	½ cup	⅔ cup
Black Raspberry	½ cup	
Apple	½ cup	¾ cup
Blueberry	½ cup	
Apple	½ cup	⅔ cup
Cherry	½ cup	
Apple	½ cup	⅔ cup
Peach	½ cup	
Apple	½ cup	⅔ cup
Pineapple	½ cup	
Apple	½ cup	⅔ cup
Quince	½ cup	
Blackberry	¾ cup	⅔ cup
Apple	¼ cup	
Cherry	½ cup	¾ cup
Currant	½ cup	
Currant	½ cup	⅔ cup
Raspberry	½ cup	
Damson Plum	¼ cup	¾ cup
Apple	¾ cup	
Elderberry	½ cup	¾ cup
Apple	½ cup	
Gooseberry (unripe)	½ cup	¾ cup
Cherry	½ cup	

Corn Cob Jelly

12 medium-sized red   1 ¼ ounce package
    corn cobs   powdered pectin
2 quarts water   3 cups sugar

Wash cobs. Cut them into fourths. Put them in a vessel of water and bring to the boiling point. Lower the heat. Let boil slowly for about forty minutes.

Strain the juice. Measure 3 cups of it into a large saucepan. Add pectin; bring to a boil. Add sugar; bring to a boil once more. Continue boiling for five minutes.

Skim the foam from the surface. Pour into sterile jars. Corn cob jelly is said to taste like mild honey.

Mesquite Bean Jelly

3 quarts mesquite beans   1 box pectin (1 ¾ ounces)
5 cups sugar

Pick mesquite beans while they are still red. Cover 3 quarts of the beans with enough water to make 5 cups of juice. Add sugar as it simmers until the juice becomes yellow. Strain it.

Follow directions on pectin juice for making jelly, but boil a bit longer than specified. Use the spoon test to check when it has jelled.

Put into sterilized jars. Seal.

Parsley Jelly (yield: six 8-ounce glasses)

3 cups boiling water   4 ½ cups sugar
4 cups chopped parsley   several drops green
    (2 big bunches)   food coloring
2 tablespoons lemon   (homemade)
    juice
1 ¾ ounces powdered
    fruit pectin

Put the chopped parsley in a bowl; pour the boiling water over it. Cover. Allow to stand for twenty minutes.

Strain the liquid through cheesecloth. Put 3 cups of the parsley juice into a good-sized saucepan. Stir in the lemon juice and pectin. Cook over high heat, stirring until the mixture reaches a rolling boil. Put in all the sugar at once and stir. Mix in a few drops of green coloring. Bring to a rolling boil again and boil hard for one minute, stirring continuously.

Take the pan from the heat, and remove the foam with a metal spoon. Quickly pour the liquid into sterilized jelly glasses. Cover immediately with hot paraffin to a depth of ⅛ inch.

Homemade Pectin

Make apple jelly stock—sugar-free pectin—to preserve for future use or to prepare jams and jellies immediately. (Most commercial pectins contain sugar.)

For your homemade pectin select small, green, immature apples, available in early summer. Being rich in pectin and acid, they make excellent jelly stock and impart a snappy, tart flavor to the finished product. Apples cut or bruised by falling from orchard boughs, and even those damaged by birds and insects, can be utilized by cutting away the imperfect parts.

Wash the fruit thoroughly, retaining only the sound portions and cutting them into thin slices. Put them in a vessel, and add 2 cups of water for each pound of apples. Cover the vessel; boil its contents for fifteen minutes. Strain the juice with pulp through one thickness of cheesecloth; do not squeeze the pulp.

Put the pulp back in the vessel, once more adding the required measure of water. Cook the mixture again for fifteen minutes, but this time over lower heat. Let it stand for ten minutes. Now strain the juice with pulp through cheesecloth, without squeezing the pulp. When the pulp cools sufficiently for handling, press any remaining juice from it. You should have accumulated approximately 1 quart of apple juice for each pound of fruit.

If you don't have immediate plans for blending the pectin with the juice of other fruits to make jam or jellies, prepare it for storage in this way: Heat the jelly stock to the boiling point; then pour it into hot, sterilized canning jars. Seal them. Invert the jars, and allow them to cool. Instead of canning the pectin, you may freeze it by letting the liquid cool and pouring it into freezer containers. Leave 1 inch of headroom to allow for expansion.

To prepare honey jelly, use 2 cups of homemade pectin to each 2½ cups of honey plus ½ cup of water. These amounts will vary a little when fruit juice is used, depending on the kind involved. Remember that the greater the quantity of pectin, the thicker the finished product and the weaker the other fruit's flavor.

Grape Jelly with Homemade Pectin

Blend the following:

2½ cups grape juice (unsweetened and, if possible, homemade)	½ cup honey 2 cups homemade pectin

Rapidly boil the mixture for ten minutes. To prevent its foaming over, stir the jelly but don't lower the heat.

Pour it immediately into hot, sterilized jelly jars. Seal them. Do not disturb the jars until the contents have partially set. To complete the jelling, refrigerate them.

MAKING VINEGAR

In the presence of a particular kind of yeast, the action of oxygen upon a solution of alcohol produces vinegar. The alcoholic liquors from which vinegar can·be made result from the fermentation of almost any fruit or vegetable juices. The chief types of vinegar are wine vinegar from grapes; malt vinegar from barley; cider vinegar from apples; sugar and molasses vinegar from sugar cane; beet vinegar; corn vinegar; etc.

Cider Vinegar

Put cider into a jug. For each quart of cider, add ½ cup of molasses and ¼ cup of brewer's yeast. Leave the container partially open to admit air. Fermentation will begin at once. The cider will become vinegar in about a week's time.

Pour off the clear vinegar into bottles and close tightly. To repeat the process, leave the lees (which provide the necessary yeast) in the jug and fill with fresh cider.

White Wine Vinegar

Crush 1 pound of clean raisins. Add ½ gallon of pure soft or distilled water and put in a 1-gallon jug, uncovered. Allow to stand in a warm place. It will turn into white wine vinegar in about a month.

Strain the clear vinegar through cheesecloth. Leave the raisins and sediment in the jug. Add another ½ gallon of water along with ¼ pound of raisins to repeat the process.

Fruit Vinegar

The juice of most fruits, such as currants, gooseberries, and raspberries, contains enough sugar to ferment and produce an alcoholic liquor for making vinegar, with or without adding molasses.

To make vinegar from fruits, extract the juice by boiling the fruit with its equal in water. Press out the juice through several layers of cheesecloth. You can do this by inserting sticks at either end of the cloth and twisting them. To each 2 quarts of fruit juice, add ¼ cup of yeast. Allow to stand in a jar or jug with the top slightly tilted to admit air. Keep it in a spot where the temperature ranges between 70° and 80° F. Or you may let the boiled fruit juice stand for two or three days to ferment before straining it. Add the yeast after the fermented liquor has been removed from the fruit pulp.

PREPARING PICKLES

Pickling is the process of preserving foods with vinegar or brine. A variation of seasonings and spices results in spiced pickles, sour pickles, and sweet pickles.

Vegetables and fruits can be pickled sliced, quartered, in halves, or whole. The most commonly pickled foods are cabbage, carrots, cauliflower, cucumbers, beets, onions, tomatoes, crab apples, grapes, peaches, and pears.

* *PREPARATION OF FOOD FOR PICKLING:* Scrub vegetables thoroughly in clear water. Next, soak them in salted water (from ⅛ to ¼ cup of salt for each quart of water) for a few hours or overnight. The salt extracts moisture from the tissues, crisping the vegetables so that they more readily soak up the pickling solution.

Fruits do not require a preliminary soaking in water and salt. Prepare them as you would for canning, and put them in the pickling solution.

* *PICKLING POINTERS:*
* Lift or stir pickles with a wooden or granite spoon.

* Cool pickles in an aluminum vessel or porcelain-lined graniteware.
* Keep in mind that too much salt will shrivel vegetables and make them tough.
* Vinegar that is too strong can bleach vegetables and cause them to soften after pickling.
* Seal pickles in stone or glass jars.

Bread-and-Butter Pickles

8 cups sliced cucumbers	1 tablespoon mustard
5 cups sliced onions	seed
½ cup finely chopped	½ teaspoon celery seed
green pepper	¼ teaspoon turmeric
¼ cup salt	¼ teaspoon ginger
1 quart water	1½ cups vinegar
2½ cups sugar	1 cup water

Put cucumbers, onions, and green peppers in a big bowl. Dissolve the salt in a quart of water, and pour it on the cucumber mixture. Cover. Allow to stand for four hours at room temperature.

Drain the bowl's contents. Place them in a 6-quart kettle. Heat the rest of the ingredients in a saucepan to the boiling point, stirring until the sugar dissolves. Pour over the cucumber mixture. Heat to a boil.

Pack in sterilized jars to within ½ inch of the rim. Seal. Process in boiling water for ten minutes.

Pumpkin Pickles

Cut a pumpkin rind into strips. Peel and cut them in 1-inch pieces. Prepare 4 cupfuls.

Combine the following in a saucepan:

1 cup sugar	6 whole cloves
¾ cup white vinegar	2 teaspoons ginger,
¼ cup dark corn syrup	freshly grated
½ cinnamon stick,	
crushed	

Bring these ingredients to a boil, and add the pumpkin pieces. Slowly cook the mixture for about forty-five minutes or until tender.

Put the pickles in a quart jar; close it tightly. Store in the refrigerator.

Sauerkraut

*5 pounds cabbage (select   5 tablespoons salt
    firm heads)*

Take off the outer leaves—wash and put them aside—and any imperfect parts of the cabbage. Quarter it, removing the core. Slice the cabbage finely with a slaw cutter or sharp knife. Toss cabbage and salt in a large bowl, mixing well.

Solidly pack it into a 1- to 2-gallon crock. Allow to stand for a few minutes. Forcefully press on the cabbage with a wooden pestle (a wooden spoon will serve) until juice makes its appearance. Cover the top with the well-washed outer leaves of the cabbage; place several thicknesses of cheesecloth over them. Lay a plate on the cloth that fits snugly within the crock. To insure that the cabbage remains beneath the liquid and that the cloth stays wet, weight the dish. A heavy stone will do nicely. Let the crock stand in a warm place (65°–68° F.) to ferment for about four weeks. When choosing the spot, take into consideration that the contents will give off a very disagreeable odor during the initial stage of fermentation. Check the crock each day. Skim off scum. Remove the cloth cover, rinse in cold water, wring dry, and replace.

After four to five weeks, the sauerkraut is ready for use and should be stored in a cool (below 60° but above 32° F.), dark place. Keep the top covered to prevent air from entering. For canning, simmer kraut and juice in a large vessel to heat; avoid boiling. Pack into clean hot jars. Fill them with juice to within ½ inch of the rim. Seal and process.

Watermelon Pickles
General Rules
* Cut watermelon rind in long strips. (Leaving on a little pink flesh lends color to the finished product.) Peel them. Cut the rind into 1-inch chunks. Prepare 4 quarts.
* In 2 quarts of cold water, dissolve 1 cup of salt. Drop in a few cherry or grape leaves to insure crisp pickles.
* Pour this solution on the rind pieces, adding water, if necessary, to cover them. Allow to stand for six hours. (For

a shorter soaking period, two to four hours, you may substitute 3 tablespoons of slaked lime for the salt and leaves. Check the bag's label to be sure the lime is intended for pickling.)

* After the soaking period, rinse the rind thoroughly, and cover it with cold water. Cook the pieces until just tender. Drain.

* Select your favorite watermelon pickle recipe, and tie the indicated spices in a bag of cheesecloth. Put it in a vessel with the rest of the ingredients mentioned in the recipe, except the rind, and simmer for ten minutes. Then add the rind pieces, and simmer them until they become transparent. Should the syrup get too thick, thin it with boiling water.

* When the rinds are clear, take out the spice bag. Refrigerate smaller amounts to be used right away. Pack the remainder of the boiling-hot pickles with their syrup into sterilized jars to within ⅛ inch of the rims. Close tightly.

Pumpkin, winter squash, and cantaloupe rind can be pickled in the same manner.

Ingredients for Spicy Watermelon Pickles

1 tablespoon salt
1 teaspoon celery seed
　　(Do not put this
　　ingredient in the
　　cheesecloth bag.)

1 teaspoon whole cloves
9 cups sugar
2 quarts vinegar

Ingredients for Lemony Watermelon Pickles

2 tablespoons whole
　　cloves
3 sticks cinnamon
2 pieces ginger root

1 thinly sliced lemon
8 cups sugar
1 quart white vinegar
1 quart water

Zucchini Pickles (yield: 6–7 pints)

5 pounds squash
4 to 5 medium onions

1 quart white vinegar
2 cups sugar

¼ cup salt
2 teaspoons celery
    seed

2 teaspoons ground
    turmeric
1 teaspoon dry mustard

Cut the unpeeled zucchini into ¼-inch slices. Thinly slice the onions, enough to make 1 quart. Mix the squash and onions in a big bowl.

Combine the remaining ingredients in a saucepan, mixing them well. Bring to a boil. Pour the bubbling liquid on the vegetables in the bowl. Leave it for one hour; stir now and then.

Now put the bowl's contents into a vessel. Bring to a boil; simmer for three minutes. Then let the simmering continue as you quickly fill hot sterilized jars to within ½ inch of the rim. Be sure that the zucchini and onion mixture is completely covered by the vinegar solution.

Spiced Crab Apples (yield: 6 pints)

4 quarts crab apples
5 cups brown sugar
2 cups vinegar
1 tablespoon whole cloves

2 sticks cinnamon
1 tablespoon whole
    allspice

Wash the crab apples, but do not pare them. Prick their skin a few times with the tines of a fork. Remove the blossom ends. Mix the remaining ingredients, and simmer them for twenty minutes. Add several apples at a time; simmer until tender.

Put the apples in hot sterilized jars and cover with syrup. Seal.

For spicier apples, include a bit of ginger root and one blade of mace with the other spices when preparing the syrup.

Strain the leftover syrup to pour on vanilla ice cream.

Pickled Prunes

1 pound prunes
2 cups light brown sugar
1 lemon
1 cup tarragon vinegar

8 cloves
1 cinnamon stick
1 dried red pepper

Soak the prunes overnight. The following morning, simmer them until plump and tender in just enough water to cover. Add the remaining ingredients, except the red pepper. Cook until glossy; then put in the dried pepper.

Seal the prunes in a 1-quart jar.

Chow Chow *(yield: 9–10 pints)*

1 peck (12½ pounds) green tomatoes	1 tablespoon cinnamon
8 large onions	1 tablespoon allspice
10 green bell peppers	¼ teaspoon cloves
3 tablespoons salt	3 tablespoons mustard
6 hot peppers, chopped	several bay leaves
1 quart vinegar	1¾ cups sugar
	½ cup horseradish

Chop tomatoes, onions, and green peppers. Mix them in a bowl and cover with the salt. Allow to stand overnight.

Drain the mixture, and add the hot peppers (chopped), vinegar, and spices tied in a bag of cheesecloth. Bring the ingredients to a boil.

Pack the chow chow in clean jars and process for fifteen minutes.

MAKING MINCEMEAT

Apricot Mincemeat *(yield: 3 quarts)*

Coarsely grind the following, even the sugar, if need be:

1 pound dried apricots, soaked overnight	1 pound apples, peeled, cored, and chopped
1 pound pitted dates	1 pound seedless raisins
1 pound currants	2 cups brown sugar
2 cups suet	¼ cup almonds

Add to these ingredients the juice and rind of one lemon and 2 tablespoons of grated nutmeg. Use at once, or can at ten pounds pressure for ten minutes.

Green Tomato Mincemeat

1 peck green tomatoes, finely chopped	½ peck apples, finely chopped
1 tablespoon salt	2 pounds raisins

4 pounds brown sugar   2 tablespoons cinnamon
1 cup weak vinegar   2 tablespoons cloves
1 cup suet, finely chopped   1 tablespoon nutmeg

Put the finely chopped tomatoes in a large vessel. Cover the contents with cold water; add salt. Heat to boiling. Drain. Cover with cold water; heat to boiling. Repeat the procedure a third time, cooking the tomatoes until tender. Drain.

Add the remaining ingredients. Cook them gently. Once the apples are tender, fill sterilized jars with the mincemeat. Seal at once.

Traditional Mincemeat

4 pounds lean beef, chopped
2 pounds beef suet, chopped
1 peck sour apples, peeled, cored, and sliced
3 pounds sugar
2 quarts cider
4 pounds seeded raisins
5 pounds currants
1½ pounds citron, chopped
½ pound dried orange peel, chopped

½ pound dried lemon peel, chopped
1 lemon, juice and rind
1 tablespoon cinnamon
1 tablespoon mace
1 tablespoon cloves
1 teaspoon pepper
1 teaspoon salt
2 whole nutmegs, grated
1 gallon sour cherries and their juice
2 pounds broken nut meats (if desired)

Slowly cook these ingredients for two hours. Stir them often.

Fill sterilized jars. Seal.

MAKING CATSUP

Apple Catsup

½ bushel sour apples
1 cup sugar
1 teaspoon pepper
1 teaspoon cloves
1 teaspoon mustard

2 teaspoons cinnamon
1 tablespoon salt
2 onions, finely chopped
2 cups cider vinegar

Wash, quarter, pare, and core the apples. Put the apple pieces in a vessel, and cover them with boiling water. Bring to the boiling point, and then simmer the fruit until soft; by this time almost all the water should have evaporated.

Rub the vessel's contents through a sieve, making 4 cups of pulp. Combine the remaining ingredients, and add them to the pulp. Bring the mixture to the boiling point and simmer for sixty minutes.

Bottle and seal the apple catsup while it is hot.

Grape Catsup

20 pounds grapes	1 tablespoon allspice
5 pounds sugar	2 tablespoons cloves
2 quarts vinegar	1 grated nutmeg
1 tablespoon cinnamon	

Wash grapes, and remove their stems. Barely cover the fruit with cold water, bring to the boiling point, and simmer until softened. Press it through a sieve; discard seeds and skins.

Put 10 pounds of grape pulp and the other ingredients into a kettle. Bring to the boiling point; simmer until the consistency of catsup is reached.

Fill and seal bottles.

Raspberry Catsup

4 quarts ripe raspberries	1 cinnamon stick, in
4 cups cider vinegar	pieces
½ teaspoon white	6 cloves
mustard seeds	2 cups sugar
1 slice ginger root	

Put the fruit and vinegar in an enameled pot. Simmer gently for sixty minutes. Strain through a fine sieve, pressing the pulp through with the back of a wooden spoon.

Rinse out the pot, and return the puree to it, adding mustard seeds and spices. Cook slowly for twenty-five minutes. Again strain and then measure.

To each quart of berry puree, add 2 cups of sugar. Simmer over a low fire, stirring continuously until the mixture is thick and smooth.

When the raspberry catsup is cool, bottle it.

Tomato Catsup (yield: about 1 quart)

¼ cup cider vinegar
1 3-inch cinnamon stick
    (broken in small
    pieces)
½ teaspoon whole
    cloves
½ teaspoon celery seed

6 large ripe tomatoes
    (red)
½ cup water
¼ cup minced onion
3 tablespoons sugar
1 teaspoon salt
dash cayenne pepper

Put the first four ingredients into a saucepan. Boil for one minute. Take from the heat and pour into a container.

Cut tomatoes into quarters, after removing their stems, and place them in the saucepan. Add the onion and water. Heat to the boiling point, using a wooden spoon to stir and mash the tomatoes. Reduce the heat. Simmer about twenty minutes, stirring now and then to avoid sticking. Rub through a sieve. Return the strained juice to the saucepan. Blend in salt, pepper, and sugar. Simmer for about forty minutes or until reduced to one half, stirring occasionally. Strain the mixture of vinegar and spices into the pan. Simmer from ten to thirty minutes more, depending upon the consistency of catsup you prefer.

Take from the stove and cool. Fill a clean container with the catsup, closing it tightly. Store in the refrigerator.

MAKING SOY SAUCE

Prepare soy sauce in autumn after the soybeans have been harvested. Boil them, using any preferred amount, until thoroughly cooked. Put the hot, wet beans through a meat grinder having very fine cutters. Keep the liquid along with the mash. Form the wet pulp into a cone shaped like an inverted flowerpot.

Spread a clean, white towel over a window screen (or fruit-drying rack), and place the mass on it to dry. During this time, any excess juice will leach out.

Lay down two strips of unbleached muslin, about 6 inches wide and 2 feet long, so that they bisect each other. When the cone has dried to a rather hard consistency, set it where the cloth strips meet. Bring up their ends, tie them together, and suspend the bean mass in a warm place while fermentation begins. After several weeks, take it down and put it in a cotton or muslin bag. Store the package in a warm spot through the winter. To avoid damage by insects or mice, it may be hung from a hook.

In spring, break the bean mass into a few chunks; put them in an earthenware crock. Fill it with water, and add salt to taste plus several lumps of charcoal, which will absorb gas and any impurities. (Activated charcoal can be purchased from chemical supply houses or wherever water treatment products are sold.) Set the crock in the sun for a few days to encourage further ripening of the contents. The water will turn black, and moldy pieces of the soybean mass will rise to the surface.

When the few days are up, ladle the liquid into a pot, adding a little garlic. Boil it, skimming off the scum during cooking. Once the liquid becomes sufficiently concentrated, cool, bottle, and store your patiently awaited soy sauce.

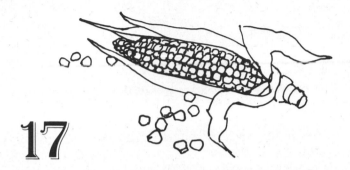

17

FROM THE DRY HOUSE

DRYING FOODS

Drying vegetables, fruits, and herbs is the cheapest way of preserving food. It also requires little space and fills some needs more readily than frozen or canned foods.

A few generations ago, drying herbs, fruits, and vegetables was a standard way of keeping edibles. Metal racks 3 feet square and equipped with tiers of trays were used for drying sweet corn. The trays could be rotated from top to bottom, hastening the drying process. Corn cut from the cob was spread evenly and thinly on a cloth to prevent the kernels from slipping through the slatted trays. The bottom tray was about 10 inches above a fire or stove, which was used to enhance drying during rainy periods. The procedure was usually carried out in the kitchen or smokehouse. In dry weather, foods were spread or hung outdoors. Pumpkins were cut in circles and the rings hung on stretched lines. Sometimes they were cut in strips and strung on heavy twine. Green beans, snapped into pieces and strung on twine, were called "leather breeches." Folks often constructed small buildings designed for drying fruits. Known as "dry houses," they contained slatted trays attached to the walls, with a small stove for heating the interior.

Sun-Drying Method

Sun drying requires time and care. Spread foods on trays, cookie sheets, cake pans, wire racks, or butcher paper; space the pieces for air circulation. Shield them from insects with cheesecloth or wire screening. Most vegetables require about two days to dry properly. Foods should be stirred and inspected frequently during the process. They must be brought in from rain and night dew.

Here are ways to successfully dehydrate certain foods by sun drying them:

* *CABBAGE:* Select well-developed heads. Remove the outer leaves. Cut the cabbage in ¼-inch-thick strips. Spread them on trays. For 1 pound of dried cabbage, you will need 18 pounds of fresh.

* *CORN:* Choose corn at its sweet, best-eating stage. Discard the husks. Blanch the vegetable for three to five minutes in boiling water. Cool rapidly in cold water. Remove the kernels from the cob. Spread them on trays to dry in the sun.

* *PEAS:* Pick peas in their ripe stage, not too old or too immature. Shell them. Spread the peas on trays placed in the sun for thorough drying. Approximately 3½ pounds of fresh peas make 1 pound of dried.

* *PUMPKIN AND SQUASH:* Cut pumpkin and squash into slices ½ inch thick. Since they keep well without processing, you may not want to bother with drying them. However, it's a long time between autumn harvests.

* *TOMATOES:* Bright sunlight is essential for drying tomatoes. Slice them thickly, and spread them on drying trays. To prevent mold from developing, turn them now and then. When leathery dry they can be packed in containers. Sprinkle a bit of salt between each layer.

Storing Sun-Dried Foods

Store dried foods only after they are completely cool. Package them in plastic or paper bags, and close them securely. Put the bags in insect- and rodent-proof containers. Store them where it is cool and dry. If you live in a humid climate, store them in glass jars. You may keep dried foods in your freezer, particularly if insects are a problem.

Reconstituting Dried Vegetables for Cooking

Prepare dried vegetables for cooking by first soaking them; onions, cabbage, and finely chopped peppers are the exceptions.

To each cupful of cabbage, add about 7 cups of water. Slowly bring to a boil in an uncovered vessel and boil for thirty minutes. Add salt and preferred seasonings. Dried cabbage in chicken or beef stock with a dollop of margarine makes a hearty, delicious soup.

Corn requires a preliminary soaking of two to four hours. For 1 cup of corn, use 2 cups of water.

Peas should be soaked for about twenty-four hours.

Pumpkins and squash need soaking overnight. Add 10 pints of water to 1 pound. They are then ready for use in breads, cookies, pies, or in any recipe calling for the canned or fresh kinds.

Tomatoes need a period of twenty-four hours or more for softening. Before soaking them, rinse them a few times under cold water to remove any excess salt.

All of these dried vegetables make excellent casserole dishes, either in combination or separately.

Oven-Drying Method

If your area lacks fairly long periods of steady, hot sun, prepare foods by the oven-drying method.

Meticulously pick over all foods to remove blemishes. Blanch vegetables before drying them. To avoid vitamin loss, blanch by steaming rather than boiling. Use disease-free herbs, and select fruits at their ripest stage when sugar content is highest. Prevent discoloration by treating fruits with ascorbic acid solution.

Spread the food evenly on cookie sheets. Dry them in the oven for twelve to twenty-four hours. (Corn may require more than twenty-four hours.) Use an oven thermometer to maintain the temperature between 90° and 115° F. Do not allow the temperature to exceed 120° F. Stir the food from time to time with a spatula. Turn the pieces over, and transfer those in the center to the outside edges. When done, vegetables should be brittle; the fruit, leathery.

Here are ways to successfully dehydrate certain foods by oven drying them:

* *CARROTS:* Wash carrots well. Leave them whole and steam for twenty minutes. Lay them on paper towels to dry. Peel and cut them in slices ⅛ inch thick. Spread the carrots on a cookie sheet. Dry them in the oven until brittle and a deep orange. Don't let the temperature exceed 120° F.

* *CORN:* To avoid the necessity of soaking dried corn prior to cooking it, use this old-time recipe for oven drying the vegetable: Cut enough sweet corn from the cob to equal 16 cupfuls. (Speed the operation by utilizing this handy implement: Take a metal shoehorn and keenly sharpen its wide end. The curve of the shoehorn conforms to the shape of the cob so that its sharpened edge can speedily slice off kernels to just the right depth and over a wider area than a knife.)

Put 4 ounces of cream, 6 tablespoons of sugar, and 4 teaspoons of coarse canning salt into a kettle; add the unblanched corn. Boil these ingredients for twenty minutes. Stir continuously to prevent sticking.

Remove the mixture from the stove, and spread it on shallow pans. Put the corn in an oven set at its lowest temperature. Stir frequently.

Once the corn is dry and somewhat crisp, transfer it to clean paper bags. Close the bags securely, and hang them in a dry place to finish the dehydration process. When the kernels rattle in the bags, they are ready to be stored in tightly closed jars.

At serving time, no presoaking is necessary. Heat the vegetable, using a small amount of milk rather than water to enhance its flavor.

* **ONIONS:** Onions do not require steam blanching. Peel them and slice thinly. Separate the rings, and spread them on a cookie sheet. Dry in the oven until very crisp at no more than 120° F. Crumble the onions, and put them in airtight containers.

* **GRAPES (Raisins):** Wash grapes; stem them. Lower them in a colander into briskly boiling water just long enough to split their skins. Spread on paper towels to dry. Place on a cookie sheet in an oven set no higher than 120°F. Remove when pliable.

* **APPLES:** Pare and core tart cooking apples. Slice them ¼ inch thick. For each 5 quarts of sliced fruit, mix 2½ teaspoons of ascorbic acid in 1 cup of water. Sprinkle this over the fruit slices, completely coating each piece. Spread on a cookie sheet and dry at a temperature not exceeding 120° F. Remove from the oven when springy and pliable.

* **HERBS:** Collect herb leaves for drying just before the plant blooms. Wash the leaves quickly in cold water. Using paper towels, blot them dry. Remove the leaves from the upper two-thirds of the plant. Spread on a cookie sheet. Dry them at an oven temperature not exceeding 120° F. To check to see if they're done, pinch the leaves. If they are brittle and crumble, take them from the oven.

To dry the seeds of herbs, pick the whole plant. Put it upside down in a paper bag. Make holes at the top of the bag to allow air circulation, and hang it up. As the flower heads dry, the seeds will fall into the bag.

Put the seeds in airtight containers. Store them in a dry, dark, cool place.

Storing Oven-Dried Foods

Allow the foods to stand for complete cooling. Then store them in airtight containers. Keep them in a cool, dark, dry place.

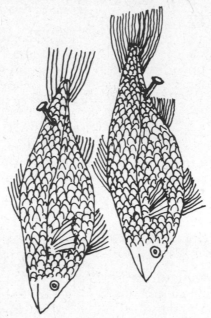

18

MEAT, FOWL, AND FISH

SMOKING MEAT, FOWL, AND FISH

Smoking meat, fowl, and fish converts them into food with a special taste and texture, appealing to the most discriminating gourmet.

The process is a slow one and requires a smoker. Small-scale smokers can be purchased in hardware stores or made at home. Use a semi-enclosed box with some sort of heating element in the bottom, such as a hot plate, to support a pan of wood chips. The chips should be slowly heated and a temperature maintained somewhere between 150° and 200° F., 190° being considered most favorable. Do not use chips from the wood of evergreen trees. Hardwood chips, such as hickory, keep the flames down and generate more smoke. Soak the chips in water for thirty minutes before use. Dried corncobs can substitute for the chips. As the wood chips smolder, the food gradually absorbs the smoke, which imparts a delectable flavor. Heat and smoke can be controlled by some kind of adjustable vents. To maintain steady temperature, use an oven thermometer. A meat thermometer will help you determine when the meat is done.

Smoked Roasts (Beef, Lamb, or Pork)

The smoker should be preheated to 225° F. Rub the roast with a mixture of salt and your favorite spices, or with seasoned salt alone. Insert a meat thermometer in the middle, away from bone and fat. Smoking time will depend on the size of the roast. Be sure that pork attains an internal temperature of at least 170° F.

Smoked Ribs or Chops

Trim fat from the ribs or chops, and rub them with seasoned salt. Hang the meat or lay it on racks in the smoker. Smoke for about two hours at 80° to 85° F. Slowly raise the temperature to 250° and smoke for an additional thirty to forty-five minutes. The meat is done when it begins to fall from the bone. During the last fifteen minutes of cooking, baste the ribs or chops with barbecue sauce, if desired.

Smoked Sausage

Any sausage can be smoked; smoking will flavor the meat, not cook it.

Suspend uncooked sausages from hooks in the smoker. Smoke from one to two hours at 70° F. Then cook according to the recipe.

Put bulk sausage in loaf pans in the middle of the smoker rack. Smoke from one to two hours at 70° F. Then cook according to the recipe.

Jerky (yield: 1 pound)

4 pounds lean beef	2 tablespoons lemon
⅓ cup soy sauce	juice
3 tablespoons vinegar	1 teaspoon onion powder
2 tablespoons sugar	1 teaspoon seasoned salt

Select very lean meat for making jerky, and carefully trim away any fat. Partially freeze the meat. Cut it (across the grain for flank steak) in very thin slices.

For mild-flavored jerky, sprinkle one teaspoon of pepper and one teaspoon of seasoned salt for each pound of meat.

Smoke it immediately. For a stronger flavor, blend all the other ingredients, and marinate the meat in this mixture either for a few hours or overnight, keeping it in the refrigerator. Turn the meat a few times.

Thoroughly drain the meat, and arrange it on greased racks that are slightly separated to permit circulation of air. Smoke it until brittle and dry for approximately twenty-four hours at 85° to 90° F.

Smoking Pork in a Smokehouse

* **PRELIMINARY PREPARATION:** Each cut of pork may be wrapped in cheesecloth to protect it from soot, but this measure is not essential. Run wire or string through the meat, and loop it around cross poles in the smokehouse. Hang hams with the hock downward in order to retain juices. Allow free circulation of smoke to all areas of the meat by spacing the pieces.

* **FUEL:** The ideal smoking temperature ranges between 110° and 120° F. Sawdust, chips, or small pieces of wood from alder, apple, beech, hickory, maple, or oak make good fuel. The wood of all nut and fruit trees is suitable, as are corncobs. Never use resinous wood. Since smoke, not heat, is desired, keep the lit fuel smoldering by lightly sprinkling it with water whenever it flares up.

* **SMOKING TIME:** The longer the smoking period the better. During prolonged smoking the meat dries slowly, and the acid of the smoke permeates each piece. Quick smoking affects only the ham's exterior; the smoke's acid coats it but does not penetrate its fiber.

Hams may be smoked either for eight to ten hours or for a few weeks, depending on the quality desired. Generally, hams are satisfactory in about five days, bacon in three.

Smoking time can be determined by color. Meat that is mahogany-colored all over, either light or dark in hue, may be removed from the smokehouse. The darker the meat, the longer it will keep.

* **STORING:** Wrap the meat pieces in cheesecloth and then newspaper. Place them in paper bags, tied closed. Store the smoked meat in a cool (43° F.), dry place.

Smoked Fowl

Small game birds—ducks, pheasants, and quail—can be successfully smoked. Smoking will render them tender and succulent. The average pheasant requires about ten hours of cooking time, perhaps a bit longer. You will need to add wood chips three or four times during this period. Smoke should trickle constantly through the vents. If you prefer a heavy smoked flavor, continuously add wood chips to the pan; for moderate flavor, a handful now and then is sufficient.

Some game birds can be put directly into the smoker. However, for the best results, brine them first. This applies as well to domestic chickens. Place the bird to be smoked in a glass or crockery vessel. Cover it with water. For every 4 quarts of water, put in 4 cups of cider, several dashes of lemon juice, ¼ teaspoon of maple flavoring, 1½ cups of curing salt, ½ teaspoon of ginger, ½ cup of brown sugar, and 3 tablespoons of pepper. You can either cold soak the bird overnight in this brine or simmer it in the solution for approximately five minutes. When it is ready for smoking, dry it in the air for an hour, or wipe it with a towel. Combine brown sugar, garlic powder, and black pepper. Rub the bird generously with this mixture.

Thread a long, heavy string through the body, and truss up the legs, using the excess string to hang the bird in the smoker. Maintain the temperature as close to 190° F. as possible. For each pound of bird, allow one and a half hours of cooking time. To determine how well it's done, twist a leg. If it moves easily, the bird is ready for eating.

You might like to give the brine an oriental flavor. Mix ⅓ cup of soy sauce, ⅓ cup of sherry, ⅓ cup of water, ¼ cup of honey, and ½ teaspoon of powdered ginger, all over low heat. Let the mixture cool. Leave the bird whole, or cut it in pieces. Marinate it in the refrigerator for at least eight hours, turning it several times.

When readying a bird for smoking, don't discard the giblets. They can be put to good use as tasty snacks. Prepare livers for smoking by putting them into boiling water and cooking them until all redness disappears. Drain and smoke. Hearts and gizzards do not require this preliminary boiling. Coat the gizzards, hearts, and cooked livers by shaking them in a plastic bag containing a mixture of the following seasonings: pepper, table salt, sugar, and garlic salt. Put the giblets on the racks inside the smoker for forty-five minutes to one hour at 80° F. Then raise the temperature to 225° or 250° for thirty to sixty minutes more.

Take out the giblets; put them in a jar, adding a little vegetable oil. Roll them about in the jar until well coated. Keep the jar refrigerated for twenty-four hours to insure the best flavor.

Smoked Fish

For mildly salty, spiced fish, marinate for several hours; for more spiciness, let it stand in the marinade for at least six hours or overnight.

| 10 fish fillets of firm flesh | ½ cup sugar |
| 1 quart water | ½ cup salt |

one or two of these seasonings:

garlic or onion salt	hot pepper sauce or dried
black or white pepper	red pepper flakes
leaves of bay, dill, or	lemon slices or grated
tarragon	lemon peel
ground mace or ginger	

Mix the water, sugar, salt, and seasonings in a bowl until the salt and sugar dissolve. Put in the fish. Cover. Then weight the cover down to keep them beneath the brine. Refrigerate the fish either for a few hours or overnight.

Drain the fillets, and thoroughly rinse them in cold water. Pat dry with paper towels and place on a wire rack to dry in the air for thirty minutes to one hour. Grease the smoker racks, and lay the fish on them, skin down, spaced for air circulation. Smoking should begin at 90° F. After fifteen minutes, slowly raise the heat to 135° to 140° F. and smoke for one to two hours.

When the fillets are golden brown and flake at the touch of a fork, they are ready to be eaten; or they can be tightly wrapped and stored in the freezer.

Smoked Oysters

Shuck and wash oysters. Mix 1¼ pounds of salt in 1 gallon of water. Soak the oysters in this brine for five minutes.

Drain them well. Lightly coat the oysters with salad oil. Lay them on a well-greased rack wide enough apart to permit air circulation. A wire cake rack may be used if the spaces of the smoker rack are too wide. Smoke the oysters for fifteen minutes at 180° F.

If they are not eaten immediately, they can be refrigerated for a few days. They will last for two months when stored in containers in the freezer.

SAUSAGE MAKING

Sausage comes from the Latin word *salsus,* meaning "salted"; that is, preserved meat. Here is the general procedure for making sausage.

Divide in half the amount of meat required for the recipe you have chosen. Put 3 rounded tablespoons of it in a blender, adding 1 tablespoon of crushed ice. Cover and liquefy at high speed for five seconds. Shut off the blender, uncover it, and move the meat to the blades, using a rubber spatula. Blend five seconds more. Turn off the blender, again moving the meat to the blades if need be, and add a little more ice. Blend five seconds more or until the contents have a peanut-butterlike consistency. With the spatula, scoop the meat into a large bowl. Repeat this procedure until you have smoothly blended half of the meat. While allowing the blender to cool, measure all other ingredients into the bowl with the already processed meat. Now process the rest of the meat in your blender, and mix it thoroughly with all the ingredients in the bowl. Use your hands or a spoon (you may also find a potato masher handy for this) to insure that the seasonings are evenly blended.

Tie the end of a sausage casing with a string, and firmly pack in the meat. (Buy synthetic casings. They are easily stored and cannot spoil. The size generally preferred is 24 inches in length and 6 inches in diameter.) Try to squeeze out as much air as possible as you work. Tie the tip close to the meat, and snip off the casing. Cook according to the recipe you have selected. Or, if the recipe indicates, put the mixture into a loaf pan instead of casings and cook as directed.

Pork Sausage

12 ½ pounds fresh pork
   (approximately
   11 pounds lean
   meat and 1 ½
   pounds fat)
¼ cup salt

¼ cup brown sugar,
   firmly packed
1 ½ tablespoons sage
1 tablespoon black
   pepper
1 tablespoon red
   pepper

Trim away excess fat from the pork. Cut the meat into 2-inch cubes. Spread them on a piece of waxed paper. Blend the remaining ingredients, and sprinkle the mixture over the meat. Grind the seasoned meat twice in a meat grinder, and thoroughly mix it with your hands to help distribute the seasonings and fat. Stuff into casings.

Canned Pork Sausage

Shape the pork sausage into small patties. Bake them for twenty-five to thirty minutes at 350° F.

Then place them in quart jars. Pour in their juice to cover. Seal the jars and process for fifteen minutes at ten pounds pressure.

Grandma's Cracklings Sausage

The crisp bits of skin and meat remaining after hog fat has been rendered are called cracklings. Grandmother used them as an ingredient in homemade sausage, that is, if she could keep the family from pilfering too many of those crunchy snacks right from the kettle.

Here is her recipe: With each cup of cracklings, mix 1 cup of grated potato. Season the mixture with salt, pepper, and grated onion to taste, adding any preferred herbs. Grandma favored marjoram and thyme.

When well mixed, the blend should be put in bread pans and baked for one hour at 350° F. Then cool and chill it.

To serve, cut the sausage in slices, and fry them for an old-time country breakfast.

Bologna (Fine-Cut Sausage)

3 pounds ground beef (75% lean)	1½ teaspoons ground coriander
2 pounds ground pork	1½ teaspoons ground cardamom
1 tray ice cubes, crushed	1 teaspoon dried sage
1 cup instant powdered milk	¾ teaspoon ground allspice
3 tablespoons salt	¾ teaspoon ground mace
1 tablespoon white pepper	1½ teaspoons sugar

Heat the oven to 275° F. Follow the general rules for preparing the meat mixture as already described. Pack the mixture into the casings, tying and cutting them.

Firmly press each stuffed casing into a loaf pan. If the casings fail to fit snugly against the ends of the pan, fill any empty spaces with wadded aluminum foil to keep the sausages tightly in place. Insert a thermometer in the middle of one. Place the pan in the center of the oven. Bake for two hours or until 160° F. registers on the thermometer.

Take the meat from the oven. Remove the thermometer. Allow cold water to run over the sausages for several minutes to cool them. Refrigerate them until serving time.

Braunschweiger (yield: 1 ½ pounds)

½ pound ground pork liver
½ pound ground pork
½ pound ground beef
1 medium-sized onion, minced
2 tablespoons powdered milk
½ teaspoon sugar
½ teaspoon pepper
¼ teaspoon ground cardamom
¼ teaspoon ground mace
¼ teaspoon margarine or butter
1 teaspoon salt

When grinding your own meat, use the grinder's fine cutter. If you have your meat man do the job, ask to have all the meats ground together twice.

Heat the oven to 275° F. Follow the general rules for preparing the meat mixture as described previously. Use less seasoning rather than a generous amount. Check the flavor of your sausage meat just before filling the casings by frying well 1 tablespoon of it. Add more seasonings if you find it too bland. Pack the meat into a loaf pan. Place a piece of waxed paper over it, and press down firmly and evenly. Remove the paper, and insert a thermometer in the middle of the mixture.

Set the loaf pan in a larger baking pan in the center of the oven. Fill the larger container with water to a one-inch depth. Now and then check to see that the water does not boil. If it does, lower the temperature. Bake for one to one and a half hours or until the thermometer reaches 160° F.

Take the loaf out of the oven, and remove the thermometer. Place the pan in a container or sink of ice. Cool it rapidly, and put it in the refrigerator until serving time.

To store the Braunschweiger, remove it from the pan,

wrap it in foil or transparent wrap, and keep it in the refrigerator, where it will remain edible for one week. It will keep in the freezer for six months.

Venison Sausage

When making venison sausage, first weigh the venison to determine the amount of pork required. Use two parts venison to one part pork. The pork will compensate for lost venison fat (which many people dislike), keeping the sausage moist and imparting a pleasant flavor. Your butcher can supply you with pork trimmings, a combination of fat and pork meat, and with casings, if you intend to make link sausage.

After mixing the venison and pork, grind the meat twice to insure a good blend. A hand grinder is adequate unless you are processing more than 100 pounds, in which case a power grinder is practical.

Spread the ground meat on a table or counter top, and flatten it into an immense meat patty, some 4 inches thick. Sprinkle it with 1 tablespoon of black pepper and 2 tablespoons of salt (or garlic salt) for each 5 pounds of meat. If you prefer hot sausage, add 1 tablespoon of chili pequins (very small red peppers), dried and crushed.

Roll the meat into logs, 3 inches thick and 1 foot long. Wrap them well; freeze for future use.

Bulk sausage may be cooked by cutting it into ½-inch-thick patties and frying them, seven minutes to a side, in an ungreased skillet.

To make link sausage, prepare the casings. Soak them for five minutes in warm water and rinse; turn them inside out and repeat the soaking and rinsing.

Attach the stuffer spout. Gather up a casing (as you would when putting on a sock), and slip it on the spout. Approximately 3 inches of casing should extend from the spout opening. Tie the lower end of the casing with a string. When 3 to 4 feet have been stuffed, tie the filled casing in individual sausages, using strong cotton cord. Cut the casing in lengths of 24 inches. Tie the ends of each 2-foot length together so that it resembles a loop.

You can broil or barbecue the venison sausage, fifteen minutes to a side. It can also be boiled for twenty to thirty minutes or fried. Before serving the sausage, prick the casings to release pressurized juices.

If smoked meat is desired, keep it in the smokehouse for twenty-four to forty-eight hours. Smoking should be done only in cold weather. Cook the sausage thoroughly before serving it.

CURING PORK

* *METHODS:* Meat can be cured by two methods: the wet cure involves immersing the meat in brine; the dry cure entails rubbing the meat with a salt mixture. The wet method is often preferred for smaller cuts, the dry cure for larger pieces.

Whichever method is followed, each piece of meat must first be weighed, rubbed with fine salt, and allowed to drain, flesh side lowermost, for six to twelve hours.

Procedure for Wet-Curing Pork

Pack the meat in earthen or glass crocks (never use metal with brine); fill them up with water. Take out the meat, and empty the water into a vessel. For each 100 pounds of pork, assemble the following: 9 pounds of medium-grain salt (10 pounds in warm weather); 4 pounds of unsulphured molasses (you may substitute 4 pounds of maple syrup or 2½ pounds of brown sugar for the molasses); and 2 ounces of saltpeter. Add these preserving ingredients to the vessel of water, and stir with a wooden spoon.

Fill the crocks with pork, placing the largest pieces on the bottom. Cover them with the curing brine. Put lids on the crocks, and weigh each down with a stone or some heavy object to insure complete submersion of the meat. Store the crocks in a cool place.

Once a week, pour off the brine, remove the meat, and replace it, changing the position of the pieces. Return the brine to the crock. If scum develops on the brine's surface, empty the crocks and wash them and the pork thoroughly. Repack the meat in fresh brine, if possible. Otherwise, use the original solution by boiling it and skimming off impurities.

* *CURING TIME:* Large pieces of meat need four days in the curing solution per pound of pork. Smaller pieces require three days in the brine to each pound. Record on a chart the

weight of each cut and its calculated date of removal.

When the meat is taken out, soak it in clean water for thirty minutes.

Procedure for Dry-Curing Pork

Thoroughly mix the following ingredients for each 100 pounds of meat:

> 6 pounds salt (In warm
>   weather use 8
>   pounds.)
> 2 pounds molasses, maple
>   syrup, or brown
>   sugar (If the salt
>   content is
>
> increased, use 2 ½
>   pounds.)
> 2 ounces saltpeter (found
>   in drugstores or
>   meat-packing
>   plants)
> 5 ounces black pepper

To this blend you may add any preferred seasoning, such as pickling spices, sage, or savory. Using a kneading motion, rub the curing mixture on all meat surfaces. Work it in well around the bones.

Pack the pork in a crock (or barrel) with the larger pieces on the bottom, smaller ones on top. Remove the meat after several days, and repack it. This step insures that the cure completely coats all pieces.

* *CURING TIME:* The curing process will require two days per pound of each cut. Keep a chart of weights and the duration of curing periods for individual pieces.

Country Ham

> 1 ham (10–15 pounds)   4 quarts ginger ale

Place the ham in a very large pot of water heated to just below the boiling point. (If you lack a vessel of adequate size, use a clean lard can.) Allow to boil for ten to fifteen minutes. This will remove excess salt from the exterior of the ham. Take out the ham; discard the water.

Return the ham to the pot, and fill it to the halfway mark with hot water. Pour in 4 quarts of ginger ale and cover loosely. Bring to a rolling boil and continue boiling for thirty minutes. Ginger ale will develop the ham's flavor.

Lay down several thicknesses of newspaper; place the pot containing the ham on them. Cover the pot (or lard can) closely with its lid. Now bring the newspapers up and around the pot's sides and top, and bind them in place with twine. Cover with blankets and quilts. Allow to stand for ten to fourteen hours, depending on the size of ham. A 13-pound ham will need about ten hours.

Remove the skin and cut away fat. Serve your country ham baked or fried.

Country Ham and Grits with Red-Eye Gravy

Cut country ham in slices ¼ to ½ inch thick. To prevent curling, slit the fat around the edges. Cook the ham slices slowly in a heavy skillet, turning them a few times. When the ham is brown, add a little water and simmer for several minutes. Take the ham from the skillet, and keep it warm.

Cook the gravy until it turns red. You may add a small amount of strong coffee to darken the color. Accompany your country ham with grits, serving red-eye gravy over both.

Corned Beef

Put 1 quart of water into an enamel pot with sufficient salt to enable an egg (still in its shell) to float. Remove the egg, and add a bay leaf, 8 peppercorns, and 2 tablespoons of pickling spice mix. Bring the contents of the vessel to a boil; then simmer for ten minutes. Let the liquid cool to room temperature.

Place a 4- to 6-pound beef brisket in a good-sized crock. Pour the cooled brine into it. Cover the crock with foil topped by a weighted plate. Allow to stand for forty-eight hours. After that, wash the meat, and simmer it again for approximately three hours.

Bake the corned beef in a 300° F. oven for one hour. Coat the cooked meat with a glaze of mustard and brown sugar. Serve warm or cold.

Hog Jowl and Black-eyed Peas

Black-eyed peas are good any old time. But in Texas they are especially good on New Year's Day—for luck. Including them in your dinner on the first of January is supposed to insure a favorable year.

So, for good luck and good eating, prepare your black-eyed peas in this way:

½ *pound hog jowl*   *salt to taste*
¾ *pound black-eyed peas*   *1 onion*
1 or 2 jalapeño peppers

Cook the hog jowl until partially tender. Add the remaining ingredients. Slowly cook until the peas are just done, being careful not to overcook them.

Headcheese (Pork)

Scrape and clean a hog's head, washing it thoroughly. Shove a hot poker into the nostrils and ears. Cover the head with lightly salted water in a large vessel. Put in onion and bay leaf. Simmer until the meat comes away from the bones, usually within several hours' time. Then drain the vessel's contents, saving a small amount of the liquid.

Remove all meat from the bones, discarding any gristle, and shred or chop it coarsely. Season it to taste with sage, thyme, salt, and pepper. Press the meat into a crock, and add a little of the pot liquor in which it was simmered. Cover the crock; place a weight on the lid. Allow to stand in a cold spot for three days.

When the headcheese has solidified, slice it for serving cold.

Headcheese (Veal)

Quarter a calf's head. Remove eyes, ears, brains, snout, and the greater part of the fat. Soak the four pieces in cold water to withdraw blood. Then put them in a kettle with enough cold water to cover and simmer until the meat separates from the bones.

Drain—setting aside the liquid—and dice the meat. Cover it with the stock, adding herbs, salt, and pepper. Cook for thirty minutes. Transfer to a mold. Cover with a cloth, putting a weight on top. Chill.

Cut in slices to serve.

Old-fashioned Scrapple

Cut a 5- to 6-pound pig's head into four sections. Cover them with water and boil until the meat falls from the bones. Drain, saving the pot liquor.

Eliminate any gristle, and run the pork through a meat cutter. Add water to the stock, making 4 quarts in all. Put in the meat and sausage seasonings. Stir in enough cornmeal or buckwheat to give the consistency of mush. Let the mixture boil for several minutes.

Empty it into greased loaf pans to cool. Cut the scrapple in slices, and fry it without lard until crisp and brown.

Easy Scrapple

Make a thick porridge by cooking 1 cup of rolled oats in 2 cups of water. In another saucepan, cook 1 cup of cornmeal to like consistency in the same way. Then combine the two cereals. Mix in 1 pound of sausage meat plus some additional sausage seasoning.

Pack the blend into a crock and chill. When the scrapple is firm, slice and fry it thoroughly. Serve it plain, or trickle homemade maple syrup over the slices.

Aging Game

Aging tenderizes meat and improves its flavor. Hang game meat in a cool place, such as a garage or a basement, where the temperature remains in the low 40's. Air must be kept circulating around the meat. To effect this, hang a small electric fan close by.

Inspect the game two or three times each day. Check for souring, particularly in cracks and folds of the meat. If you detect a sour odor, trim off the area involved, and clean the place with a half-and-half solution of water and vinegar.

The length of aging time ranges from two to fourteen days, depending on personal preference; however, about five days generally suits the taste of most folks.

Venison Mincemeat

Make mincemeat of irregular venison cuts that are not suitable for any particular game recipe.

3 cups venison, chopped fine or ground	1 cup butter
	1 cup strong coffee
9 cups apples, chopped fine or ground	3 teaspoons salt
	2 teaspoons cinnamon
3 cups each of raisins, sugar, cider, molasses	1 teaspoon cloves
	1 teaspoon nutmeg

Blend all ingredients in a large pot. Bring to a boil. Then lower the heat, and simmer the mincemeat for four to five hours.

Put it into hot, sterilized jars. Seal and cool. Venison mincemeat may also be frozen.

Two Small-Game Recipes (yield: 6 to 8 servings)

2 good-sized squirrels or 2 rabbits (even better, 1 of each)
2 tablespoons butter
1 large onion, chopped
½ pound smoked ham, diced
1 bay leaf
1 celery top
1 hot red pepper pod
1 parsley sprig
1 cup lima beans
1 cup corn
1 cup sliced okra

1 teaspoon salt
1 teaspoon pepper
2 quarts water
4 medium-sized potatoes, cubed
1 teaspoon soy sauce
dash Tabasco sauce

} tie in a cheesecloth bag

2 teaspoons Worcestershire sauce

Wash the game, and pat it dry with paper towels. Cut it into serving sizes. Melt the butter in a large stew pot, and cook the chopped onion. When they are soft, put in the meat. Fry it until brown, about three minutes on each side. Mix in the ham. Add the water, salt, and pepper, and the cheesecloth bag containing herbs and vegetables. Cover the pot. Simmer until the meat is tender, for approximately forty-five minutes to an hour, stirring occasionally.

Now put in the vegetables. They may be fresh, canned, or frozen. Fresh vegetables should be added in this order: corn, lima beans, potatoes. After twenty minutes add okra, tomatoes, soy, Tabasco, and Worcestershire sauces. Stir and cook until the potatoes are tender. Take out the cheesecloth bag. Do not add water; the stew should be very thick. It may be served over white rice.

3–5 pounds small game meat
½ cup butter (or margarine)

1 large garlic clove, minced
1 large onion, chopped
2 cups water

1 teaspoon sweet basil
1 cup white wine
1 28-ounce can whole
     tomatoes

2 cups chicken stock or
     broth
salt and pepper to
     taste

Cut the meat into serving pieces; sprinkle it with salt and pepper to taste. Melt the butter in a pot, and brown the meat with garlic and onion. After the meat is nicely browned and the chopped onion is tender, add the white wine, basil, tomatoes and their liquid, chicken stock, and water. Cover. Simmer until the meat is tender, from forty-five to ninety minutes.

During the last twenty to forty-five minutes, put in any desired vegetables, and cook them for the required amount of time, adding liquid if necessary.

How to Pluck a Duck

For a fast, clean duck-plucking job, follow these steps:
* In a bucket of boiling water, melt 1 pound of paraffin wax. Fill a second bucket with ice-cold water.
* Cut off the feet and wings of the duck. Use the head as a handle.
* Remove the roughest feathers from back and breast. This job should take no more than one minute.
* Grasping the head, plunge the body to the bottom of the bucket of hot water and pull it out through the film of wax on the water's surface. Repeat this procedure a total of three times to thoroughly coat the duck.
* Immerse the bird in the bucket of cold water to set the wax. Take it from the water to let the wax harden completely in some cool place. When properly hardened, the wax coating should feel cold to the fingers and crack down to the skin when the bird is flexed.
* With the duck's back in your palms, split the coating along the breast with your thumbs. It should come away in about six large sections, taking all down and feathers with it. Around the legs, work your thumb beneath the wax, and separate the skin from the wax. Removing the entire wax coating plus down and feathers should require less than sixty seconds. An essential for success is making certain that the wax coating is thoroughly hard and cold before removal.

Grilled Bluefish

4 pounds bluefish, dressed   salt and pepper to taste
    lemon juice
    melted butter (or
        margarine)

Stuffing:

2 tablespoons chopped   ¼ cup chopped parsley
    onion   4 ounces crumbled blue
½ cup chopped celery   cheese
½ cup butter   1 tablespoon lemon juice
2 cups herb-seasoned
    bread crumbs

Rinse the fish; pat it dry. Lightly season the inside with lemon juice, salt, and pepper. Spread butter in the middle of a good-sized sheet of aluminum foil, and place the fish on it.

To prepare the stuffing, sauté onion and celery in butter until tender. Put in the crumbs; toss to absorb the butter. Mix in the parsley and blue cheese. Moisten the stuffing with lemon juice and approximately ⅔ cup of water.

Fill the cavity of the fish with the stuffing. Close the opening by drawing the skin together and binding with soft string. Butter the top of the fish. Sprinkle with lemon juice, salt, and pepper.

Bring the sides of the foil over the fish and close them with a double fold. Seal the ends in double folds. Place on a grill over a medium fire for ten minutes on each side; turn a third time and grill for an additional ten minutes.

Serve stuffed bluefish garnished with parsley and lemon slices.

19

SWEET THINGS

SUGAR
Making Sugar from Beets

So highly valued was sugar several centuries ago that it was listed as a wedding present, along with precious gems and jewels, for a future queen of Bohemia and Hungary.

You can produce this once–greatly prized commodity at home from sugar beets. Scrub the vegetable well, and chop it into small pieces. Cook them in water to extract the juice; then strain the juice. Cook down the resulting syrup. Let it cool to crystallize.

Your homemade sugar will not be pure white, and a slight beety flavor will linger. It will be nutritionally superior, however, to treated commercial sugar.

Sugar Substitutes

Each of the following is a sweetening equivalent to 1 cup of white sugar and may be substituted for it when preparing food or drink:
   * ½ cup of firmly packed brown sugar

* ¾ cup of strained honey, minus 3⅓ tablespoons of liquid per cup of added honey
* 1½ cups of molasses or sorghum, minus ¼ cup of liquid for each cup added
* 2 cups of corn syrup, minus ¼ cup of liquid per cup added
* 1½ cups of maple syrup, minus ¼ cup of liquid per cup added

CONFECTIONS

Granny Barlow's Bran Brittle

1 cup granulated sugar	3 tablespoons corn syrup
½ cup brown sugar	½ cup water
1 cup bran	½ teaspoon lemon extract
2 tablespoons butter	

Cook the sugars, syrup, and water to 290° F. on your candy thermometer. Take the pan from the fire, and stir in the butter, bran, and flavoring.

Pour the mixture on a greased slab. Roll it very thin, using a greased rolling pin. When it cools, mark it into bite-sized squares.

Butterscotch Apples

2 cups sugar	1 teaspoon lemon extract
1 cup corn syrup	¼ teaspoon salt
½ cup water	red apples
¼ cup butter	

Combine the sugar, corn syrup, water, and salt in a saucepan. Cook the mixture until the sugar dissolves, stirring constantly. Then, without stirring, continue to cook the syrup to the hard-crack stage (295° F.). Add butter and cook until your candy thermometer reaches 300° F. Stir in the lemon extract.

In the stem end of each well-washed, unpeeled apple, insert a wooden skewer. Dip the fruit in the hot syrup. Stand the apples on a wire cake rack for drainage of excess syrup as they harden.

Cracker Jacks (yield: 2½ quarts)

2 quarts popped corn	1 cup molasses
2 cups shelled peanuts	½ cup sugar

Blend the popped corn and peanuts in a pan. Mix the molasses and sugar in a deep saucepan, and cook the syrup until it becomes threadlike when dropped in cold water or until the candy thermometer registers 234° F.

Pour the hot syrup over the popped corn and peanuts blend, mixing well. When the candy is cold and firm, break it into chunks.

Fruit Leather

Fruit leather, a nutritious, lightweight food, is an excellent addition to the outdoor menus of hikers and campers. Making this old-time confection is a good way to utilize overripe fruit.

Put 5 cups of any ripe fruit (apples, apricots, prunes, persimmons, etc.) in a saucepan. Add 1 tablespoon of lemon or lime juice and sweetening (preferably honey) to taste. Simmer until the mixture has the consistency of thick oatmeal. Stir and mash constantly to prevent burning and promote thickening.

Spread the thick fruit sauce on cookie sheets to a depth of ¼ inch. Dry it in the oven at 120° to 150° F. for about 4½ hours, leaving the door slightly open. If the day is sunny and warm (over 80° F.), dry the fruit paste in the sun for about 9 hours, covering it with cheesecloth to screen out insects.

Keep fruit leather in a dry, cool place until ready for use. It lasts for thirty weeks at a room temperature of no more than 70° F.; it can be stored in a refrigerator for months and in a freezer for years.

The idea for preparing food in this manner stems from certain Indian tribes who made plant leather. They cooked the bee plant to a soup, removed the stems, and boiled the mixture until it became a thick paste. It was then sun-dried in sheets and stored for future camp use or on-the-trail consumption.

Fruit leather is not only a staple food for outdoorsmen. By adding five parts water to one part leather and churning the mixture in a blender, you can turn it into a delicious beverage. It can also be used in cooking, and as pie fillings and dessert toppings.

Lemon Gumdrops (yield: 60 pieces)

1 6-ounce bottle liquid
   pectin
¼ teaspoon baking
   soda
¾ cup sugar
¾ cup light corn syrup
1 ½ teaspoons lemon
   extract

1 teaspoon grated
   lemon rind
3 drops homemade
   yellow food
   coloring
sugar

In a one-quart saucepan, mix the pectin and baking soda. Mix the ¾ cup of sugar and the corn syrup in a 2-quart pan. Cook both mixtures simultaneously over high heat until foam leaves the first mix and the second comes to a fast boil—within three to five minutes. Stir both vessels often. Continue stirring as you slowly empty the pectin mixture into the sugar mixture in a steady stream. Boil for one minute, stirring constantly.

Take from the stove and add lemon extract, lemon rind, and coloring. Put it in an 8-inch-square pan at once. Allow to stand at room temperature for about two hours. When the candy is cool and set, cut it in 1-inch cubes. Roll them in sugar. Keep gumdrops in the refrigerator.

Lollipops (yield: about 80)

4 cups sugar
2 cups light corn syrup
1 cup hot water
preferred extracts
(lemon, orange, etc.)

homemade food
   coloring
7 dozen wooden lollipop
   sticks

An old slab of marble is handy for making lollipops. (A baking sheet can substitute.) Coat it with oil. Line up the skewers on it, about 4 inches apart, with their points all in the same direction.

Combine the sugar, corn syrup, and water in a four-quart pot. Cook them until your candy thermometer registers 270° F. (the soft-crack stage). Then reduce the heat and continue cooking until the thermometer reaches 310° F. (the hard-crack stage). Take from the heat; let cool for several minutes. Divide the mixture in half. Add any preferred flavorings and, if desired, the homemade food coloring. Stir to blend thoroughly.

When the candy thermometer falls to 280° F., drop table-spoons of the syrupy mixture on the points of the lollipop sticks. Let stand until completely cold and hard.

Maple Sugar Candy *(yield: about 2 pounds)*

2 pounds homemade   ¼ teaspoon cream of
   maple sugar   tartar
                             1 cup water

Butter the rim of a good-sized, heavy saucepan. (This will keep the contents from boiling over.) Put in all three ingredients, and bring them to a boil, stirring continuously. Cook until your candy thermometer registers 234° F. (the soft-ball stage). Let cool.

Now work the mixture with a wooden paddle until it becomes creamy and thick. Turn it into maple sugar molds. (If they are not available, twelve 2-inch cupcake tins will do nicely.)

When the candy is completely cold, invert the molds to remove their contents.

Marshmallows

2 tablespoons gelatin   ⅛ teaspoon salt
¼ cup cold water   1 teaspoon vanilla
¾ cup boiling water   powdered sugar
2 cups sugar

Soak the gelatin in the cold water. When it has absorbed all the moisture, add the salt and vanilla.

Boil the water and sugar to the soft-ball stage (280° F.). Slowly pour this syrup over the gelatin, continually beating the mixture with a wire whisk until it is thick and cool.

Lightly butter a shallow pan; dust it with powdered sugar. Turn the confection into the pan. Smooth the surface evenly; dust it with powdered sugar. Allow to stand overnight.

The next morning, cut the candy in small squares, and roll them in powdered sugar.

Honey Marshmallows

1 tablespoon gelatin	1 cup honey
¼ cup cold water	

Thoroughly soak the gelatin in cold water. Dissolve it over hot water. Warm the honey, and add it to the gelatin. Beat the mixture for ten minutes in a blender until very fluffy and light. Spread it on a buttered pan. Allow to stand for twenty-four hours or longer.

Cut the confection into squares with a knife that has first been dipped in cold water. Store in airtight jars or tins.

Old-fashioned Pulled Confection

2 cups water	chunk of butter (as big
4 cups sugar	as an egg)
¾ cup vinegar	2 teaspoons vanilla
1 cup cream	

Put all ingredients in a vessel. Boil them until a test sample "cracks" in water. Then pour the mixture out on a buttered platter.

When the candy is cool enough to handle, pull it (as you would for taffy) until white.

Old-time Sugar Candy

Combine the following ingredients in a pot: 1 cup of water, 6 cups of sugar, and 1 cup of vinegar. Put 1 teaspoon of soda in just enough hot water to dissolve it. Add this solution plus 1 teaspoon of butter to the vessel.

Boil the contents for thirty minutes without stirring. Sugar candy may be flavored to taste.

Popcorn Balls (yield: 12 to 15)

1 ½ cups popcorn	1 cup sugar
4 tablespoons butter (or	⅓ cup corn syrup
margarine)	1 teaspoon salt
⅓ cup water	1 teaspoon vanilla

Pop the corn, and remove imperfect kernels. Set the popcorn aside in a large bowl.

Mix the butter, water, sugar, and corn syrup in a saucepan. Cook the blend to the medium-crack stage (280° F. on your candy thermometer). Remove from the stove. Add the salt and flavoring.

Slowly pour the syrup over the popped corn, stirring constantly to evenly coat all kernels. As soon as the popcorn is cool enough to handle, shape it lightly into balls with oiled or slightly floured hands. Place them on waxed paper, wrapping them individually.

Potato Candy

Boil and mash a medium-sized potato. Mix in sufficient sugar to make it stiff. On a dough board sprinkled with powdered sugar, roll out the potato mixture. Spread on homemade peanut butter. Roll it up jelly-roll style. Slice in ½-inch pieces to serve.

Spun Carnival Candy

2 cups sugar
1 cup water

⅛ teaspoon cream of
tartar

Combine the three ingredients in a saucepan, and boil them without stirring until the candy thermometer reaches 310° F. Immediately put the pan in a larger pan of cold water to halt the boiling; then set it in hot water. Add homemade food coloring if desired.

Lay broom handles across chairs set three feet apart. Spread newspaper beneath. Dip a sugar spinner into the syrup, and quickly wave it back and forth over the broomsticks. From time to time gather up the spun sugar, and pile it on a cold platter or shape it into nests. Should the syrup become sugary, melt it over heat for a moment.

Spun sugar candy can be eaten alone or used as a garnish for ice cream.

Taffy (yield: ½ pound)

1 cup light corn syrup
½ cup sugar
1 tablespoon vinegar

1 teaspoon butter
flavoring

Lightly butter a platter. Combine the first four ingredients in a saucepan. Boil them until your candy thermometer registers 252° F. The mixture should now be firm.

Pour it on the platter. When it is cool enough to touch, add several drops of any preferred flavoring and pull the taffy with thumbs and forefingers until it is light. Pull away bite-sized pieces; wrap them in squares of waxed paper.

Vinegar Candy

2 cups sugar	2 tablespoons butter
½ cup vinegar	

Melt butter in a saucepan. Add the sugar and vinegar. Stir until the sugar is smooth and the mixture starts to boil. When it is bubbly, put a drop in cold water. If it congeals, becoming brittle, empty the mixture onto a buttered pan.

When it is cool enough to pick up, pull it into strands, as you would taffy. Then cut it into bite-sized pieces with scissors or a knife. Place them on buttered plates to cool further.

CAKES, COOKIES, AND FROSTING

Carrot Cake

1 ½ cups cooking oil	2 teaspoons baking
1 ¾ cups sugar	powder
4 eggs, separated	2 ½ cups whole wheat
¼ cup hot water	flour
1 teaspoon nutmeg	1 ½ cups grated raw
1 teaspoon cinnamon	carrots
½ teaspoon ground	½ cup raisins
cloves	

Bake carrot cake in a preheated 350-degree oven. Grease and flour a 10-inch tube pan.

Beat the oil, sugar, and egg yolks together. Stir in the hot water until the sugar dissolves. Mix in the spices, baking powder, flour, carrots, and raisins. Blend well.

In another bowl beat the egg whites until they are stiff but not dry. Gently fold them into the batter. Empty the batter into the prepared cake pan, and bake it for seventy minutes or until done.

Grandma's Gingerbread

½ cup shortening	1 cup molasses
½ cup sugar	2 eggs

2 ½ cups flour
  1 teaspoon salt
1 ½ teaspoons soda
  1 teaspoon ground
      ginger

2 teaspoons ground
    cinnamon
½ teaspoon ground
    cloves
1 cup buttermilk

Cream the shortening and sugar; blend in the molasses. Add the eggs, one at a time, beating after each addition.

Combine the flour, salt, soda, and spices. Alternately add the dry blend and the buttermilk to the creamed mixture.

Grease a 9-inch-square cake pan. Spoon in the batter. Bake in a 350° F. oven for forty minutes or until done. Cool.

Oatmeal Cake

  1 cup oats (quick
      cooking)
1 ¼ cups hot water
  1 stick butter (or
      margarine)
  1 cup white sugar

1 cup brown sugar
2 eggs
1 ⅓ cups flour
1 teaspoon soda
1 teaspoon cinnamon
1 ½ teaspoons salt

Pour the hot water over the oats; allow to stand for twenty minutes. Cream the butter and sugar together, and stir in an egg at a time. Add the oatmeal mixture. Sift the dry ingredients. Stir them in, blending thoroughly.

Grease and flour an 8-inch-square pan. Pour in the batter. Bake in a 350° F. oven for thirty to thirty-five minutes until done. Cool and frost.

Sugarless Frosting

Mix 4 tablespoons of cornstarch and 8 tablespoons of cocoa powder. Stir in 8 tablespoons of honey. While stirring continuously, slowly add small amounts of evaporated milk until the frosting reaches the desired consistency.

Country-Boy Ginger Snaps

  1 cup molasses
½ cup butter
3 cups flour, sifted

½ teaspoon soda
1 teaspoon ginger
2 scant teaspoons salt

Put the butter and molasses in a saucepan; boil them for two minutes.

Mix and sift the remaining ingredients. Add them to the contents of the saucepan. Beat well.

Chill the mixture overnight. Roll the dough out thin, and cut it with a cookie cutter or knife.

Bake on buttered cookie sheets in a 375° F. oven for about ten minutes.

Yogurt Cookies *(yield: about 60)*

½ cup cooking oil	1 teaspoon baking
1 cup sugar	powder
2 eggs	3 cups rye flour
½ teaspoon salt	1 tablespoon grated
1 cup homemade	orange rind
yogurt	

Grease two baking sheets.

Beat oil, sugar, and eggs in a big bowl. Add the rest of the ingredients, stirring and blending well.

Drop dough by the tablespoon on the cooky sheets, spaced roughly 1½ inches apart. Bake in a preheated 350° F. oven, until lightly browned, about 10 to 12 minutes.

PUDDINGS

Molasses-Cranberry Pudding

2 cups cranberries	1½ cups flour
½ cup boiling water	1 cup sugar
2 teaspoons soda	½ cup butter
¼ cup molasses	½ cup cream
¼ cup corn syrup	½ teaspoon nutmeg
1 egg, well beaten	½ teaspoon vanilla

Chop the cranberries. Mix the soda into the boiling water; pour it over the berries.

Beat the egg well. Blend it with the molasses and corn syrup. Add the mixture to the cranberries, and stir in the flour. Blend well.

Pour into a well-greased pudding mold. Steam for three hours.

Cream the butter and sugar. When they are of a creamy consistency, add the cream. Cook until fluffy in a double boiler, beating continuously.

Mix in the nutmeg and vanilla. Serve as sauce over the hot pudding.

Persimmon Pudding

1 cup persimmon pulp	½ teaspoon vanilla
1 tablespoon butter, melted	1 lemon
	1 orange
1 ¼ cups flour	1 cup sugar
1 teaspoon soda	1 egg
½ cup milk	2 tablespoons hot water

Sift together the flour and soda. Blend this dry mixture with the milk, persimmon pulp, melted butter, and vanilla.

Pour into a well-greased pudding mold; cover. Steam for 2 hours.

Lightly beat the egg. Cook it in the top of a double boiler along with the grated rind and strained juice of the citrus fruits, the hot water, and sugar until the mixture develops a creamy consistency. Serve the sauce hot over the steaming persimmon pudding.

Chocolate Pudding (yield: 4 servings)

Sift together the following ingredients:

¼ cup flour	dash of salt
6 tablespoons sugar	4 tablespoons cocoa
⅔ cup powdered milk	

Store the blend in a tightly closed jar until ready for use.

To prepare pudding, empty the mixture into a saucepan. Gradually add 2 cups of water and 2 tablespoons of margarine, blending thoroughly all the while.

Put over a low flame and stir until the pudding thickens and starts to bubble when stirring is arrested for a moment.

Turn off the heat; blend in 1 teaspoon of vanilla. Cool.

INDEX